RELIGION AND CULTURE SERIES

Joseph Husslein, S.J., Ph.D., General Editor

ST. REGIS
A Social Crusader

By the Same Author

A MODERN GALAHAD: ST. JOHN
BERCHMANS

SAINT JOHN FRANCIS REGIS

A reproduction of the oldest portrait of the saint, painted from life by order of the Bishop of Le Puy, and handed down in his family for three centuries.

St. Regis

A Social Crusader

ALBERT S. FOLEY, S.J.

THE BRUCE PUBLISHING COMPANY
MILWAUKEE

Imprimi potest: THOMAS J. SHIELDS, S.J., Prov. New Orleans
Nihil obstat: H. B. RIES, Censor Librorum
Imprimatur: ✠ MOYSES E. KILEY, Archiepiscopus Milwaukiensis
September 5, 1941

B
R337f

ST. REGIS: A SOCIAL CRUSADER. So the author has fittingly entitled his book.

In the role of social apostle Regis can best be understood by all the world. Not less than Vincent de Paul is he the saint of social work. More even than Ignatius of Loyola does he stand out as the heroic protector of those enmeshed in the net of social vice.

Indeed, for a modern model of the Good Shepherd, bruised and torn in His search for the lost sheep, the painter need do no more than fix his eyes on this priest of sturdy peasant stock.

But in the list, too, of noted names in labor history that of Regis must rank among the first. True, he was no agitator or class-conscious propagandist, but his own knew him and received him with open arms — the poor mountain folk and country people, the share-croppers of their time. These worshiped him, and so did the unwashed multitudes of the city who ran after him and crowded every hall and every church in which he preached. His methods of combating unemployment and solving the most vexing labor problems, such as no one else would touch, were not only marvelously successful but also eminently scientific. Truly a Christian social apostle, he had his own wonderful way of ever looking after the bodily no less than the spiritual welfare of men.

An admirably correct picture is given by the author, not merely of the man himself, but of his physical and geographical environment, of the historical background of his time, and finally of the character of those hardy, rough, un-couth, but sturdy mountaineers and peasant people with whom above all else he loved to deal. And his success with them, that has made him for all time their unforgotten apostle, was due in large measure to the fact that he himself embodied the best and most sterling qualities of that splendid type of mankind.

Yet the influence of St. Francis Regis was not to be confined to his own small mountain section of France. It was by God's Providence to spread over all the earth. The hallowed spot in Lalouvesc where he laid down his life for his flock after labor, risks, and hardships utterly incredible, and where in death his remains were resolutely guarded by the mountaineers, was to become a famous shrine of pilgrimage.

Hither, for instance, on May 3, 1800, a beautiful and accomplished French lady made her toilsome journey up these rugged mountain heights. She had been a Visitandine nun in the days before the Revolutionists suppressed all religious orders in the land. Now, at the closed door of the desecrated church she pleaded for light to know God's will, pleaded with the saint who had been one of her special patrons that he might now intercede for her. And from Lalouvesc she returned with a heart overflowing with love of the poor and a missionary zeal that consumed her. Before she died, fifty-two long years later, Rose Philippine Duchesne, for she it was, had become the Xavier of that body of consecrated women of which St. Madeleine Sophie Barat was the Ignatius. She crossed the seas to America and became the foundress of many houses of the Religious of the Sacred Heart.

Six years after that visit to Lalouvesc came a young seminarian, climbing those heights with heavy heart, Jean-Baptiste Vianney. But that name had then no meaning. His poor head could never learn even the little Latin needed to complete his priestly studies — and yet, with the Reign of Terror over, there were now so few priests left in France to teach the Gospel to the poor! From Ecully, near Lyons, he had begged his way to the shrine of the great friend of peasants and the poor. And did St. Regis help him? History answers that question. As the Curé d'Ars, he is known today throughout Christendom. But during all his own wonderful apostolate the example of his Jesuit friend guided his methods and undertakings. Grown old, he wished to offer St. Regis some return and so commissioned his spiritual daughter, Catherine Lassagne, to make for him a pilgrimage of gratitude to Lalouvesc.

Similar examples can be multiplied. Thus we have the young French priest who came to pray for his sister's cure, vowing that in return for this favor he would become a missionary in America. The miracle was not refused, and Father Mathias Loras took sail for the United States. In 1830 he became the first president of the seminary-college at Spring Hill, and in 1837 was consecrated the first Bishop of Dubuque, Iowa. Today it is hoped that in due time he will be raised to the honors of the Church's altars.

But there are two instances in particular of a strictly social nature that may not be overlooked here. The first is the miraculous cure, on June 30, 1824, of the Parisian lawyer and judge, M. Gossin, former councilor of the Paris Court. His life, which he wished to dedicate to social work, had been seriously threatened by disease, and he vowed that if restored to health he would organize his efforts throughout Paris. His "work of St. Francis Regis" mainly consisted in combating the libertinage caused by the wretched poverty of the people, with not money enough in their purses to have their daughters legitimately married. He secured dowries, rectified unions, and legitimated the children. Marriage licenses and certificates of birth had been so highly taxed as to be out of the reach of the poor. Special arrangements, therefore, were made by him with official bureaus. In Paris alone the Society of Regis, during the first half century of its existence, validated 85,000 marriages and legitimated 15,000 children. The movement spread through Belgium, Italy, and other European countries. Even in England and Germany the name of Regis was a synonym for rehabilitation of the married lives of the poor. The movement, indeed, was one of the most truly human and realistic radiations from Lalouvesc. In all of these the spiritual was ever combined with the social, as should be the case with all social work that aims to be complete.

The second working-class activity to be mentioned here is the congregation called The Worker Brothers of St. Francis Regis. It was started under the saint's inspiration at Le Puy, where Regis himself had labored so zealously for the social-spiritual well-being of this city. The purpose was to conduct agricultural schools for orphans, teaching them religion and training them to earn their living. Five such schools were opened in Le Puy alone. Today several of these houses exist in Canada. Thus the spirit of Regis is active through the centuries.

And here I must content myself with naming just one more organization linked most intimately with the memory of Regis. As time went on, the number of pilgrims at Lalouvesc, on certain days, had grown so large that a plan was conceived by Father Jean Therme, while saying Mass at the saint's tomb, of erecting a special establishment for women pilgrims. So was founded the House of Regis, which became the home of Mother Thérèse Couderc and the cradle of the Society of the Cenacle. The sole purpose of this fine organization is to give retreats to women. Thus one more splendid work took its beginning at Lalouvesc, and the Society itself quietly but effectively extended the apostolate of St. Regis into many lands.

Readers, in fine, may not be surprised if I say that in the

catalogue of saints few names can be found that have been so widely applied to institutions of every kind, by Catholics and non-Catholics in the United States, as the name "Regis" or "St. Regis." In American City Directories we find such entries as St. Regis apartments, St. Regis hotel, St. Regis college, down even to St. Regis swimming pool. Yet of the thousands who daily see that name emblazoned on signs or over doors and gates through which they must pass, few doubtless could tell the story of the fascinating and almost romantic life of Regis.

Typical of our neglect hitherto to make properly known to the world this saint of the strenuous life, is the story told of a New Yorker who purchased property on Lake St. Regis, in the upper portion of his state. Curious to learn for whom that body of water was named he made inquiries of his neighbors. No one knew. He pushed his search further, and only when he returned to his metropolitan city could he find who the saint was after whom not only Lake St. Regis, but the neighboring mountain also was called.

Let us hope, then, that, with the publication of this book and its wide distribution through the years to come, there will be no further difficulty hereafter in receiving a satisfactory answer to the question, "Who is St. Regis?"

Joseph Husslein, S.J., Ph.D.
General Editor, Religion and Culture Series

St. Louis University,
April 5, 1941.

Contents

ST. REGIS
A Social Crusader

CHAPTER I

CITY OF THE FIRST CRUSADER

DURING the late sixteen-twenties, under the distant and preoccupied rule of Richelieu, Le Puy-en-Velay, the quaintest and most picturesque hill town in France, slumbered in unruffled security amid the highlands of the Massif Central. Pillowed comfortably upon the spacious bosom of Mount Anis, the city drowsed lazily while the rest of France was convulsed in the last of the great civil and religious wars. With its stout walls intact, its sentinels keeping continual watch from the summit of the mount, and its gates ready to be shut at a moment's notice, Le Puy reposed in its accustomed peace.

Life coursed slowly in the ancient arteries of this medieval keep. The easy paced, self-contained routine of the Commune, under the nominal control of the prince-bishop, was pursued equably with unchanging rhythm. The townfolk plied their bourgeois trades, celebrated their traditional festivities with wonted merriment and dancing, held their twelve annual fairs for the sheer pleasure of haggling over bargains, and handed down from generation to generation the legends and memories of their city's bygone glory.

Like an aging queen in her dotage, Le Puy lived in reverie among the souvenirs of a glorious past. The place had been the Lourdes of the Middle Ages, honored by all France as the City of Mary, the Loretto of the Gauls. Within the walls of her world-famous basilica, majestically situated on a prominent ledge halfway up the mount, Le Puy still guarded and cherished its dearest possession — a unique Black Virgin. Legend declared that it had been carved by Jeremias the Prophet. St. Louis the Crusader had borne it to France in the thirteenth century and had personally donated it to this shrine where the Virgin had wrought so many wonders.

The first of these was hid in the distant mist of legendary antiquity. Companions of the Apostles themselves were believed to have erected a chapel over a great stone after the Blessed Virgin had miraculously cured an invalid prostrate upon it. The fame of the shrine spread rapidly in the course of the following centuries. Hither popes journeyed as simple pilgrims. Here kings and nobles laid precious gifts at the foot of the altar. Here saints and sinners alike felt close to Mary, and chivalrous warriors dying afar off begged to be buried within the shadow of the cathedral walls. Eventually the Virgin of Le Puy became Notre Dame de France and queened it over the whole land from her niche above the main altar.

These and other memories of her brilliant days of old lived in the minds of the good people of Le Puy. But of none of their past glories were the townfolk more proud than of that in which Le Puy reached the zenith of her spiritual leadership. It occurred in the year 1095. A worried but hopeful pilgrim toiled up the hundred steps to the sanctuary of the Virgin and prostrated himself for long hours of prayer upon the miraculous stone. It was no other than Pope Urban II. Rising up at last he carried in his heart a great resolve. He would summon a council to Le Puy for the purpose of launching the First Crusade.

Unfortunately, the cross-shaped cathedral of Le Puy was not well suited to the needs of a general council. Undeterred, the pontiff designated Clermont in Auvergne as the scene of the epoch-making assembly. Three months later all

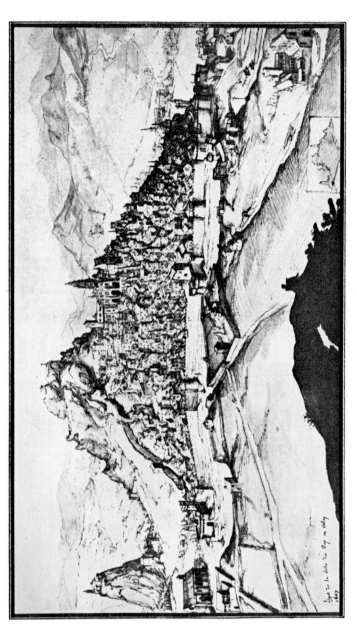

Le PUY-EN-VELAY IN 1607

A view of the western side of that picturesque hilltown where Regis taught

Christendom was represented there when Urban proclaimed his historic challenge and appealed for men to take the cross in defense of Christianity.

In that magnificent gathering it was Le Puy that assumed the leading role in the person of the high-spirited Adhemar du Monteil. As soon as the pope's astounding plea was ended, the prince-bishop of Le Puy leaped to his feet. Rushing to Urban he at once volunteered to swear the oath and march forth on the crusade. Gratefully the pontiff embraced him as the first crusader and appointed him, in his own stead, spiritual head of the expedition.

Returning to Le Puy in a blaze of enthusiasm, Adhemar preached the crusade so effectively that red cloth enough could not be found to make crosses for the thousands who pledged themselves to the cause. From his own diocese alone the prince-bishop mustered a force of five thousand men and prepared to lead them to the wars.

Etched forever on the mind of Le Puy was the scene of their departure. Standing aloft on the miraculous stone in his cathedral, Adhemar stirringly addressed his soldiers, and then bade affectionate farewell to the people he was to leave behind. That done, he faced toward the altar above which was enshrined Our Lady of Le Puy. His hand rose in salutation to his Queen, and his voice burst out into that mighty anthem, ever afterward known as the Antiphon of Le Puy: "Hail, Holy Queen, Mother of Mercy, our life, our sweetness, and our hope. . . ." In a full-throated chorus, the crusaders joined in with their leader, adopted this as their favorite hymn, and by their fervor and zeal spread it through the whole crusading host.

Adhemar gallantly sacrificed his life beneath the walls of Antioch. But his memory continued to live on at Le Puy, where for centuries afterward his statue still commemorated Le Puy's spiritual leadership of France in that golden era of Christianity.

Not long after this, Le Puy's star began to wane. Material ambitions replaced the spiritual ideals of the citizenry. The *Cours de l'Épervière,* literary academies devoted to the honor of Mary, had become *Cours d'amour,* attracting troubadours and trouvères from all over Europe and rivaling Toulouse in brilliance and color. In quest of their Magna Carta of political and economic independence, the citizens further stained the honor of the city of Mary. Instead of obliging their prince-bishop, Robert de Mehun, to agree to their rights as the English barons at that time were forcing King John to do, Le Puy wantonly murdered him, even defying the pope until their demands were heeded.

But the citizens had reason to hang their heads even lower in shame over the part they played in the bloody Albigensian crusade. The Council that condemned the Albigenses was held at Le Puy in 1181 under Cardinal Henri. This prelate called for a crusade of prayer, peace, and preaching, to combat the heresy. But instead, Bertrand of Chalençon, bishop of Le Puy, and Arnaud of Cîteaux raised armies and bathed Languedoc in the blood of the heretics. Finally Simon de Montfort completed the perversion of the intended spiritual crusade by turning it to his own political ends.

Le Puy preferred to forget this unsavory episode. In glossing over it, local legend claimed for the city the only redeeming personage in the whole disgraceful expedition — St. Dominic, the sole crusader who carried the cross instead of the sword, who preached peace and tolerance, poured balm into the wounds inflicted by the others, and, by means of his great Order of Preachers, restored the faith to the Midi. The fourteenth-century tradition at Le Puy localized in the basilica on Mount Anis the famous vision which St. Dominic is said to have had. Here, the legend maintained, Mary appeared to him and commissioned him to preach the rosary and its mysteries to the misguided Albigenses.

Thus did Le Puy try to salve its conscience and conserve its popularity.

By the year 1627, however, Le Puy's star had definitely set. Save on the rare occasions of the *Grand Pardon,* in years when March 25 coincided with Good Friday, pilgrims no longer thronged in thousands to the sacred temple. No miracles were reported. The age of faith had passed. The city had even been subjected to the indignity of a siege during the Wars of Religion. Its vaunted treasures had barely escaped profanation at the hands of some bandit Huguenots. But though it still possessed the outward, material legacies of the Middle Ages, its spiritual heritage had been lost. None of its inhabitants looked for a return of its medieval wonders.

Yet one day, in the late spring of 1627, the town buzzed like a beehive with some new spiritual excitement. It seemed as though the good Virgin enshrined above had again smiled upon her favorite city.

A young boy, Jacques Guigon, son of a city councilman, had been at the point of death from a violent case of fever and dysentery. The gray-bearded doctors had struggled in vain to ward off the onrush of death, until finally they gave up hope. The Last Sacraments were administered, and it remained a question of a short time only before the end. Pious aunts were still burning vigil lights for him before the altar of Notre Dame. His schoolmates at the Jesuit College, across town, continued their prayers for his recovery. But all seemed to no avail. Even the family despaired of him and kept a sobbing watch at the deathbed with no hope in their hearts.

The lad's life hung by the slenderest thread. He had, in fact, lost all interest in living. The long siege of fever had wasted his strength, had glazed his eyes into a blank, unrecognizing stare. Jacques was not even aware of his mother, kneeling beside him, clutching his arm in a futile effort to keep her boy from slipping away from her. But to his father and to the other weepers at the bedside, it was apparent that death was upon the boy.

Of a sudden, the deathly silence of the sickroom was broken. "Have courage, my boy," a voice said. "You will not die!"

Startled, and almost resenting the intrusion, the watchers glanced toward the speaker — a tall figure in black, standing like an apparition in the dark doorway and shimmering in the mist of their tears. They did not recognize his familiar face until he stepped into the room, smiling upon the boy who sat up in bed and beamed on him in return. "Why Père!" Jacques gasped; "I'm so glad you came."

Before another moment elapsed, the significance of this sudden change in the dying boy flashed upon them. His mother felt his feverish hand grow cool and normal. She touched his forehead — it was placid again. He was cured. In an ecstasy of joy she threw her arms about him and kissed him, tears of gratitude streaming down her cheeks the while.

Words choked in their throats as boy and mother looked upon the friend who had brought this great blessing. They could not speak, but young Père Regis, Jacques' teacher at the Jesuit College across town, understood their intentions and so reminded them: "It is not I who am to be thanked. It is God." But they nevertheless smothered his hands with kisses of joy until he tore himself away, forbidding them to mention anything about himself in connection with the sudden cure.

Next morning the entire family climbed the steep, stair-like approaches to the basilica to give thanks to our Lady and to God. A mild sensation was created when Jacques and the family walked into the main nave and knelt beneath the hallowed statue. The pious folk, gathered there for their morning orisons, had difficulty in restraining their curiosity while the Guigons heard Mass and offered their thanksgiving.

Once they had emerged from the church they were besieged with queries. "How did Jacques recover so quickly?" "Wasn't he dying yesterday?" "Was it a miracle?" — But to all the Guigons refused answer. They did admit that it was a sudden cure, but they had been pledged to secrecy by their benefactor.

The mystery made the local gossips all the more alert. The story of the indubitable cure of young Jacques traveled rapidly through the city. By nightfall they had fixed upon the "miracle-worker."

Across the street from the Guigons' home dwelt an elderly lady. She had seen a young Jesuit hurriedly departing from the house with his lay brother companion. With that for a clue, the curious spinster soon learned that the boy's professor, Père Regis, had paid him a visit. The mystery was solved. Even the Guigons admitted it when asked point-blank, but they insisted that it be kept a secret as much as possible. Soon the whole city believed that the young Jesuit, though not yet ordained priest, was a true man of God, a saint.

For the past two years Regis had been quietly and humbly laboring in their city. He had been seen in company with the priests of the College, visiting the sick, going about on college business, or leaving for and returning from missionary excursions in near-by villages. He had been hitherto just another of the familiar blackrobed figures, but now, unwittingly, he became the "cynosure of neighboring eyes."

People hurried to their gabled windows when they heard he was passing by. His tall, lithe, imposing figure became recognized and admired. Men stopped him on the narrow, winding footpaths that served for streets. After the interchange of a few words they could not fail to notice his equally striking features. Quiet, deeply penetrating eyes were overarched by somber, placid brows. A winsome smile played about his lips as he spoke. But what to the discerning was the most marked feature of his countenance was the determined line of his jaw, outlined beneath his sparse beard. He had a distinctive personality. And his shadowless gaze revealed him as a true man of God.

From casual inquiry, the townspeople soon learned that his home had been a small hamlet at the foot of the Pyrenees. His family were noble, landed gentry, connected with some of the prominent lines of the Midi. He had renounced all this when he entered the Society of Jesus upon the completion of his college work at Béziers. But nothing in his course had indicated to his fellow Jesuits that one might expect a miracle at his hands or through his prayers.

Indeed, at the College itself there were other Jesuits who gave more promise and seemed more holy than the young scholastic. The Father Rector, Arnaud Boyre, had recently won wide renown for unmasking a pseudo-mystic. Another priest, Father Antoine Lamour, had been singled out by the bishop as his personal preacher. Still others, as the Father Minister, Arnaud Dupin, the professors, Fathers Francis Juyé, Francis Bernard, and Etienne Deleuze, were already manifesting that holiness and devotion to the people which would make them victims of charity in the plague of 1629–30. But young Père Regis was only a scholastic, teacher of the lowest class in the school, and seemingly bereft of the qualities that made for a career as a pulpit orator.

Withal, the boys who attended class in the proud new College on the Rue de Fava Grèze, had readily recognized the sincere and radiant holiness of the young professor. With their uncannily keen faculty of appraising genuine and unfaked piety, they secretly revered him, and honored him as a forthright man of God.

The return of Jacques Guigon to school within the next week after his cure confirmed their suspicions of Regis' sanctity. In their knots of conversation about the college courtyard, before and after class and during recreation, the boys heard over and over from the lips of the fortunate youngster the story of his cure.

Thenceforward their eager eyes were constant in surveying the young scholastic. His every move in class and about the school came under their close and penetrating scrutiny. They noticed him in church especially, as he knelt motionless in prayer, his face suffused with the fire of his spirit, his head raised in rapt attention, his eyelids closed in the deepest reverence.

One of the boys began noting down the various virtues he observed in young Père Regis. He soon discovered enough matter to fill a whole notebook. In later life he treasured this as a sacred memento of his saintly professor. When more than eighty years old, after years spent as superior of a Benedictine monastery, he declared that there was enough evidence in the book to justify his canonization. Unfortunately, the notebook has been lost since then.

Still, by all other accounts, young Francis Regis was a winsome and effective teacher. Nor was this a simple matter in the classrooms of those days. In the first place, there was the pressure from above. Father Jerome Sauret, the Prefect of Studies, was strenuously endeavoring to raise the standards of the school in an effort to make it the best in France. Already the cityfolk had built a magnificent building to house the eleven hundred students. The academic life had to be brought up to match it as well. Indeed, four years later Hugues d'Avignon would write that "whether for its admirable buildings or for its flourishing scholastic life, it is estimated as one of the most celebrated in all France."

Meanwhile, it was no easy task to mold the minds and the behavior of the motley mixture of youngsters that made up his class. As in most Jesuit colleges that had been reopened in France after Henry IV lifted his ban on the

Order, the College of Le Puy embraced within its ranks children of every type of family. Mixed in among the hundreds of boys was a small contingent of nobles, dainty and scented little Fauntleroys whose liverymen or nurses called for them each day at the end of school hours. At the other end of the social ladder was a large bulk of farmer lads, some as cloddish as the soil itself, stolid, rugged youths, with square, inelegant heads. Between these extremes were the sons of the bourgeoisie — of merchants, property holders, public officials, innkeepers, professional men, butchers, bakers, candlestickmakers. All the varied professions and occupations that rounded out the complete, self-contained city were listed beside the names of the boys' parents.

In any one class, such as Francis' Third Grammar, the range of intellect and of home training would run from maximum to minimum, and not always conjointly. But even with the most intractable, Regis was patience itself. He did not curry their favor by giving them an easy time, but he sympathetically and understandingly helped the lagging along the arid and stony paths of rudimentary grammar.

His own experience had taught him the secret of success in handling boys. In his early youth, Francis had been utterly unnerved by the harsh treatment he underwent at the hands of the village Ichabod who wielded a menacing ferule. Young Regis had become unhappy and unresponsive, dejected and mentally paralyzed under that mode of dealing with pupils. He had come out of his shell only upon a change of the teacher's tactics. As a result, when he himself began to teach later, he relied heavily upon encouragement and stimulation to draw the best out of his boys. His personal fascination and charm of character, his southern vivacity and liveliness of imagination were all called into play to absorb the interest of the students in the healthy competitions prescribed by the *Ratio Studiorum*. Even the most backward responded under his warm and considerate manner.

This in itself was no small accomplishment. The boys up in the cold climate of the Massif Central were of a naturally less exuberant temperament than those of the smiling South or of the coastal regions. In the mountains up here, winter set in before school began in October, and lasted until long after it was balmy spring down in the valleys.

It is all the more remarkable that the young professor could stir these unimaginative youngsters by the seemingly spontaneous moralizations so dear to the ingenious school-masters of the seventeenth century. Yet such is the simple fact. One of them, Pierre Guillelmy, son of the city gold-smith, recorded it years later. "The Père, often interrupting his prelection, exhorted us, incited us, inflamed us. . . . And his advice was so well fitted to our capacity. There was no way of not paying full attention to the words that flowed from his lips. Each of us, in incredible silence, hung upon the least words he spoke with so much ardor, especially when his thought was to inspire us with devotion to the Mother of God and with love of the most Holy Eucharist."

The weekly periods devoted exclusively to *ferverinos* and to catechetical instruction were events in the lives of the students. His words made indelible impressions upon those young and pliant minds. The Benedictine referred to pre-viously still remembered them more than a half century later. "Even now," he remarked, "they serve me as incite-ments to virtue."

Already was Francis beginning to exhibit that penetrating forcefulness of speech which was destined to be the main source of his effectiveness in later life. Simple, straight-forward, unaffected, his words burst from the abundance of his heart and struck the boys with the directness of his man-to-man address. Moreover, Regis knew how to be vivid and concrete in the presentation of his matter. If he wished to inculcate contriteness of heart, he did not elaborate on the abstract qualities of the virtue. He personally made an act of contrition with the boys. His own sincerely shaken voice, his patent sorrow, even his unabashed tears showed them exactly what he meant.

Speaking of devotion to the Guardian Angels, he could illustrate their providential care by the story of his own preservation from death when he was a boy like them. On one occasion, at Béziers, he had gone for a fishing trip with some of his fellow students. After their lunch they stretched out for a siesta beneath a tree on the banks of the river Orb. Francis automatically commended himself to his Guardian Angel, and then dropped off into a deep sleep. Arising while in that state, he unconsciously walked toward the steep bank of the river. One step from its edge he was suddenly and inexplicably awakened. He confidently believed that his angelic protector had saved him from certain drowning. His sincere conviction and earnestness impressed the boys with the point he wished to make, though they probably paid more attention to the revelation of their saintly professor as somewhat of an angler, an occasional sleepwalker, and an amateur swimmer.

Into the sources of his effectiveness — his deep spiritual life, his constant prayer, his fervent and almost daily Communions — we are not allowed to penetrate. That he steeped his soul in God and in things divine is evident from the effects he produced. Not otherwise could his spiritual exhortations have given him so perfect a control over his class. At school itself, when the pupils emerged from his classroom their behavior was pronouncedly different from that of other boys. It eventually happened that at the College and even about town, when people saw a boy more composed, more devout, or more intelligent than others, they spontaneously declared: "There goes a pupil of Père Regis!"

No matter how winning his ways, however, there were

times when the waywardness of an individual student rendered them unavailing. One case in particular has been recorded. A youngster, known for his truculence, persisted in annoying the class and the teacher with those minor disturbances boys delight in perpetrating on the sly. Regis had warned and pleaded with him, but all in vain. The boy continued his misbehavior. Finally the blow fell. Francis decided to hand the offender over to the official corrector — an outsider, in those days, whose occupation was the birching of such undisciplined imps.

While Regis was giving the necessary instructions, the little rogue performed behind the professor's back the contemporary equivalent of thumbing his nose. Out of the corner of his eye Francis caught the impudent gesture. He quickly turned, and the lad ducked for cover behind a desk.

Instead of unleashing a fury of indignation, Regis stood in silence, biting his lip in deep chagrin and trying to fight back the tears that glistened in his eyes. The boy's unredeemable contumaciousness smote him like a blow beneath the heart. Here was one lad he had lost, perhaps irreparably. His own personal dignity and feelings did not matter. The tragedy of the thing was that his chances for winning that particular youngster to Christ were gone. He blamed himself as much as he did the boy, and that night kept a long vigil before the altar and laid the discipline heavily upon his shoulders in atonement.

The significance of the incident was not lost on the rest of the class. It was plain to them that Regis had at heart their own good, not his own reputation or success, nor even the high standards of the school in themselves. This personal interest in them was a revelation to their young minds. The average seventeenth-century Frenchman, unsentimental as ever about family relations, believed that it was the purpose of a boy's being to be spanked. Once able to leave home, the middle-class boy was packed off to school and forgotten until old enough either to be apprenticed or to help in his father's business. What little money the family could save was put aside for the girls' dowries, with the result that the boys' interests were of secondary consideration, if indeed they were not completely neglected.

It was consequently an almost unbelievable experience for them to find in their professor a fatherly friend who actually smiled at them, who, as one boy phrased it, showed the same regard for them individually as if they were all princes of the blood. They warmed to the considerate, impartial, and elevating treatment he accorded them.

If Francis had any favorites at all, they were not the few nobles who disdainfully sat in the same benches with the rough lads from the poorer districts. Rather, he looked with extra compassion upon these latter — youngsters whose worn and patched clothes were a terrific psychological handicap for them at school. In behalf of these, we are told, Regis went in person here and there about town to beg money and clothes from the shopkeepers and the richer folk. He needed only to present his case to them in order to procure what he wished. The good folk saw in him what the people of Paris were even then seeing in St. Vincent de Paul — a true saint who thought of nothing for himself, but all for his poor.

Many a boy who was about to leave school because his last and only pair of trousers had been worn shabbily thin was thus saved by the paternal solicitude of the young Regis. But Francis unfailingly spared the boy's feelings as much as possible. His aid was always given in secret, so that the lad could still hold up his chin among his companions, could continue to aspire toward making something of his life instead of running the streets with the friendless and unfortunate waifs of the city's slums.

Thus with poor, middle class, and rich alike, Francis was eminently popular. The boys of his class and of others as well came to love the tall, athletic, and kindly Jesuit. Eagerly they sought out his company whenever he appeared in the courtyard during the noon recreation, or on the afternoons of the half holidays which they occasionally enjoyed. One would imagine that the extended class periods, which lasted from seven until twelve in the morning and from one until almost four-thirty in the afternoon, would have surfeited the youngsters with the school and with everything connected with it. Still, the fact is that they liked to comrade with Regis even out of class time. Fortunately, they did have many holidays. Hardly a week went by without affording them at least one day off, besides their usual Thursday *congé*. At Le Puy itself, there were almost sixty holydays of obligation in the ecclesiastical year. If these were major feasts, they meant full holidays. Minor feasts brought the boys relief from class while they attended their usual morning Mass, and the afternoon was devoted to play.

The boys enjoyed spending their off hours in playing about the large courtyard. This was one of the few cleared spaces in the cramped town where they could get together for games. Unfailingly, Regis was with them here, keen on watching them as they engaged in pall-mall; in *paume,* their current form of tennislike handball; in marbles and in quoits. They even had a sport that matched, in description at least, modern basketball. Francis had introduced among them still other games which he had learned down south as a boy, or had picked up in Gascony and Auvergne where he had previously taught.

With this feature principally in view, the Jesuits had insisted upon a suitable site for their school before they consented to open a college at Le Puy, in 1588. Father Louis Richeome, the provincial, delayed two years in signing the contracts, until the city fathers bought up an entire block on a comparatively level place in town — and so, *L'île Chambon,* as it was called, became a busy playground.

Another feature of Jesuit extracurricular care for their charges was the country house. Out across the valley of the river Borne, north of the city, they had secured a villa, and here the boys from the city streets had opportunity to play their more expansive games, soccer-football, discus throwing, slingshooting, and races of all kinds. It did their souls good as well as their bodies to be freed for a day from the stifling slums that constituted the greater portion of Le Puy. Moreover, it provided the Jesuits themselves with ample occasion for studying the boys and aiding in their character formation. Regis, like most of the Jesuits of that day, took seriously to heart the responsibilities of his position as master, and managed to be out among his pupils whenever pressure of other duties allowed.

In at least one of these extracurricular occupations, as we might call them, Regis succeeded in interesting the boys themselves. On some of the major feasts and even on regular Sundays when the weather permitted, Francis was deputed to preach or teach catechism in a near-by town. A few leagues up the gorges of the Loire was Solignac; not far off, Bains; and north over the Borne Valley, Polignac — outlying parishes to whose spiritual interest the Jesuits were obliged to contribute, since the major part of their tithes were donated to the support of the College by the Countess of Polignac. Toward the little churches in one or other of these, Francis and his devoted pupils would hike on a Sunday or feast-day afternoon.

Once there, the boys joined the congregation that gathered for the sermon or instruction, the like of which they never heard from their poorly educated Mass priest. Just as the boys in class, so the peasants in turn hung upon the grace-laden words of the speaker and treasured up his least utterances. Francis poured out his soul in the simple, moving talks he prepared for them. Here he was in his element. All the unction and fervor of his own deep spiritual life flowed uninhibited upon the spiritually starving peasants of the little flock.

Nor was it lost on them. "It was like the Gospel," remarked one of the boys upon his return to school next day. "After the sermon one woman cried out, 'Blessed be the mother who brought into the world such a son!' And then she added, 'Happy am I to have heard him preach.'"

The whole outing was not less beneficial to the boys themselves. Claude LaBroue, describing one of these missionary trips with Regis, states: "I still remember how those poor people adored him. They publicly averred that no sermon had ever made such an impression on their souls. The Holy Spirit spoke in him. Before receiving the power of the keys and Holy Orders, he already mightily swayed men's consciences and hearts."

It was congenial work for Regis. Like all his other similar catechetical excursions during the past nine years of his life as a Jesuit, it strengthened in him the conviction that he was best fitted to labor among these poor people, whose language he could speak, whose needs he understood, whose hearts he was able to touch. Everywhere throughout the neighboring mountain districts there was profound need of just such apostles, and Regis felt a yearning to devote his life to the tremendous task of reawakening the faith in these regions.

His ardent zeal led Regis to volunteer often for these extra missions. What time he did not give to them was devoted to mingling with the boys, accompanying them on their own outings, or aiding them in various ways. One of his fellow Jesuits noticed this and upbraided Regis one day for spending himself so completely upon them. "You ought to employ your time better," the friend admonished him; "you ought not waste in behalf of your pupils all those leisure hours that might be used to make progress in learning that would redound to your credit."

Francis took the gentle hint well enough but remonstrated: "Well, I perform what duties obedience imposes on
me; but, candidly, if I am happy enough to comply with
what God demands of me, I shall not in the least be concerned about the shame of being thought unlearned."

Clearly, Francis himself perceived what God was demanding of him, and his five years of teaching had instilled
deeply into his mind the principle that Emerson was later
to phrase so aptly: "In dealing with the boy, my Latin and
my Greek, my accomplishments and my money stead me
nothing. But as much soul as I have avails." And so he persevered in lavishing all the time and attention he could
upon his charges. One observer has insisted that Regis thus
accomplished a vastly greater amount of good for the boys
by his private conversation than he did by his routine classwork with them.

Nor does one search long to discover the motives that impelled Francis toward this added concern for his boys. If
the teaching he gave them in class was to have any permanent value, it was imperative that his influence reach as far
as possible into their lives outside. Parental neglect at that
time was traditional, and the parents unreasonably expected
the school to turn out boys of good character while they on
their part did little or nothing to cooperate. Besides, a great
number of the boys were out-of-town students who were
lodged in groups at approved boarding houses or with private families about town. But, despite the efforts of the
college authorities to secure some cooperation from these
hosts, little in the way of positive help could be hoped for
in that regard.

Hence, whether the boy resided at home or boarded out,
he was exposed to all the dangers and pitfalls of the wide-
open city life. At that particular time, after almost fifty
years of continual civil wars, morality was at a low ebb.
Dueling was still the vogue. A local chronicler records as

many as thirty murders that went unpunished within the span of a few years. Dissipation of every sort had prepared the way for them, and the police were seemingly powerless to cope with the situation effectively. Richelieu was obliged to send a special investigator to enforce the laws. The conditions he found were appalling. "The morals of the people of Le Puy," it was later said, "were so corrupted that, instead of doing honor to their faith by edifying conduct, they dishonor it by a licentious life."

It is a sad commentary on the times that the Fathers at the Jesuit colleges throughout France were obliged to secure the passage of laws to protect their boys against conditions such as these. They obtained injunctions forbidding the hosts of young boarders to allow them to carry arms, or to go out after nine o'clock. Another law was enacted against cabaret owners who exploited these lads. Still another was passed prohibiting women of evil life from coming within ten blocks of the colleges. But these laws were futile in face of the lack of enforcement. The net result was that the boys ran wild.

Regis had himself witnessed the current trends of college life as a student at Béziers. Your seventeenth-century collegian was not content with the ordinary range of school pranks. True, he did not consider it beneath him to band with his friends in winter and pelt passers-by with barrages of snowballs, to beard the gendarmerie by mobbing pedestrians at night, by breaking windows in private homes and — most delicious of all — in the college itself, by invading the graveyards and upsetting the tombstones. But usually these budding Cyranos and d'Artagnans sought out more exciting diversions. They found slumming the gallant thing to do. They delighted to spend evenings in wineshops, swapping stories with older, more reckless swashbucklers. And they unfailingly but stupidly proved that they were grown up, by drinking into a daze what little brains they had.

Nor did they stop there. Quarrels and challenges in school or outside easily resulted in duels, sometimes fought in the very street in front of the college. It is amazing to read instances of lads of fifteen with the blood of their comrades on their hands. If they were thrown into jail for dueling or rioting, it was a harrowing night for the jailers. The students were fond of capturing the guardhouse from the police and barricading themselves in it against all comers.

Even the Jesuits themselves were not spared. A group of them sallied forth one day to stop a students' riot just outside the college gates. They were themselves mauled by the rioters, and rescued only when the rector sent an armed group of domestics to deliver them. Again, after a student had been arrested for violating a law the school authorities had caused to be passed, the collegians rose in their wrath and kidnaped one of the Jesuit scholastics and one of the boarders, holding them as hostages until their schoolfellow was released.

The strangest phase of the whole school scene seems to be the apparent indifference shown by the townfolk themselves. They evidently expected the boys to sow their wild oats and to carry on the colorful traditions of the Middle Ages, especially those of the Latin Quarter of Paris. In this regard the seventeenth-century student, at least before the rise of the Sun King and the betterment of manners that accompanied his reign, lived up to, and even exceeded expectations.

While he was himself a student at Béziers, Regis had discovered that nothing short of segregation from them could save him and his companions from contamination. He had therefore grouped together the boarders who roomed with him and by his quiet but effective influence persuaded them to follow him in keeping to an exact order of the day, similar to that the Jesuits were to enforce when they eventually began to conduct their own residential schools. The results he had achieved there he now repeated on a much larger scale at Le Puy. Enriched spiritually as he had been by his years of Jesuit training, he more expertly spread about him the atmosphere of clean living and drew the boys to abandon the ways of the older generation of students and strike out anew along the lines of conduct he traced for them.

The younger boys at Le Puy had need abundant for just that mighty effort to break with the past. There, a few years before Francis' arrival, the whole community had been shocked by two of the students. Father Boyre, the rector, had been summoned hurriedly to the parlor one day, where he found a young girl, Agnes Galand, bruised and in tears with the horrors of her recent ordeal. She had been well known to Father Boyre for some time, since he was her spiritual director, her confessor, and to him she had revealed all the extraordinary gifts God had lavished upon her. Already she had received mystic revelations, presaging the future of exalted holiness that lay before her, when as Mère Agnes de Jésus at Langeac, in Auvergne, she would experience visions and ecstasies, would be impressed with the sacred stigmata, and would inspire M. Olier with the resolve to found the Sulpicians.

Yet that day, as she sobbingly had to tell Father Boyre, two of his students had made a vicious attempt on her virtue, while she was visiting her godmother with whom they were lodging. She had managed to escape only by throwing herself from the height of the stairs and imperiling her life and limbs in the process.

Nor was this an isolated instance. During Regis' own time one of the older boys had been apprehended in the act of committing a grave and scandalous fault. In the blunt and coarse ribaldry of the times, the story had soon made the rounds, so that even the youngsters of Regis' class knew of it the next day. Notwithstanding his own reticence, Francis inveighed against the sin with such fiery words that he "engraved profoundly on our souls a horror of that vice," Pierre Guillelmy admitted later. "Not for one day after that did I lose the memory of the moment when I saw him so inflamed, and when I felt implanted in me, by the grace of God, the detestation of this sin."

Confidence in that same grace of God was the only thing that buoyed up Francis' heart when, at the end of the school year of 1627, he bade farewell to his boys and to Le Puy, and set out upon the ancient pilgrim road southwest toward Toulouse for his study of theology. Regis trusted that God would perfect in them the work started through the instrumentality of his own teaching and example. But he feared, too, for those youngsters whose lives would have to be lived out in a city where every street had two dead ends, with slums and hoodlums to match.

As he traveled over the undulating plateau, toward the mountains that rimmed it in the distance, memories of his two years crowded in upon Francis. Some, like that of the cure of Jacques Guigon, consoled him to the utmost; but others made his heart heavy with anxiety for the future of his boys.

Reaching the edge of the Velay plateau, Francis turned for one last look at the city of Mary, with its famed basilica resting like a many-colored jewel upon Mount Anis. Setting it off with somber brown and green patches of farm and vineyard, the billowing hills of the upland basin rolled around it on all sides. Here and there giant, mesa-shaped crags of basaltic rock stood like petrified icebergs in what had once been a vast ocean of alluvial lava overflowing from the extinct, snow-capped Vesuviuses that battlemented the horizon. The whole scene resembled a dreamland of Doré's most fantastic creation, with Le Puy in the center, reigning as queen of this weird domain.

Regis lifted his heart in prayer once more to the Virgin

enshrined in this mystic and fascinating sanctuary. Silently, he begged her to raise up another great crusader, as she had so often done before, and to inspire him with the mighty ambition of quickening the dead consciences of the people of her own city, wakening their dormant faith, and bringing life and warmth again into their devotion to her and to her divine Son.

His prayer was destined to be answered. Within a few years Francis himself would return to Le Puy as a spiritual and social crusader to rout the forces of evil that were holding it in thrall, and to re-establish in truth and in fact the reign of Christ in the hearts of the people.

CHAPTER II

THE PALE HORSEMAN STRIKES

INTO drab, gloomy, melancholy Toulouse Francis Regis and his companion trudged wearily late one evening in September, 1627. With the shadows of dusk enshrouding the city, they wound through the labyrinth of cobbled streets toward the tower of the Renaissance Hotel de Bernuy in the Rue des Balances — now the Jesuit College. Upon reaching its handsome entrance, Francis paused for a glance down the street toward the old Novitiate building, just a few blocks away. The familiar red-brick walls were faintly limned in the gathering darkness, but the blurred sight of them was enough to make him feel that his return was a spiritual homecoming. He was once more near the cradle of his soul.

The scene of his first arrival at Toulouse flashed before his mind. Eleven years previously, in the foggy cold of a bleak December day, a shy, ungainly lad of nineteen, he had descended from the stagecoach before an unsightly building fronting on the square of the Round Chapel. Rising out of the mist, gaunt and forbidding as a haunted house, the Novitiate had seemed at first sight a dismal, inhospitable place. It was so utterly different from the cheeriness of the College at Béziers and from the lightsomeness of his own native Fontcouverte that Francis had felt depressed. But gulping down his natural dismay, he had knocked upon the gate and been admitted.

The welcome he received had soon changed his spirits.

26

The warmth, geniality, and genuine fellowship that greeted him dwarfed all else into insignificance. He soon felt at home in the group of young men whose complete detachment from the cares and comforts of earth filled them with a happiness that was contagious.

A similar welcome now awaited Francis and his companion behind the doors of the Hotel de Bernuy. Familiar faces, some of whom he had not seen for years, appeared to greet him. There was stout Ignace Arnoux, an affectionate friend and ardent admirer of Francis; Bertrand Parra, cast in the same mold as Regis and destined for a parallel career; Michael Charbonnier, an angelic youth still, of whom it would be said that when he was not treating of God with souls, he was treating of souls with God; Jean Vieules, Malycen, Cladel, Broquin — all crowded around to embrace their old friend and bid him a hearty welcome.

In the courtyard that evening Francis and his confreres sat reminiscing and detailing stories of their experiences during the past years. The arches of the portico rang with merry laughs and happy chatter. But there were somber notes at intervals in the conversation. Francis inquired about his friend Arnaud Boret, the saintly old councilman who had surrendered all his wealth and had been admitted to live among the novices years before. He had died recently, revered by all as a saint. He had been the inspiration of the novices with his holy presence and spiritual conversation, and had taught them unforgettable lessons in the art of winning souls while he conducted catechism classes for simple folk and children in the near-by church. Francis himself averred: "I count my acquaintance with this saintly old man among the principal blessings of my youth."

Regis slipped easily into the routine of class and study, of prayer and recreation that was marked out for the thirty theologians of the College. He plunged eagerly into the last stage of his preparation for the priesthood, and progressed apace in his study of theology. Together with his companions, he pilgrimed often to the tomb of the greatest of theologians, St. Thomas Aquinas, in the spired church of the Jacobins close at hand. That very year, 1628, the Dominican chapter general had decreed the erection of a magnificent monument to the remains of the Angelic Doctor, and the silver casket with the sacred relics thenceforth reposed in a richly ornamented tomb.

All in all, everything pointed toward a most happy year for Francis. Toward the end of the first quarter, however, a summons reached him from his former novicemaster, Father Pierre LaCase, now residing in the Professed House across town, and governing the whole province of Toulouse.

At a loss as to the reason for the unexpected call, Francis hastened to answer it. He had loved the venerable old Gascon priest and was ready to do anything he could to prove his gratitude for the spiritual guidance received through him.

"Word has just been received from Auch in Gascony, Francis," Father LaCase began after a hearty greeting. "One of the teachers there has been taken desperately ill and will be unable to do any more work this year. Someone of the theologians must be sent to fill his place, as I have no one else available. Will you be willing to make the sacrifice?"

The question came like a bolt out of the blue. Francis paused for a moment to grasp its full significance. It would mean the postponement of his ordination for another year, even though he had already taught his full five years and a few months more for good measure. A similar contingency had arisen a decade before at the end of his novitiate, when one of the Auch scholastics had left the Society. On that occasion Francis had been most willing to accept the appointment, despite the fact that he had not yet taken his vows. But this was different. The priesthood toward which he had been yearning so fiercely would have to be sacrificed for ten months more. But if he did not accept, one of his brethren would be obliged to face the same disappointment.

"If God demands the sacrifice of me," he answered simply, "I am ready to go — today."

Father LaCase embraced his former novice. "I knew I could depend on you, Francis. God will not fail to be generous to you for your generosity toward Him."

Francis hurried back to the College, gathered up his few personal effects, bade farewell, and sallied forth westward for Auch.

A day's journey, and the little archiepiscopal town rose in its familiar outlines before Francis. Peacefully crowning a modest row of hills on the side of the river Gers, it presented an imposing sky line featured by the lordly cathedral and the stately buildings of the Jesuit establishment close to it. Regis was not long in adapting himself to his new surroundings.

No specific details of his year of teaching here have been preserved for us. Certainly, a new and wide variety of experiences opened up for him, in charge, as he now was, of the spirited cadets of Gascony, immortalized in the Cyrano de Bergerac legend. One of the students at the College then was Carbon de Casteljaloux, captain and leader of Cyrano's own famed regiment. Another, Beatz de Castelmore, was later to be the uncle of the famous fourth musketeer, d'Artagnan.

One lasting benefit we know that he derived from Auch. While there he became intimately acquainted with the saintly Father Francis Tarbe, professor of philosophy and spiritual father of the community. Regis discovered in him an ideal spiritual director. To him he freely unburdened his soul, with him he discussed his progress in the way of God and received valuable advice. Hence, great was his delight when at the end of the session Father Tarbe was transferred with him back to the theologate as spiritual father.

Together, then, they left for Toulouse, late in September, 1628. Absorbed in spiritual conversations, they hardly even noticed the unusual number of travelers departing from the capital city of Languedoc. But no sooner had they stepped off the Garonne river bridge into the center of Toulouse than they became aware of the reason for this exodus. A deathly pall of silence brooded over the city. The otherwise bustling streets were almost deserted. Here and there, as they hastened toward the Jesuit College, white and red crosses on the portals of various houses attracted their attention. They were signs of the dreaded invasion of the plague that had paralyzed the city.

At the College the pair learned that the efforts of the magistrates to check the epidemic had been unsuccessful. For six weeks they had been fighting a losing battle. The first case reported was that of an inmate of the *Couronne-d'Or*. He had died August 19. Attempts were made at once to isolate subsequent cases by transferring them to huts outside the city, in a place called the *Sept-Deniers*. But the virulent attacks of the pestilence spread like wildfire. The populace became panicky. Already vast numbers had abandoned the doomed city. More and more families were fleeing to the comparative safety of the countryside. A few days previously, the rector of the Novitiate, Father Pierre Verthamond, had ordered his charges to pack up their belongings and take refuge in the villa beyond the city walls.

Similarly, too, orders were given to close up the theologate in the Rue des Balances and remove the students to the country house in the hills about a mile from the city. Francis, of course, was with them. Here temporary arrangements were soon completed and the normal routine of prayer and study resumed.

Unfortunately, the coming of winter did not bring the hoped-for surcease in the ravages of the plague. The harvesters that year had brought no grain to the blighted city, and

all other trade had been frightened away as the speedy
rumor of the epidemic spread through the surrounding
territory. Famine stalked the streets, and soon the first of
those fifty thousand fated to die in this extended calamity
had been laid away in their shallow graves.

The few magistrates who remained were hopelessly unable to cope with the emergency. They consequently summoned to their aid the valiant contingents of the religious
brotherhoods and confraternities who pledged themselves to
hospital work and service of the stricken poor. Clad in their
penitential garb, with masks and hoods used for further
protection, these spectral figures moved about the abandoned
streets with their death carts, ringing a doleful bell that
signaled the living to give up their dead. Soutaned priests
hurried about the city, pausing to bestow the last absolution
on a lone pedestrian as he slumped down dead in the street,
then rushing on to make the rounds of those houses whence
cries for help issued.

But while love of God drove abroad these heroic souls,
nothing but imminent starvation could draw the vast majority of the frightened people out of their homes. As the winter
advanced, food shortage became still more acute. Famished
mobs in search of provender plundered with impunity the
houses of the rich. Their frantic scouring of the larders and
cellars in the mansions of wealth merely increased their
desperation. No food was to be found. Desolation and despair engulfed them. Often, in a macabre orgy of mad passion, those attacked by the plague or perishing from hunger
snatched a few fleeting hours of vicious pleasure from their
ebbing lives, and then surrendered to the march of the
visitation.

At night, from the surrounding hills, the refugees gazed
down upon the dark charnel house of death and decay that
now was Toulouse. Gone were the glee and gaity of carnival.
No fireworks or lanterns or brilliant bonfires dispelled the

gloom. Rather, the lurid light of the flambeaux burning in-
cense, balsam, pitch, or resin in a pitiful attempt to purify
the pest-laden air, lent a Stygian glow to the whole scene.
Onlookers from the Jesuit farmhouse where Regis was stay-
ing could see the luminous mists hovering over the city like
the pale horseman of the Apocalypse, snuffing out the life
of the inhabitants.

All through the winter the epidemic spread throughout
the south of France. More than sixty Jesuits out of the scant
three hundred priests, scholastics, and lay brothers, volunteered to serve the plague stricken, although one only was
accepted for Toulouse, Father Odo de Gissey, famed all
over the continent for his scholarly writings. Already, before
the end of 1628, almost a score of Jesuits had died as victims
of their heroic zeal in the contaminated areas. At Le Puy,
three had sacrificed their lives, seven at Cahors, and others
throughout Languedoc.

Details concerning these martyrs of charity reached the
theologians in their temporary quarters outside Toulouse.
The news sounded strangely unreal, incredible, bizarre. It
simply did not fit into the idyllic scenes that surrounded the
villa and sparkled in the crisp winter sunshine of the Midi.
But of the theologians not a few felt their souls burn with
desires to carry on the glorious tradition of the Society of
Jesus and to devote themselves to the perilous service of the
plague victims. Francis Regis was one of those who fretted
at their inactivity. It seemed cowardly, craven to be supinely
indifferent at this time of calamity, to flee from the battle, to
desert the sick and dying just when these needed spiritual
and bodily help most urgently.

Through the months of late 1628 and early 1629, Francis
repeatedly besieged his superior with requests for a chance
to risk his life in the stricken city. Scarcely a week passed
without the repetition of his entreaties. Yet every time Father
Solanet, his superior, was obliged to answer with refusals.

The magistrates would not allow anyone to re-enter the closed gates of the city. Moreover, by the middle of March, Father Solanet had received a letter from the General of the Society in Rome, approving his removal of the students from the city. This he quoted to Francis often in order to silence his importunate pleadings. There could be no question of his serving the unfortunate sufferers until after his ordination.

Regis was thus left with only one way to aid the prostrate city. That was by prayer. His zeal for the relief of the diseased prompted him to redouble the fervor of his already intense life of prayer. We are told that his roommate in the straitened quarters of the country house noticed how, after a brief period of rest at night, the ardent scholastic was wont to arise and spend the remainder of the time on his knees, pouring forth the most appealing petitions to God. Night after night this practice was observed. Finally, his companion thought himself obliged to mention this unusual and dangerous habit to the spiritual father of the scholastics. But the saintly Father Francis Tarbe, already aware of Regis' high destiny and spiritual achievements, simply remarked: "Avoid troubling his prayer, and do not prevent his sweet communion with God. The time will come, believe me, when the sanctity of your companion will be a glory to the Society."

It is regrettable that Father Tarbe, who knew the interior fire blazing in the heart of Francis, did not leave any further remarks about his saintly friend, whom he was destined to outlive, becoming later the Provincial of Toulouse. But we must be content to draw the veil of silence over the sacred scenes of those nightly trysts with God, "too pure for the touch of a word." God was gently but unmistakably leading another chosen soul in His own wonderful way.

Thus Regis worked and prayed all through his first year of theology. His hopes of being permitted to prove the love he protested for God never fully died down. But they seemed

almost completely frustrated during the early summer of
1629. In the meanwhile the interminable plague showed
signs of lessening. In June the novices reoccupied their building on the square of the Round Chapel. The superiors were
on the point of recalling the theologians to the College when
the epidemic broke out anew with doubled intensity.

The peak of the summer heat marked a new high point
in the mortality caused by the disease. Throughout the rest
of the summer and the following winter the pale horseman
rampaged through the Midi. At Toulouse, however, the contagion was not as severe as before, or at least new cases were
ferreted out more quickly and quarantined more effectively.
Father Solanet was able to reopen the old Hotel de Bernuy
for his theological students.

Now, too, many more of the priests of the Professed
House at Toulouse were permitted by the public authorities
to minister to the sick. The result was that during the term
1629–30 a number of Regis' fellow Jesuits were added to the
list of victims of charity. One of his personal friends, the
newly ordained Father Jean Vieules, succumbed on November 5. At the end of the same month, Brother Chantaloube,
the faithful porter at the College, likewise met his death in
the heroic work.

The scourge was striking closer home that year. To the
sixteen Jesuits who had died in the first wave, thirty-five
more were added in 1629, and before the whole prolonged
visitation was over ninety-seven names were to be marked
down in the Society's necrology as its victims.

During his second year, Francis continued to champ at
the bit, impatient to be given a chance for martyrdom. He
even requested to be sent out as a companion of the priests
who were obliged to bring Viaticum to the wretched huts in
the *Sept-Deniers,* or in the other hospitals about the city. But
Father Solanet was adamant to his arguments. "Wait until
after your ordination," he would insist. "Only the priests

are of use to the sick now." Francis cited the precedent set
by Aloysius Gonzaga in dying for the plague stricken while
only a theologian, but to no avail. Regis would have to continue his studies and be ordained before superiors could
think of him as a candidate for the service of the
quarantined.

According to the regular canonical procedure, Francis
could not be ordained before the end of his fourth year, in
1632. By that time it might be too late to be of any help
here. True, the plague continued unabated all through 1629.
But it would almost certainly have died out by the end of
another two years.

So, then, in the early months of 1630, Francis' thirst for
martyrdom inspired a different desire — to have his ordination advanced at least a year, or even two, if possible. He was
practically assured, though not with certainty, that he would
benefit by the privilege of being raised to Holy Orders at
the end of his third year. The established custom in the
Society was to ordain at that time those theologians who
had taught more than three years. Regis had been a teacher
for six full years, three at Billom, two at Le Puy, and one at
Auch. He was accordingly entitled to ordination in 1631.

It was at Communion time, during those early months
of his second year, that Francis felt the desire for ordination
and for martyrdom urging him so strongly that he decided
to beg for the privilege of becoming a priest in that year.
The loss of so many priests from the inroads of the plague
favored his chances. The need for workers in the ordinary
duties of the ministry was increased, for many of the older
priests were chaplains at the hospitals, and some of the newly
ordained, destined to fill their places in the Colleges, had
fallen prey to the plague.

Upon approaching the Provincial, Father LaCase, to discuss the matter, Francis had the advantage of asking no
more than to be ordained with his own class. He reminded

the superior that he had sacrificed his chance for ordination that year by heeding his request for a teacher at Auch three years before. Now it was Father LaCase's turn to repay the generosity of his obedient son. Would he be willing to obtain from Rome permission for an early ordination?

Father LaCase could not refuse. He agreed to write for the special privilege. But he forewarned Francis that an anticipated reception of Orders would seriously interfere with his theological studies. In all probability, urgent calls for his priestly ministrations would render it impossible to study sufficiently for the examination necessary to attain solemn profession of four vows. For Francis, this was but a minor consideration. He was more than willing to sacrifice life itself for his fellow men. The loss of his chances for the highest grade in the Society was light compared to that. Only let him have the opportunity of showing that greater love for his Friend and for the least of His brethren, and he would have no further request.

News soon arrived from Rome to the effect that the Provincial could allow Regis to be included in the number of those to be ordained for the coming Pentecost, May 19, 1630. Almost before he could realize it, the time of his ordination was upon Francis. It drew nigh so suddenly that for a while he experienced fears and scruples lest he be unprepared for it. In the white light of the presence of God, the honest eyes of the saint discovered hitherto hidden imperfection in his all but immaculate soul. He hesitated about taking upon himself the heavy responsibilities of the priesthood while still in that state. But Father Tarbe quieted his fears. As his spiritual father, he assured Francis that God was pleased with his soul. He urged him to abandon himself confidently to God's holy will and trust implicitly in the power of His grace.

Among those who had impressed on them the sacred seal of the priesthood that Pentecost by Archbishop Charles de

THOVLOVSE.

1 Saint Sernin, 2 Porte du Faubourg, 3 Les Cordeliers, 4 Tour de Batzada, 5 S¹ Pierre, 6 S¹ Pierre et Les Freres Prescheurs, 7 Moulins de Batzada 8 Porte de Batzada, 9 Pologe du Betzaux 10 La Dauradi, 11 Filtre refugte du vieux pont 12 Le pont neuf 13 La Dalbade 14 S¹ Inan 15 Bastide 16 Ibel neuf 17 L'Hospital pour le Dauhpin 18 S¹ Nicolas 19 Reduit.

SEVENTEENTH-CENTURY TOULOUSE

Contemporary sketch showing the many church steeples of the city to the left, and the suburb of St. Cyprian with its hospital of St. Jacques in the right-center.

FONTCOUVERTE: REGIS FAMILY CHÂTEAU

Montchal, none was more happy or spiritually elated than Regis. It was the most memorable day of his life, but again no revelation of his experience during that time has been put on record. We possess only a short note written to his mother on the Thursday of Pentecost week:

Madame,

Since so it has pleased my Superiors, I shall say my first Mass next Sunday, a day dedicated to the Most Holy Trinity, and I shall continue celebrating it all the days of my life, as long as my health permits.

Should you have doubts as to my affection for you, and as to the desire I have of corresponding with your wishes, I assure you that I will remember you when offering these most august sacrifices to the Divine Majesty.

Ordination and first Mass both took place in Toulouse itself, where ever since mid-April the epidemic had been on the wane. It flared up again in the heat of midsummer, but there were sufficient priests at the Professed House to care for the emergency cases without calling on the newly ordained. According to one account, however, Francis did see some brief service during this phase of the endless calamity. Yet the cherished prize of martyrdom eluded his grasp. One of his companions, Jean Malycen, who is reported to have left in writing a testimony to Regis' work among the plague victims, himself succumbed. That was tragedy enough. But still greater was the death of Father Charles de Lorraine, former prince-bishop of Verdun, who had fled to the Society to avoid the cardinalate. He had been put at the head of the Professed House in the latter part of 1630. A few months later, he, too, was a martyr of charity. So heroic and devoted had been the brief period of his service that the whole city, though hardened to the sight of death by the thousands witnessed recently, publicly mourned his passing.

For Francis there remained only the necessity of resuming his study of theology. God was preserving him for a more formidable foe than the phantom horseman who rode the streets of Toulouse.

But now suddenly, toward the end of 1630, Regis' studies were brought to an abrupt termination. From an unexpected quarter had issued a pressing demand for his attention. Father Solanet had learned of a disturbing family quarrel among the Regises at Francis' birthplace, Fontcouverte, in southern Languedoc. Relatives had requested that Francis be commissioned to settle the dispute. Accordingly, Solanet wrote to the General for advice about the matter. Father Vitelleschi referred the case to the Provincial. The upshot was that, about Christmas time, Regis was sent as a messenger of peace to his home town. It was his first visit there since his entry into the Society, fourteen years before.

All during this time, from his constantly changing residences, Francis had kept up a correspondence with his mother, *Madame la mère*. In fact, when the invasion of the plague had disrupted communications, Francis had been deeply worried about the fate of his family. He had learned the distressing news that the epidemic had decimated the population of Carcassonne and of Narbonne. Hence, he greatly feared that Fontcouverte, situated halfway between these two, was itself tainted, perhaps wiped out by the plague. His joy was consequently unbounded when he heard that the place had been spared, and it still glowed in his heart as he hurried through the foothills of the Pyrenees toward the scenes of his younger days.

At length, across the meadows that were bare of their usual crops, arose the little feudal town, consisting of only a score or more houses clustered around an ancient château. The stout walls of the enclosure bulwarked the town behind a protecting moat. Stray groups of thatched peasant dwellings, standing outside its walls along the roadside, were quickly passed by Francis as he sped toward the ancient drawbridge and its protecting ravelin. Once within this

medieval entrance, the scene he had known so well in child-
hood and boyhood greeted his eyes. The old château, in its
gray grimness, rose on the right of the miniature square, its
central section well within the shadow of towering wings.
Opposite it, facing the square on the northwest corner, reposed the modest stone chapel, plainly but sturdily built out
of the native rock, together with the sentinel-like campanile
standing guard beside it. The antique presbytery still ad-
joined the church, occupying the space between it and the
house on the northeast corner of the square, the home in
which Regis himself was born. In this unadorned stone
house, and not in the château itself which the family did not
purchase from the Benedictine convent of La Grasse until
1602, Francis had first seen the light of day, January 31,
1597.

Thither he rapidly walked. One brief moment, and again
he was in the bosom of his family, tenderly embraced by his
mother, greeted with overflowing happiness by his father
and his three brothers, Charles, Jean, and François. It was
still the plain, homely household of a good, solid, landed
gentry, more interested in their family's titles to the neighboring farm lands than in the many connections they had to
the titled nobility of the Midi. But over the family now
hung the shadow of the quarrel that had brought Francis
down from Toulouse.

After he had settled himself in the residence of the local
priest, had said his first Mass and preached his first sermon
in the chapel, Regis undertook the arbitration of the family
differences.

The exact nature of these difficulties is not known. To be
sure, there was ample matter for dispute between his father
and his uncle, Bartholomew, who had conjointly purchased
the old château, the latter taking the southern half with its
wing, and leaving the northern end for Francis' father. The
unsatisfactory arrangements may have caused trouble now

that the oldest of Regis' brothers was on the point of being married and claiming his share in the paternal estate. The fact that old Jean de Regis did deed over half his property to Charles in 1631 indicates that he was the favorite, while two younger brothers may well have been in urgent need of placation at the prospect.

Whatever the disagreement, Francis amicably settled it and brought peace and concord once more to Fontcouverte.

But he was not satisfied with reordering material interests only. To his effort as peacemaker he added much spiritual work in the first fervor of his newly acquired priesthood. For the benefit of his family and that of the hundred and thirty residents of the neighboring homes, Francis conducted a series of sermons that amounted to a full-fledged mission. Likewise, he stirred out of their spiritual lethargy a company of soldiers quartered in the environs for the winter. But his most exquisite care was bestowed upon the poor, the field laborers, and the simple countryfolk of the neighborhood.

On one of his excursions to bring the spiritual joys of the Christmas season to some peasants in the vicinity, Francis discovered an exhausted and abandoned beggar, the lone inmate of a wretched hut along the roadside. The meager rations upon which he subsisted had been insufficient to sustain his strength. He was reduced to a helpless condition, sleeping upon the bare earth in his hovel and indifferent as to life or death. Francis immediately secured relief for him. On his own shoulders he carried a mattress to the pauper's hut, earning thereby the scoffs and jeers of some ribald soldiers who loafed about the town. Even his own brothers did not refrain from upbraiding Francis for bringing disgrace upon the family in the eyes of the other residents of the town. But Francis blithely soothed their ruffled dignity. He had seen a fellow man in dire straits. He simply could not wait until someone else could be found to carry his burdens for him. Direct, immediate action was imperative. So he had done the work himself.

Before he left for Toulouse in the early weeks of 1631, both the family and the soldiers had formed an exalted opinion of their visitor. Soon their impressions of Francis were noised about the neighborhood, reaching the Jesuit community at Carcassonne, and eventually the ears of the Provincial himself.

A short time afterward, Father LaCase wrote to Vitelleschi remarking on the signal fruits of Regis' visit to his home:

> Father Francis Regis has very successfully brought to an end the family disputes, and has left in his native place a true fragrance of holiness. His example of rare virtue and his pious undertakings, as well as his sermons impregnated with the spirit of Jesus Christ, have gained many souls to God. His fellow townsmen have been charmed with the zeal he manifested for their salvation.

Thus the excursion to his home town, which might have been just a holiday for renewing old acquaintances, proved to be a significant event in the life of the young priest. It called attention to his gifts as a missioner and singled him out as a holy and effective campaigner for Christ. A few more months of training and he would be fully prepared for the struggles that the future would soon bring.

The last stage of his formal preparation began soon after Regis had taken his place at the College on the Rue des Balances. Because of the vacancies in the ranks of the Society, caused by the death of ninety-seven victims of charity, the General authorized a curtailment of studies in the case of those almost ready for the ministry. Indeed, even novices, with only six months of training, were dispatched to teaching posts in the Colleges. Francis himself was withdrawn from his theological studies and associated with a small group of priests who combined the exercises of the tertianship with ministerial work in and about Toulouse. All the tertians pursued the full course of the thirty-day retreat required by the rule, and applied themselves to the other experiments of the third year of probation.

It was during this last year at Toulouse that Francis finally achieved the satisfaction of his years of yearning to serve the plague victims. The period from May to October, 1631, witnessed a recurrence of the fearful paroxysm that had convulsed the city periodically during the past thirty months.

The meadow of the *Sept-Deniers* became once more an inferno of the condemned. In May, 1631, only eight persons still survived out of the thousands quartered there in noisome, pest-laden shacks. But within the next few months scores were banished from the city to this quarantine camp daily. Willing or unwilling, they were herded out and forcibly imprisoned behind the high fences of that desolate lazaretto. Soon there were more than twenty-five hundred confined there to await death.

The proportions which the new attack assumed once more struck panic into the hearts of the Toulousans. Laws were swiftly enacted to compel the hospitalization or expulsion of the diseased. A wave of denunciations swept over the city. Anyone showing the least sign of sickness was delated to the magistrates and carted off to the lazar-houses without further investigation. Often, perfectly healthy persons, despite their cries and pleadings, were corralled with the really stricken and marched out at the point of the sword. Hardly a house in the city did not have a dread white or red cross upon its façade, chalked there by some panicky citizen who suspected the dwellers of having contracted the plague.

Across the Garonne, in the suburb of St. Cyprian, the large hospital of St. Jacques was packed with the sick. The incredible number of nine thousand sufferers is said to have been crowded into its wards, its galleries, and its areaways. Many hundreds of these had finally succumbed to the

inroads of the famine that was consequent on the failure
of the crops. Those who had fled Toulouse at the new outbreak were forced to return in search of food. With them
came peasants and villagers, perishing for lack of sustenance.

Amid these stark scenes of terror and suffering, Francis
Regis and his fellow tertians moved like angels of peace,
toiling ceaselessly to bring relief to bodies and souls that
were tortured to the breaking point. With a vast, self-for-
getful, Christlike tenderness, he made the rounds of the hospital and the lazaretto, carrying the Bread of Life through
those death houses, whispering words of comfort and absolution to the tossing, moaning figures, and spreading the
fragrant odor of love and mercy through those dank, fetid
holes of agony. His heart was wrung with anguish for the
afflicted wrecks of humanity he everywhere encountered,
and he spent every ounce of his energy to ease their last
moments and help them safely over the merciful threshold
of death.

Eagerly would he have sacrificed his own life to rescue the
least of these wretches from their agonizing deaths. But he
was spared. His companion and fellow worker, Father
Jean Cladel, was smitten one day, toward the end of the
epidemic, and Francis assisted him also in his last moments,
jealous almost of the heroic joy with which the newly ordained priest departed to meet the great Christ for whom
he had laid down his life.

Francis lived on. There were other thousands of suffering
people, prostrate under a spiritual plague more deadly than
the bubonic. For the relief of these Regis was destined to
labor during the nine remaining years of his priestly life.
The same broad, all-embracing human sympathy that had
characterized his selfless service of the citizens of Toulouse
would reach out toward countless other souls before the very
intensity of his love for God and men would wear out his
strength.

CHAPTER III

Start of the Crusadings

HIS full year of tertianship had not as yet been completed when Francis was again summoned to the office of Father LaCase in the Professed House across town. The Provincial had another challenging proposal with which to test the generosity and obedience of his former novice. Down in Pamiers, a small episcopal see fifty miles directly south of Toulouse, one of the three Jesuits engaged in missionary work and in teaching had contracted the plague and had died. Father LaCase stated the bare fact to Regis, and with equal dispassionateness informed him of his appointment to the vacancy. Francis did not hesitate a moment. He bade adieu to his Superior, and before long was on his way to his new destination.

Two days later, as Francis mounted the last stretch of road that led up into the hills upon which Pamiers was located, it was difficult for him to believe that war and famine and pestilence had struck even into this remote corner of the realm. Everything round about seemed peaceful and bright in the brisk October sunshine. To the south and west stretched rolling hills toward the distant, snow-capped Pyrenees, a vast amphitheater of mountains where the Midi achieves its most throbbing beauty. The extensive plain below, which Regis had traversed on his way from Toulouse, was a superb tapestry of verdure when seen from this vantage point, with the Ariège River winding like a silver thread through the multicolored pattern. To the east the fertile expanses of Mirepoix and Mazères were rich with vineyards as far as the eye could see.

Yet the ugliness of civil war and the gloom of the plague had alike visited this enchanting spot. Pamiers lay prostrate, like a conquered warrior, despoiled of arms and reduced to a skeleton by wounds and suffering.

On re-entering his city after the defeat of the Protestants, in 1628, Bishop Henri de Sponde had shed bitter tears. Everything was in ruins — churches, convents, and Catholic homes. Undaunted, he undertook his work of rebuilding. The Carmelites, Franciscans, and Poor Clares reconstructed their own pillaged convents and aided the bishop in his labors of spiritual rehabilitation. Besides these, Bishop de Sponde secured from Toulouse two Jesuit missionaries, Fathers Jean Bayol and Gregory Clavelier, who laid the groundwork for a school at Pamiers, while at the same time conducting missions there and in the rest of the diocese.

Upon his arrival in the town, Francis learned that the epidemic had been successfully checked after decimating the populace. Classes had been resumed in the school and Francis was immediately loaded with the task of teaching rhetoric to the small group of pupils there assembled.

It was pioneer work. This year was the first in which the higher class was taught, and the accommodations for pupils and professors were almost primitive. In a dilapidated old building, only three unornamented, meagerly furnished rooms were used for classes. Upstairs, in the priests' quarters, the furniture was equally scarce. The near-by chapel of the old school had been so wrecked by the Huguenots that the Jesuits cleaned out the stable in which the Duke de Rohan had kept his horses, and made use of it for Mass and spiritual exercises. But after the harrowing experiences in Toulouse within the past year, Francis experienced no difficulty in bearing up under these inconveniences.

The nine months of his stay at Pamiers were not without their meed of spiritual labors as well. After class and on holidays, and especially during the vacations, Regis joined his fellow missioners in apostolic work throughout the diocese. Ample outlet was afforded his pent-up zeal. Francis ranged far up into the Pyrenees, preaching the word of God even in towns near the Spanish border. There is also record of his presence in Carcassonne, and perhaps in Fontcouverte itself, during the winter of 1631–32, but no specific details have been preserved. Suffice it to say that he justified Father LaCase's confidence in his abilities as a missionary, and merited from him at the end of the year promotion to one of the most important posts in the Province — that of *operarius,* "worker," in the second city of Languedoc, Montpellier.

Father LaCase apparently did not even await the end of the school year to give Regis this wider field of labors. Toward the beginning of the summer of 1632 a substitute for him was found and dispatched to Pamiers to relieve Francis of his duties there. This move is all the more noteworthy in view of the general condition of the Province at that particular time. Under Father LaCase's jurisdiction were the colleges of Rodez, Cahors, Auch, Mauriac, Béziers, Aubenas, Le Puy, Billom, and Tournon, besides those of Toulouse, Pamiers, and Montpellier. To provide staffs for all these institutions taxed the limited man power of the Province, especially as the plague had reduced from three hundred to two hundred the total of all, including lay brothers who did not teach.

Moreover, the plague victims happened to be precisely those men most valuable to the colleges. Superiors had written to the General complaining that while the less competent held a cautious silence, the more zealous and energetic professors and administrators had come forward and volunteered for service among the stricken. As a consequence,

Father LaCase expressed his fears that the Province would not be able to live up to the obligations contracted with the various cities of the Midi. The Jesuits had pledged themselves to the work of conducting all these schools on condition that the city authorities provide adequate endowments and build suitable buildings. The municipalities had fulfilled their part of the bargain. But now it seemed as though the Jesuits would not be numerous enough to carry the heavy load of the twelve colleges.

On his part, Father Vitelleschi, in encouraging Superiors to allow even their most promising subjects to undertake the hazardous work among the plague sufferers, had promised that he would secure help from other Provinces. Yet very few men had been transferred to Toulouse by 1632. Hence, it is a singular tribute and testimony to Francis Regis' outstanding promise as a spiritual force that he was selected for Montpellier.

On his way thither, Francis had the happiness of revisiting once more his alma mater, the College of Béziers. In the newly erected chapel of the institution he offered Holy Mass as a supreme act of thanksgiving to God for the vocation he had received in this very place.

It was like drawing a long, deep breath of refreshingly pure air to move once more in the atmosphere in which he had spent the happiest years of his life. Béziers was synonymous with mildness and sweetness, for it was a happy city, built upon a high plateau overlooking the river Orb, and within sight of the blue Mediterranean. Within its confines Francis had lived for four carefree, contented years. His character had imbibed from these pleasant surroundings some of the beauty and fragrant peace that pervaded them. There, too, his natural piety had found free play while he lodged in a boarding house immediately back of the Church of St. Felix.

Francis spent only a brief while in renewing these memories. Early next morning his eagerness for his new undertaking accelerated his pace eastward toward his goal.

The redoubtable walls of Montpellier, that had resisted the besieging army of Louis XIII ten years before, still stood impregnably upon an imposing eminence. Swelling proudly to the view like a great capital rather than a provincial town, it seemed symbolic of the Protestant defiance that had wrested from the king himself pardon for the defenders and generous terms of peace. True, since that time, Richelieu had risen to power and had ridden roughshod over Huguenot rights. Just that very summer of 1632, the great cardinal had gone one step farther. In an effort to break forever the back of Calvinist resistance in southern France, Richelieu had injudiciously striven to abolish by edict the ancient privileges of Languedoc and to arrogate to his own chosen intendants the collection of all levies previously gathered by the practically autonomous Estates of Languedoc.

The first months of Francis' residence in Montpellier were critical times. The Midi seemed on the verge of another civil war. Moreover, Gaston d'Orleans, the king's brother, had raised the standard of revolt in Lorraine. By forced marches he had come to Languedoc. His seditious uprising profited by the local hostility to Richelieu. Some notables joined forces with him, including five bishops and the famed Duke de Montmorency. Furthermore, the king himself had assumed command of the army that advanced on Lorraine to smash rebellion there. In July, he deputed Schomberg and the Huguenot LaForce to advance against Gaston and Montmorency. The opposing armies met at Castelnaudery near Toulouse and the rebels were crushed, Montmorency being wounded and captured, Gaston barely escaping with his life. The intriguing pretender then sued for peace. Richelieu and Louis XIII traveled to Montpellier to conclude the negotiations and to strike terror into the hearts of those Montpellierans who still preserved their hostility to the regime.

The king and his retinue were feted with gala demonstrations during the fortnight of their stay in the second capital of Languedoc, in September, 1632. The treaty was ratified with great solemnity, and Gaston d'Orleans was given a contemptuous pardon. But the nobles of Languedoc who had supported him were compelled to pay a severe price. The wounded Montmorency was placed on trial before his peers of the Parliament of Toulouse and was summarily executed. Other notables were heavily fined and deprived of their privileges of autonomy. Henceforth an intendant appointed by the crown controlled at the point of the sword the destinies of Languedoc.

In this atmosphere of smouldering hatred for State and Church, Francis Regis assumed his place in the ranks of those who were laboring for the restoration of the Church in Montpellier. The good work accomplished by Bishop Pierre de Fenouillet after the signing of the Treaty of Montpellier in 1622 was negatived by the outbreak of the new civil war in 1625 and the plague in 1628. But with the advent of peace and security, the bishop could now hope for substantial and lasting gains. Already the transfer of the Royal College to the Jesuits in 1629 had assured adequate attention for the youth of the city. But to win back the hostile majority of the people was still a problem for de Fenouillet. There was hardly any point in rebuilding the sixty-four churches destroyed by the Huguenots in the wars if the faith were not at the same time implanted once more in the hearts of the inhabitants. The bishop had himself witnessed the heart-breaking sights that marked the fury of the 1621–22 uprising. Many of the churches and convents that had been erected anew within the past decade were then ruthlessly destroyed again by the "Mass-breakers," as the Protestants nicknamed themselves.

The wholesale conversion of the Huguenots seemed out of the question, though Richelieu himself hoped for it indirectly through the winning over of their ministers. But what was of even greater importance, was the actual need of a wholesale conversion of the Catholics whose amazingly un-Christian lives had opened the way for the inroads of heresy and indifferentism.

Fortunately, at Montpellier as elsewhere, the perennial vitality of the Church asserted itself. The age of Richelieu became an epoch of intense religious revival. The vast spiritual and social crusade that was the Counter Reformation in France burgeoned forth from the dead bones of sixteenth-century ecclesiastical decay.

It would be fatuous to attribute to any one man or group of men the whole success of this tremendous movement. But in honoring men like Regis the Church honors the entire host of mighty warriors who achieved at least comparative victory for the faith in those trying times. To be sure, the work of Francis Regis at Montpellier was ordinary enough, and luckily, was repeated a thousand times over in the many cities and villages of the realm. The field of his activity embraced church, school, and home. In each of these there is little that is characteristic or outstanding, save perhaps the zest and energetic impetuosity manifested in his work.

Like the Curé d'Ars, who in fact two centuries later modeled much of his apostolate on that of his patron Regis, the young *missionarius* inaugurated his apostolic endeavors by means of simple, unadorned, matter-of-fact talks in church. The same sincerity and unmistakable appeal which was later destined to make little Ars the focal point of hundreds of pilgrimages, appeared with startling freshness in the sermons of Regis. One had only to listen to the frank, direct, living messages that arose from the heart of this man of God, in order to be convinced that here was the word of God and the road to life. Confessions were wrung from thousands. Conversions multiplied. Christian life was revived.

Nor is it possible to analyze or dissect the living voice of Regis. It is a part of the genius of Christianity that no bombastic faker can deliver its message convincingly. To be able to preach Christ and Him crucified one must first live the Gospels deeply and fully. Francis' secret of success was no mechanical method of sermonizing. It was the spirit of Christ Himself breathing through his very lips.

A famous preacher of the times, Guillaume Pascal, paid tribute to Francis' unrhetorical discourses during the autumn of 1632. Father Pascal was himself in demand all over France for his ability as a preacher, yet he admitted, after listening to one of Francis' talks: "How futile are our preoccupations with polishing and adorning our sermons! Look at the crowds that rush to the simple catechism lessons of this man and the conversions he produces, while our affected eloquence obtains no results of any permanence." Still, Father Pascal, called the "advocate of the poor," was himself so persuasive that he is said to have "wrung pity from the most hardened hearts, and money for alms from the most miserly."

The same might be said of Francis himself at Montpellier the short time he labored there. He capitalized on the popularity and vogue he enjoyed among rich and poor alike in order to promote much needed schemes for the relief of the downtrodden. In a day when organized charity of the medieval type had fallen into desuetude and that of the modern world was still awaiting St. Vincent de Paul and his Ladies of Charity, Regis epitomized on a small scale both the old and the new in his work throughout the slums of Montpellier. As he had done at Le Puy and at Fontcouverte, he canvassed the homes of the well-to-do Catholics begging alms in money and in kind for his poor. At times he might be seen, like a junkman, walking down the street with all manner of supplies slung over his shoulders and filling his arms. But the clothing, the shoes, the old mattresses, and the innumerable other odds and ends he collected were a god-send to the wretched poor.

Soon his rich friends became accustomed to expect Francis every Saturday and on the vigils of great feasts, for it was then that he made his rounds in quest of alms and clothing. His acquaintance with doctors and apothecaries, moreover, enabled him to secure from them free services and medicines for the sick. In behalf of these, he also gathered a group of volunteer nurses who alternated in caring for the cases that were abandoned by relatives or left alone by fate.

Unfailingly, Francis combined soul healing with allevia-tion of bodily distress. His eloquent charity opened the way to the heart of many a pauper sickened of life and perhaps despairing of God as well. So when Christ came anew into their lives in the person of Francis, practising the lessons of charity he preached to others, new hope and gladness dawned in their spirits.

There were times, however, when his charity was greedily accepted but his spiritual ministrations rejected. But such occasions were rare. A Huguenot servant maid, jailed for theft, was condemned to be whipped. On his rounds through the prison, with a group of ladies whom he had persuaded to prepare meals for the prisoners, Regis encountered the hapless maid. After seeing to it that she was fed, he turned his attention to her soul and urged her to abandon her heresy. She agreed, on condition that Francis should secure her reprieve from the disgrace of the public whipping post. Regis personally pleaded for her before the magistrate and succeeded in begging her off. But once released, the girl returned to her obstinacy. She refused to heed his appeal or to live up to her promise. Of a certainty, Francis realized her promise did not bind in full rigor. So he did not repent the act of charity he had done, but he was downcast by her resistance to grace.

With other heretics Regis achieved much happier results.

Many of the residents of Montpellier had abandoned the faith as a matter of policy during the Huguenot supremacy. Others, for lack of good priests and of proper training, had simply drifted away. Francis and his confreres experienced little difficulty in reconciling great numbers of them to the Church.

His methods were characteristic of the forthrightness and directness of his whole personality. We are told that he brought the full force of his personal magnetism to bear upon the Huguenot people with whom he came in contact. Under some pretext or other, he found occasion to visit them personally in their homes. Once there, his winsome manners captivated them, and no less his undeniably spiritual appearance. Most priests the Huguenots had seen were of a type not well calculated to offset the malignant accusations hurled against the Romish clergy by the Protestant pastors. But here was the living ideal of the best in Catholic priestliness — a man chaste, mortified, sincere, and Christlike in his every action. His charity toward them, and toward those pastors who were the bitterest opponents of everything Roman, convinced the Huguenots that Regis was interested in themselves and their spiritual welfare only, and not in the domination of the hierarchy as such.

It is unfortunate that descriptions of his convert work have come down to us only in the vaguest and most general terms. His labors are grouped together with those of his fellow Jesuits in a contemporary chronicle that remarks: "Our fathers exercised their functions with success from the first at Montpellier; a great number of conversions was witnessed; the sacraments were frequented, and everyone of importance in the city was so strongly attached to us that they have continued toward us ever since then the love and esteem with which they honored us."

In still another field of conversions, Francis' passion for direct, bold, frontal action is again manifest. Following the example of St. Ignatius at Rome, Francis devoted his attention to a class of unfortunates whose problem is a perennial one. In the slums of the French city, as at Rome and elsewhere, were to be found numerous wretched creatures who, as the first biographer of Regis states, "prostituting their bodies, sought their means of livelihood by commerce in those sins that made them unworthy of life." Realist as he ever was, Francis admitted with St. Thomas Aquinas that theoretically, and as the lesser of two evils, the persistent and unhappy trade could be tolerated and even licensed by public authority. This was true enough in general. But Regis happened upon numerous particular cases, each of which represented a poignant human tragedy. Consequently, with the optimism that Christ Himself showed in dealing with the Samaritan woman and with the Magdalene, Francis undertook to rescue these unwilling victims.

On the streets where they solicited their business, Regis would accost these women with words that wakened their slumbering consciences. Touched by his appeal to their better natures, they surrendered to his urging and allowed him to lead them personally through the city and to place them in the care of some virtuous lady who offered her home as a refuge for these penitents. With the charitable lady they attended Francis' sermons, made their confessions, and set about breaking themselves of the habits of sin they had contracted. After some months of this round of religious and character-forming duties, Francis secured honorable positions for them where they would no longer be tempted or endangered. Their subsequent blameless lives were a tribute to Francis' power and to his faith in the sincerity of their conversions.

Despite his handling of numerous cases of this kind, Regis himself never for a moment lost any of the luster that his holiness had won for him in the eyes of the townfolk. Indeed, angelic as he undoubtedly was, Francis could rush in where others feared to tread. His first biographer quaintly narrates the unusual details of Regis' work in the underworld of Montpellier:

When he learned of someone in a certain house of ill repute, he would go thither himself with a holy effrontery to demand her from the master or mistress of the house. He would not leave the house without taking the unfortunate girl away with him to lead her to a place of safety or to one of those holy retreats provided for them. Much vigor and persuasion were required to surmount the avarice of those who trafficked in such merchandise; but he needed much more patience still to change the hearts of these abandoned women themselves and to make them resolve to follow him. Nevertheless, upon occasion, one or two words of his would suffice to effect this, without any other rhetoric than that of the Holy Spirit and of the interior grace which acted in their souls the moment he opened his mouth to speak to them. (*LaBroue.*)

It was dangerous work. Many a pharisaical head, like that of Simon the leper, shook with doleful misgivings at the apparent rashness of the young priest. Skeptical, cynical critics upbraided Francis for his juvenile optimism, warning him that his efforts in behalf of those incorrigible characters would be fruitless. Regis countered with St. Ignatius' own profoundly spiritual reflection: "If my endeavors are successful in hindering only one mortal sin, I deem my labor well worth while."

As a matter of fact, there were very few among the women who had entered upon the unsavory profession from their own vicious inclinations. Most of them were victims of the iron-clad caste system that manacled France at the time. An orphan girl, or one too poor to obtain a dowry either for marriage or for the religious life, was obliged to fend for herself in a world that had very few occupations for her type. Sheer necessity provided the temptation that led them to their low estate in which the softness of the climate and the men, the abundance of wild students at the famous university and medical school, and the general laxity of morals that accompanied the incessant wars afforded the girls ample opportunity to ply their trade.

Nor were Regis' conquests confined to these lower class prostitutes. Among those he won from the slavery of sin were not a few gentlewomen of the upper classes who catered to the rakes among the nobles. Of one in particular it is recorded that at Francis' instigation, she abandoned the fashionable salon where her admirers flocked, and retired to a hospital, where in widow's weeds she atoned for her disorderly life by nursing the sick and performing other acts of penance.

In the short time that Francis worked in Montpellier during the years 1632 and 1633, his converts in this field of activity reached such proportions that he contemplated the establishment of a permanent refuge similar to the one Ignatius had founded at Rome to shelter his own penitents. According to one account, Regis actually did set on foot a project of this type, committing to a group of nuns the care of the institution. But the years in Montpellier were too crowded with other activities to allow any further progress along these lines. Besides, Francis was obliged to engage in extensive mission work throughout the rest of the diocese and in the neighborhood of Nîmes. These excursions occupied the greater part of his two winters at Montpellier and helped to season him still further for the great apostolate that awaited him.

On one of these mission tours Francis traversed the Languedoc plain north and east from Montpellier even to the foothills of the Cévennes mountains which he would later scour so frequently in quest of souls. However, the small towns and villages of that region, Saussinnes, Sommières, St. Clement, Combas, and others, provided but modest opportunities for the zeal of the young priest.

At Sommières, a walled town some twelve miles from Montpellier in the district of Lavaunage, Francis encountered a Calvinistic populace as stoutly fortified against the Catholic faith as the town was against hostile foes. Still, more perhaps through his prayers than through his actual mission work, Regis was able to offset the Calvinist influence of Georges Viret, one of the Geneva triumvirate, who had passed through the town in 1562 and had effected the mass apostasy of almost the entire population within the short space of two days. Under the Edict of Nantes, Sommières had been one of the legally recognized Protestant strongholds. Its political machinations had, however, caused the withdrawal of this recognition after Louis XIII had recaptured it in stride on his way to the siege of Montpellier, 1622. A strong royal garrison was quartered in Sommières to assure its fidelity to the crown at least, if not to the Church.

But Sommières was not any less Huguenot now than before the advent of Louis XIII. Only twenty-five or thirty Catholics resided within its confines when Regis and his companion, a teaching scholastic, journeyed thither in 1633. The mission itself received merely the briefest mention in the annual letters of the College of Montpellier: "The Catholics were confirmed in their faith; some heretics abjured their heresy; a Confraternity of the Blessed Sacrament was established." However, the impetus given to the faith and zeal of the Catholics by the mission and by the establishment of the Confraternity to perpetuate the fruits of the mission, proved to be the turning point in the battle with heresy. Sommières, from being a predominantly Protestant town, became a bulwark of the faith against the militant Jean Cavalier and his raiding Camisards who, anticipating the methods of the Ku Kluxers, tried to terrorize it into abandoning the faith toward the end of the seventeenth century. To this day, the natives still attribute to Regis their return to the fold.

On the road to the next town, nevertheless, his companion

manifested his dissatisfaction with the results of the mission
and blamed Regis for his pulpit methods. He argued that the
simplicity of the language used by Francis was opposed to
the best traditions of the Fathers of the Church, and that
the word of God should be preached to the people not in a
disjointed, unadorned, and orderless style, but with a mag-
nificence and eloquence like that employed by the great
speakers of the day. In accordance with the rhetorical principles the young man had recently learned, he criticized as
well Regis' voice, gestures, and pulpit methods, until he
had persuaded the priest to carry up into the pulpit on his
next mission a more studied and ornamented sermon.

That one effort was sufficient to settle the issue. The
pompous sermon in pretty language was flat and ineffective.
Regis returned to his familiar, heart-to-heart style, speaking
from the abundance of his convictions about the great truths
of religion. The effects of that mission served to convince
him never again to use the clumsy, cumbersome methods of
the day with their conceits of language and their classical
allusions.

In the catalogues of the various houses with which he was
connected, Regis is never designated as a *concionator,* a
preacher, but always as a missionary and catechist. His eloquence did not conform to the accepted and impotent standards of his contemporaries, but the Spirit spoke through his
mouth with great freedom. His sermons were the fruit of a
life of prayer, of an extraordinary personal austerity that
allowed him usually only three or four hours' sleep a night
and imposed upon him an almost perpetual fast. His experience taught him that only by a deep and abiding cultiva-
tion of the inner life could his social activities have any
lasting influence. And even those which seemed to be
rewarded with little visible fruit, like the mission at Sommières, were in reality the source of innumerable graces for
his fellow men.

At Saussines, a small village near Sommières, Francis had some rather dangerous brushes with heretics and soldiers.

In the church where he was giving the mission, the villagers had stored their treasures and grain. Only thus could they save them from the rapacious soldiers who everywhere plundered and pillaged homes they pretended to protect. The inhabitants hoped that the so-called Catholic soldiery might have respect at least for the holiness of the sanctuary. The subterfuge only enraged these freebooters the more, and their insolence prompted them to raid even the church itself to satisfy their greed. But at the door of the church they encountered the tall, undaunted figure of Regis, crucifix in hand and defiance in his eyes. While he lived, he calmly told them, they would not profane the house of God with their sacrilegious arms. Nonplussed, the soldiers hesitated. They had come to batter down the wooden door, but were powerless to strike down this living rampart that loomed before them as a vision of courage supernatural. The lone defender vanquished the assailants by the sheer force of his moral strength. They retired without carrying out their intention, and became, together with their commandant, admirers of the missionary.

Not long after, Regis in his turn appealed to them for aid. The peasant with whom he was lodging had been informed by his Calvinist neighbors that they would sack his house and run him out of town if he did not deliver up to them a large sum of silver for ransom. Appalled, the poor man hastened to Francis, found him in the middle of a catechism lesson, and informed him what the crowd of Calvinists had threatened to do. Immediately, Regis left his work to face the mob. "Be on your guard," his host begged him; "they are Huguenots; they hate Jesuits; your presence will excite them all the more."

His host's apprehensions were justified. The mob remained unmoved notwithstanding his appeals, his cajoleries, his threats. Their unfavorable reaction was vividly impressed on Regis by the barrage of rotten onions they rained upon his retreating figure. Not so much to avenge this insult as to avert the injustice menacing his host, Regis sought an interview with the commandant of the troops. Upon hearing the story, the captain exploded. He swore he would have all the offenders hanged without mercy. But Francis calmed his fury, and, refusing to divulge either the names or the descriptions of the extortionists, secured from the commandant a promise to publish a proclamation threatening the direst penalties for those who might perchance molest his host in the future.

Soon afterward Regis returned to the College of Montpellier. In accordance with his rules, he submitted to his superior a modest but truthful account of his missionary activities, and then resumed his routine place in the community and his routine activities about the city. But the rector, Father Balthasar Carel, was so gratified with Francis' accomplishments that he called to the attention of the General in Rome the particular merits of his recent work. "The zealous missionary," he wrote, "has traveled through many places of the diocese of Nîmes and Montpellier with a wholly apostolic charity and amid unbelievable hardships; he has gained to God numberless sinners and has brought back into the bosom of the Church many heretics. Such happy beginnings promise great things for the future." Other reports also reached the General that year, retailing the phenomenal successes Francis had achieved. Vitelleschi in consequence included the following tribute to Regis in a letter written to Montpellier sometime later (April 24, 1634):

"I experienced much joy in reading the letters of the fathers consultor, especially that of your Reverence, in which was contained something of a tableau of the good that God has accomplished in your illustrious city through the enterprises of Ours. May the Distributor of heavenly gifts, from whom proceeds every grace, deign to bless this father of whom you speak, and who, you say, works so many marvels for the conversion of heretics, for the solace of the poor, and for the consolation of prisoners, that everyone is astonished to see how much the inhabitants are edified at him and chant the praises of a worker so worthy of the Society. I like to believe that he will not reserve his care only for those outside, but will likewise fan the flame of zeal within the College, so that others may accomplish works equally meritorious by following his example.

Some months prior to this eulogy of Francis as a "worker so worthy of the Society," the General had given the official approbation of his office to Regis' fitness for the Order. In a list of thirteen names dispatched to the Provincial with authorization to admit the men to the last vows of the Society, that of Francis Regis was included with the note "to be admitted without delay."

On November 6, 1633, in the little chapel of the College, Francis pronounced the final vows of a spiritual coadjutor. The eventuality foreseen in his anticipation of the priesthood had come to pass. He was not admitted to the solemn profession of the four vows — the highest grade in the Society. Nevertheless, years later he was acclaimed by the pope, Clement XI, in his Bull of Beatification, as a "professed priest of the Society of Jesus." Legend has it that the Holy Father's attention was called to the inaccuracy of the statement, but that his reply only confirmed Regis in the honor he so well deserved and so gallantly sacrificed: "He is professed, for I make him so."

At the time of his last vows, the fathers of the province of Toulouse were engaged in a controversy, the solution of which was destined to exert profound influence on the shaping of Regis' future career.

In June of that year the bishop of Viviers, a diocese that embraced the southern portion of Vivarais on the west bank of the Rhone above Avignon, had made a visitation of a part of the flock entrusted to his care. To assist him in the

work, Bishop Louis de la Baume de Suze had secured two
Jesuits from Avignon who belonged to the Province of
Lyons. Accordingly, since the diocese of Viviers was geo-
graphically assigned to the Province of Toulouse, the fathers
of this latter province complained to the General about the
breach of custom committed in thus employing men from
another province in work within their own field.

Vitelleschi soothed the indignant complainers with some
common sense and plain reasoning. He pointed out that
Viviers was much closer and more accessible to Avignon
than to Toulouse, and that the bishop had long enjoyed
very amicable relations with the Lyons Jesuits there. It was
but natural that he should ask for the services of his acquaintances. However, Vitelleschi did admit the justice of the
Toulousans' claims. Accordingly, he authorized the Provincial to offer to the bishop the service of his men for
future work within his diocese, if the bishop should ask
for them.

Early in the year 1634, Bishop de Suze again requested
the aid of the fathers of Avignon for another projected
episcopal visitation. Father Guyon, the more prominent of
the two men used the year before, was obliged to refuse the
invitation, since he had been appointed tertian master that
year. But he suggested to his good friend the bishop that he
solicit men from the province in which his diocese was
located.

Toward Toulouse, then, the bishop of Viviers directed
his petition. Father Jean Martin, the Provincial, appointed
two men from Montpellier for the special work. One was
Father Jacques Leyssène, an orator of note, who had long
years of experience to his credit. The other was a young
priest just starting out promisingly on a career of spiritual
and social crusadings, Francis Regis.

CHAPTER IV

TREACHERY

IN THE spring of 1634, shortly after the close of the Lenten season, Fathers Leyssène and Regis left Montpellier and journeyed up to the Rhone valley to the palace of the bishop of Viviers at Bourg-Saint-Andéol, about fifty miles above Avignon. Their route skirted the vast chain of the Cévennes Mountains that parallel the Rhone's west bank from Central France almost to the Mediterranean. While not as massive as the Alps that dominate the eastern horizon, these mountains loom up beyond the Rhone valley as a formidable, menacing terrain, corrugated by a labyrinth of cross ranges that bristled at the time with dense and forbidding forests.

Within the Cévennes was a land that nurtured the giants and the demons of popular legend. Its black woods, its numerous unexplored caverns, its almost inaccessible volcanic craters were an unfathomed terror to the peasants of the Languedoc plain and of smiling Provence. In other parts of France the great timberlands were being thinned out, but in the Cévennes they still stood in thickly serried ranks on hillside and in valley. Save for an occasional river valley here and there, the military roads hacked through by the Romans were the only arteries of communication. Minor mule paths and wagon roads wound precariously through the mountains to connect the scattered hamlets with the villages that crouched in the shadow of the crag-perched feudal châteaux.

These lonely castles had become, during the Wars of Religion, veritable strongholds of Protestantism. The feudal barons of the Vivarais accepted the cause of the revolters principally as a pretext for throwing off the king's yoke of obedience and taxation. Not until the year 1629, with the final suppression of the Duke de Rohan's rebellion, was Louis XIII able to make headway against these truculent rebels. His soldiers had then set to work leveling the strongest of the fortresses in the various parts of the Cévennes that had enjoyed autonomy under the old Edict of Nantes. Richelieu had abolished the legal status of this Huguenot kingdom within the realm of France by his Edict of Alais. He had begun, morever, to subsidize missionaries of various religious orders in an attempt to regain these lands for the Church. But until the coming of Regis and Leyssène, vast sections of the Vivarais were still under the influence of Calvinism.

Upon their arrival at the episcopal residence that crested the bluff above the Rhone at Bourg-Saint-Andéol, the two Jesuits received a warm welcome at the hands of its lord-bishop, Monseigneur Louis de la Baume de Suze, Ordinary and Count of Viviers, Prince of Donzère and Saint-Maurice-du-Rosne, Baron of Largentière, Lord of Bourg-Saint-Andéol. Now only thirty years of age, de Suze had been appointed bishop thirteen years before through the efforts of his predecessor and former tutor, Jean de l'Hostel, whose "coadjutor" young Louis had been ever since the tender age of twelve. However, despite his canonically dubious advancement, the new bishop had received Holy Orders in 1628, and was sincerely zealous for the betterment of the ecclesiastical state of his diocese. His official visitation, conducted the year before in tardy imitation of Borromeo, had been undeniable proof of this. It heralded his episcopate, destined to last for seventy-two years, as one quite unlike those of the absentee Italian bishops of Viviers in the past century. The confirmation of 13,000 souls during the 1633 visitation had been evidence to the people that they could anticipate a resurrection of religious life under his regime.

Regis had learned much of the young bishop during his years of philosophy at Tournon a decade before. It is not known whether he caught a glimpse of de Suze when the latter visited Toulouse during a lull in the plague of 1631 in order to make a spiritual retreat under his friend, the famous Father Charles de Lorraine. But it is almost certain that the bishop had no knowledge whatever of Regis prior to their meeting in 1634. Nevertheless, from the first, Louis de Suze was favorably impressed by the winsome character of his young missionary, while Regis, in his turn, recognized in the energetic, martial clergyman a true leader, a worthy descendant of the militant counts de Suze.

The prelate lost no time in depicting the spiritual condition of his diocese to his new acquaintances. His own personal experiences of last year had given him firsthand knowledge of the appalling plight of his flock. He himself had visited eighty towns in the northern portion of his diocese where heresy held sway, where the priests had been murdered or expelled, where churches had been destroyed and church property expropriated. In places where, a hundred years ago, a single parish of five hundred souls had been attended by ten priests, no Sacrament had been administered since the outbreak of the Religious Wars. By 1573, after the massacre of the Carthusians of Bonnefoy, of the monks at Charaix near Privas, and of a whole diocesan synod in the south of the diocese, there were not twenty priests in the entire region. Louis de Suze's predecessor had commissioned his vicar-general, Nicholas de Vesc, to visit and inspect the diocese incognito in 1583. His report was a jeremiad on the complete desolation that encompassed the Church in those mountains.

Happily, the work of reconstruction had been begun independently of the bishops and of Richelieu. Some religious orders had returned to the diocese. The Capuchins were established again at Villeneuve-de-Berg. The Jesuits had opened a modest College at Aubenas. In the former town, the capital of Lower Vivarais, the bishop himself had pontificated at services in connection with a Jubilee of 1627, during which the revived religious life of the eastern part of the diocese was displayed. Numerous Eucharistic Confraternities, founded by the Jesuits, had marched thither and had rocketed the number of communions to 50,000. Nevertheless, almost three fourths of de Suze's flock of 200,000 souls were bereft of spiritual guides.

Even in parishes which were attended by priests ordained in the past few score years, the bishop could expect no great efforts toward reconstruction. With the total liquidation of the pre-Reformation seminaries, the training of these men for the priesthood had been limited to a few months in the scantest of study before receiving each Major Order. De Suze accordingly emphasized the attention that the missionaries were obliged to give to these ill-educated priests. The double mission of gathering the lost sheep and of recalling strayed shepherds was thus confided to them.

On the trip, whose itinerary was plotted north through Villeneuve-de-Berg and Aubenas, and then west and south through Largentière and Joyeuse, the same procedure was to be followed as had proved so fruitful the year before. The two missionaries were to go on a few days in advance of the prelate's own party in order to prepare the people for his coming. They were to assemble the dispersed parishioners, to instruct them in the minimum essentials for confession and Confirmation, to prepare them for Holy Communion. Upon the arrival of the episcopal party, the Jesuits were to depart for the next center of operations and repeat their pioneering there, while the prelate completed his canonical visitation in full pontifical style.

After Mass the next day, therefore, Regis and Leyssène bade adieu to their new master and plunged into the four months' task that had been outlined for them. It was the beginning, for Regis, of seven intensive years of crusading in those rugged mountain ranges.

Detailed records of a scant three out of the fifteen weeks are still extant. But these formal reports of the official documents are much less interesting than the anecdotes and traditions about Regis that sprang up in the various places he evangelized. From these can be snatched fleeting glimpses of this tireless fighter who essayed to restore to Christendom and to Christ lands that had been profaned more viciously than the Holy Lands themselves at the hands of the infidel. Armed with the cross alone, Francis and his companion scoured the hidden depths of the forests and the open plains of the valleys to stem the overwhelming tide of heresy which had desecrated the sacred sanctuaries housing Christ's Presence in the Vivarais.

More significant, too, than any of these external details of his crusading is one fact that everywhere strikes our notice: Catholic Christianity had meant civilization for these peoples. The Reformation had been a cultural cataclysm for them. It unleashed savage passions that vented themselves first on the Church and then on the people in such fashion as to threaten the extinction of what human virtues Christ had brought into these wilds. Regis' crusade, from the start, was a social crusade for the uplift of the people, for the moral rehabilitation of their lives, and for the renewal of the civilizing influence of Christ's Church.

At one of the first stations on the tour, Francis fell athwart the ruthlessness of the Calvinists. Villeneuve-en-Berg had been a center of Huguenot marauders since 1573, when the revolters had butchered thirty priests convened there for a synod. Even the advent of the Capuchins in 1620 did not dislodge them from the possession of the Château de Pradel and of the property that had once belonged to the Church. In Villeneuve, a group of lawless Protestant horsemen was pointed out to Regis as dangerous and murderous enemies of everything Catholic. At their door were laid numerous unpunished crimes against the faithful.

Sometime later, while he was traveling near the Château de Pradel, Regis beheld this troop of Huguenots riding hard toward him from the distance. Sensing his danger, Francis hurriedly took refuge in the grounds of the château and hid himself in a haystack. In a trice, the pursuers gained the gate, charged through it after Regis, only to find that their prey had vanished. Suspecting that he was concealed beneath one of the hayricks, they plunged their halberds and swords into them on all sides. As if by a miracle, Regis was not discovered. The Calvinists rode off disappointed and Regis emerged to continue his journey. A chapel was later built on this spot that might have been the lonely and untimely grave of one more in the endless list of victims slaughtered by the insane fury of these Huguenot fanatics.

Just north of Villeneuve, in the town of Saint-Laurent-sous-Coiron, a reception was given the bishop. It is revived for us in an official report, which is worth inserting here:

On Wednesday, the twenty-fourth day of the month of May, one thousand six hundred and thirty-four, we, the Bishop, accompanied by sirs and reverend Fathers Jacques Riffard, canon and judge of his cathedral of Viviers; Pierre Symian, officiator of the same Church, doctor of Theology; and Bartholomew Faure la Farge, canon and archpriest, his secretary; and reverend Fathers Jacques Lissène and Jean-François Regis, priests and preachers of the Company of Jesus, departed from the place Saint-Gignies-en-Coyron. There came to meet us, MM. Olivier de la Teulle, prior of Saint-Laurent; Claude Hérault, priest of the diocese of Le Puy, curé of the said Saint-Laurent, accompanied by Messires Marius Brousse, notary and bailiff in the jurisdiction and command of the said Saint-Laurent; Etienne Roux, councillor; Pierre Laurens, jurisdictional attorney; another Pierre Laurens of the said place; Jean

AUBENAS AND THE ARDÈCHE VALLEY

Present-day view of the Cévennes mountain town where Regis was stationed, 1634–1635, during his missions there and in the environs.

Boyron and other parishioners of the said church. And we — having been given the cross to kiss by the said curé, and having been vested in our pontifical vestments, the canopy having been presented to us — went in procession to the parish church where were offered prayers for the living and the deceased, and where was given an exhortation by the Reverend Father Lissène, containing the causes of our visitation. . . . On the feast of the Ascension of our Lord [the day following] after having celebrated Holy Mass, we conferred the Sacrament of Confirmation on a great number of persons, the majority having confessed and received Communion, also on those of the parish of Darbres, whom according to our command, the curé had led hither in procession, as well as on those of the said parish.

The reception of the young reforming bishop appeared unbelievably cordial. But there were two good reasons why the religious life of the little town was demonstrated so brilliantly for the Ordinary. The first was the nearness of the Jesuits of Aubenas, who had been conducting missions incessantly in the environs, founding in one year (1617) fourteen confraternities of the Blessed Sacrament.

The second reason proved to be another revelation of the double-dealing current at this time among the clergy. The Augustinian prior, de la Teulle, wished to allay the suspicions of the bishop by the fine demonstration. The thoroughness of the canonical visitation, however, unearthed the fact that this same prior had enjoyed the revenues of his preferment for thirty years without troubling himself to receive Holy Orders. Monseigneur de Suze severely reprimanded him and gave him the alternative of presenting himself for ordination within twelve months or being deprived of his benefice.

The next locale of the bishop's activity was the most consoling of the whole tour. It was Aubenas, a picturesquely peaceful town, nested in the hills through which meandered the Ardèche river. It, too, had been the scene of martyrdoms during the past century. In 1592 Blessed Jacques Salès, priest of the Society of Jesus, and Blessed Guillaume Saltemouche,

his lay-brother companion, had both been slain here by
Huguenots whom they had vanquished in verbal conflict
on the mystery of the Holy Eucharist. On the site hallowed
by their blood, and in the church that enshrined their relics,
Regis prayed to these intrepid missionaries for courage to
follow in their footsteps. Conscious of his own fear that sent
him scurrying into ignominious hiding at the first onslaught
of the Huguenots, Francis humbly begged the martyrs to
nerve his soul for the perils that still awaited him. The
sequel was to reveal that his prayer was heeded.

The Jesuit College at Aubenas staged a gala welcome for
Monseigneur de Suze, inasmuch as he was one of the most
generous benefactors of the institution. Teachers and pupils,
we are informed, vied with each other in honoring him.
After a few days of episcopal ministrations, the party took
horse for the next field of action. A day's journey south
brought them to Largentière, where on June 3 the bishop,
as Baron of Largentière, was officially greeted at the cross
of Sigalières outside the gates. There the magistrates graciously handed him the keys of the city. The military monseigneur was in his element. With a wave of the hand, he
dramatically restored the keys to the Sieur Deleuze, in token
of the confirmation of all the city's privileges. The cannon
of the fortress boomed out the news, and the city's garrison
fired their salute with their muskets. Through the files of
the soldiers and the lines of the people the party moved
solemnly into the city, along its hilly streets up to the
baronial château on the hill that dominated the scene. There
the bishop made his headquarters for the next three weeks.

Radiating out from this central location, Francis and his
companion evangelized all the surrounding country to the
southern and western borders of the diocese. To the south
they ranged as far as Joyeuse, a source of sorrow and affliction to the peasants despite its name. Until recently its château
had been the retreat of the vulturous Sieur de Jagondas, who

by violence, extortion, and robbery had preyed upon the lowly folk of the valley. Richelieu's special justice, Charles de Machault, had himself condemned this noble brigand and personally led the assault on his château in which the peasants vengefully participated. But their oppressor escaped in the night, and so the people were allowed to vent their indignation in demolishing the fortifications of his former haunt.

The regions round about Largentière and Joyeuse might well have tempted the greed of a feudal baron. The country was relatively rich, less rigorous than the northerly portions of the Vivarais, and was in fact called the "Vivarais Provence." The hillsides were covered with vineyards and the valleys with olive groves. Near the bishop's own château, and in his possession, were the silver mines that had given Largentière its significant name, "the silvery."

At Chassiers, a small town in the hills across the river from Largentière, Francis struck up a close friendship with the lord of the château de Lamothe, Jean de Chalendar, a noble patriarch who had retired from active life after years of executive offices in provincial affairs. The count provided the young missionary with lodgings while he roved about his domains in search of lost sheep.

In the château de Lamothe occurred one of Regis' most remarkable conversions. It appears that the zealously Catholic master of Chassiers was particularly interested in a noble lady of the not distant town of Uzer. Count de Chalendar had introduced some savants to her in an attempt to win her from Calvinism. These worthies had argued to great lengths with the Huguenot gentlewoman, but she remained mockingly invincible. Father Regis agreed to meet the obstinate heretic. To the château she was therefore invited, and later introduced to the Jesuit. The lady, who dearly loved an evening of religious controversy, anticipated another polemic victory for her keen mind.

To her astonishment, Francis had only one thing to say:

"Well now, my good friend, you wish to be converted, don't you?" There was a moment's delay while the words and the charming manner of the priest took effect. Presently, she who had been unyielding owned herself conquered. "Ah, who would contradict you, mon Père?" she said. "You ask it with such graciousness!" The count was amazed at the power of his guest, and henceforth regarded him as an indubitable saint. He would soon repay Francis for his personal favor to him and to his friend.

A few weeks more of this vagabond missioning in the surrounding territory and in the Ile-du-Vivarais brought the visitation to a close. The bishop and his party returned to Bourg-Saint-Andéol elated at the marked success of their toilsome tour. De Suze openly acknowledged that the reforms everywhere established and the practices of Christian piety revived throughout his diocese were due to the zeal and the indefatigable labor of the younger of his two missionaries.

Before dismissing him, the bishop urged Francis to complete the full circle of his influence by giving a mission to the laity and clergy of his own episcopal city and its environs. Regis welcomed this new opportunity and launched into a vigorous attack on the evils that flourished within the very shadow of the bishop's palace. It was here that he stirred up a hornet's nest.

Out in the country districts, Regis had frequently encountered cases of curés who had fallen away from the path prescribed for the celibate and had neglected to observe their vows of chastity. Considering the times and the lack of character training in their meager preparation for orders, one cannot pass too severe a judgment upon these country clergymen. They were for the most part men whom holy Church had raised up in her desperate need for subjects to replace the thousands of her best priests who had been killed off in the Huguenot uprisings. Any and every candidate

who presented himself was accepted and ordained, whether
or not he could live up to the grand traditions of the clergy
in France.

To these men of a dark century in the Church's history
one must needs be kind. Perhaps the poor, uncultured
country curé is less to be blamed for his weakness than are
the rich nobles who everywhere else in France battened on
the Church's substance without ever taking orders or vowing chastity. At any rate, it was not of Viviers but of another
French diocese that a contemporary bishop exclaimed to
Vincent de Paul: "I am horrified when I think that in my
diocese are almost seven thousand drunken and dissolute
priests who have no vocation." In the Vivarais the scarcity
of priests itself was also a scarcity of scandals, though there
were many faithful curés who lived and died in obscurity.
Only the scandalous seem to have risen above oblivion to
brand the Church with their infamy.

Francis Regis, nevertheless, was Christlike in his tenderness in dealing with the few cases he handled. We are informed that he warned them in a humble and respectful
manner, taking care to protect their reputation by admon-
ishing them only in private, and then without passion or
offense. He quietly spoke of the scandal they were giving,
the souls they were perverting, the danger they were risk-
ing by their disordered lives. Embracing them with affection, he "compassionated their weakness and conjured them
to expiate by a penitential life the disorders of their past
life. Thus he would gain many to God, whether by his
sweetness or by the force of his discourses." (*Daubenton.*)

But there was one vicious curé in Bourg-Saint-Andéol who
had good reason to believe that he would pass the rest of
his life in the dungeons below the episcopal palace if the
bishop heard of his doings. This unworthy priest was already
frightened quite thoroughly by the fate that had overtaken
those of his fellow clerics who had refused to yield to

Regis' entreaties. Some had been silenced. Others were se-
questrated in prison. Whatever he might be able to do to
save his Judas face would have to be done quickly, in the
heat of midsummer, while the high officials of the bishop's
circle were attending the States Assembly at Tournon.

Intrigues of this kind were not unfamiliar to this curé.
With practiced ease and consummate skill, he snaked about
the city spreading dissatisfaction against the zealous missioner, whispering innuendoes about his exaggerated fanati-
cism, his overbearing fulminations, his inhuman strictness.
Presently, animosities were brewing against Regis among
the moderately good folk both of the laity and the clergy.

By August, almost a month after his return from the
visitation, de Suze was being besieged with complaints
against the Jesuit. People whose opinion the undiscerning
young prelate respected called at his castle to deliver denunciations of the indiscreet zeal manifested by the apostle.
Letters from the clergy attacked Francis as "an impetuous
and troublesome spirit," even proceeding to such lengths
as to accuse him of violating the secret of the confessional
in sermons that were "full of bloody satire and invective,
from which no one was safe."

The artful curé had cunningly calculated on the bishop's
susceptibilities. He even arranged it so that the complaints
would coincide with those weeks during which Regis was
rambling in the environs of Bourg-Saint-Andéol and not
on the scene to defend himself. Gradually, the continual
barrage wore away the bishop's faith in the young Jesuit.
The plotters became more and more brazen. Even in public
slurs were cast on the name of Regis, nasty insinuations were
muttered about his motives in sending some reclaimed
prostitutes away to other places, calumnious remarks were
injected about his unaccounted absences from the city.

When Francis reappeared in Bourg-Saint-Andéol upon
the completion of his missionary work in late August, some

well-wishing friends apprised him of the seriousness of the situation and pleaded with him to defend himself. But Regis demurred. God would take care of his defense, he asserted, since he had been advancing God's interests.

Not long after his return, he was summoned into the presence of the bishop. The young prelate, half expecting Regis to vindicate himself, vigorously rebuked him with bitter reproaches for his abuse of the authority confided to him, for his lack of appreciation of those persons who merited delicate attention. Waxing eloquent, the testy bishop summed up the case against Regis and intimated that he was regretfully obliged to dismiss him with a severe censure.

To his utter amazement, the bishop failed to elicit any self-justification from Regis. Humbly, the Jesuit submitted to the decision. "In view of my lack of enlightenment," he declared simply, "I do not doubt that many faults have escaped my notice." This was then the final proof that the bishop needed. He was convinced now that Francis must be guilty of the indiscretions alleged. It was utterly incomprehensible to the prelate's fiery, militant mind that anyone could suffer such damaging blows to his honor without a murmur, unless he were oppressed by a sense of guilt.

Louis de Suze himself certainly had never lacked combativeness. On many occasions he had struck back ferociously when attacked or even crossed. Witness the caning he administered to one of the town councilors who had the effrontery to change the places of the church pews without the bishop's permission. De Suze had invaded the very precincts of the Council Hall and had belabored the unfortunate man with a hundred blows of his heavy walking stick. On other occasions the irascible prelate stupefied the congregation in his cathedral by slapping his archpriest, by pulling the hair of two of his cathedral chapter, and by comporting himself more like a petty tyrant than a self-possessed episcopal dignitary. It is not strange, therefore, that he failed to appreciate the sublimely Christlike silence of Regis under these false accusations.

Immediately after his dismissal of Francis, the hotheaded prelate sat down and dashed off two scorching letters: one to the rector of the College of Le Puy, asking him to recall Regis under some pretext or other, since he was no longer of service to the Viviers diocese; the other he directed to the General of the Society in Rome, via Father Martin, couching his thoughts in language inspired by the heat of the midsummer, the frothiness of his own wrath, and the wily intrigues of his vicious curé in the city below.

The letters were hurriedly dispatched. Regis and Leyssène were packed off on the road to Le Puy. The sad case was considered closed.

To Bourg-Saint-Andéol a few days later came Regis' friend, Count Jean de Chalendar, homeward bound from the sessions of the States Assembly of Vivarais at Tournon. In paying his respects to the bishop, he learned of the disgrace of the missionary. From the lips of de Suze himself, the count garnered all the unbelievable details of the accusations. Bewildered, the zealous nobleman retired from the episcopal presence to ponder over the mutability of human affairs. But his years of experience with French diplomatic intrigues did not allow him to drop the matter then and there. He soon evolved a plan for investigating the roots of the whole affair. A few weeks of probing in the gossip of Bourg-Saint-Andéol uncovered the sordid source of the entire whispering campaign.

With a courage that merits note, Count de Chalendar braved the bishop's displeasure by speaking to him in no uncertain terms of the injustice he had unwittingly perpetrated on Francis Regis. With the evidence he had amassed in his own inquiries, he plainly verified his assertions and traced back to their scheming source the rumors de Suze had converted into facts. "Father Regis," he declared, "is persecuted by these libertines for no other reason than because he asserted himself emphatically against their libertinage. I have heard many of his sermons. It is true he tiraded with a holy liberty against these public scandals, but he did it always with moderation and wisdom." The Master of Lamothe left the bishop with much food for thought.

Others, too, who had been unwilling to venture near the heavy hand or the stinging cane of the bishop, were now encouraged to add their testimony to that of Lamothe. Louis de Suze was soon confronted with more than he could handle. He decided to await the return from Viviers of his aged vicar-general, Pierre Symian, on whose advice he leaned in his difficulties.

Father Symian, who also had a deep reverence for Regis, listened patiently but with astonishment as the young prelate related his puzzling predicament. Before he had finished, Symian had reached his own decision. To the repentant bishop he expressed himself thus: "I never knew a more holy man, nor one more filled with the Spirit of God. Is it not well known to what excesses the dissolute are wont to be driven against those who wish to put a check on their passions? My advice is that we cannot, without betraying the interests of God, abandon a man who is persecuted only for having forcefully defended the cause of God."

To his credit, the impulsive bishop immediately determined to recall Regis in order to make reparation for the injustice. But to carry out his decision seems to have consumed an unconscionably long time. Months were to pass before the far-reaching results of his action and his letters could be counteracted.

In the interim, Regis and Leyssène had reached Le Puy and had taken up residence there. Francis had left Bourg-Saint-Andéol in the full conviction that his costly act of humility would not be in vain. But on the journey to Le Puy

Father Leyssène prophesied dire consequences for his companion's foolhardiness in not defending himself. Leyssène argued that Superiors would be certain to deal harshly with him on account of the bishop's complaints. He protested that Regis should not have allowed de Suze to retain his false impressions of a member of the Society since they would do harm to the whole Order. But Francis, believing he had simply been following Christ in his silent acceptance of humiliation, answered that he committed the entire matter to the will of God. He did not even ask Father Leyssène to intercede for him with the Superiors.

Fortunately, at the College of Le Puy was a sympathetic Superior, his former novice master, Father Pierre Verthamond. This good priest fully understood the depths of Francis' soul and the sublime purity of his motives. He soon communicated with the Provincial, Father Martin, only to learn that the letter sent by Monseigneur de Suze to him had been forwarded to Vitelleschi. The case was therefore in the hands of the General.

Verthamond hastened to write to Rome in defense of his former novice. Under date of October 11 he informed Vitelleschi: "Everyone declares that Father Regis has a marvelous talent for the missions. He is sustained by a very ardent zeal for the glory of God, and he has never given more brilliant marks of it than when he accompanied Monseigneur the bishop of Viviers in his visitation of his diocese. I cannot estimate the great number of conversions that have been effected as well by the rare example of his life as by the efficacious power of his discourses — a thing that has made him already regarded as the apostle of Vivarais. He is a holy missionary who breathes nothing but the glory of God and the salvation of souls."

Weeks of anxious waiting elapsed, more worrisome for Father Verthamond than for Regis himself. Francis was resigned to God's will. He stayed on at the College, uncertain of his status, inactive, even unclaimed by any of the houses of the Province, since his name does not appear in any of the College catalogues for that year.

Finally, the summons came from Bourg-Saint-Andéol. Once more, Regis traveled down into the diocese of Viviers, and humbly received the public marks of reparation that the bishop bestowed upon him. For the present, however, the prelate had no further need of his services. Francis returned to Le Puy to await further developments.

Those weeks of seclusion in the city that had mothered so many of his apostolic desires made Regis question the desirability of labor in a country where the whispers of an evil tongue could destroy months of intolerable toil. He weighed the meaning of the stab in the back he had received that year from one who should have been crusading, like himself, for the same kingdom he was preaching. And the arbitrary, whim-guided rule of the bishop also caused him to ponder whether any lasting good could be accomplished under this regime.

On the other hand, the vision of the New World arose before him with its limitless opportunities for evangelic endeavor under Superiors fired with his own ideals. The Jesuits of France were starting anew in that virgin field from which they had been expelled by the English in 1629. Last year and this, many of the old missionaries had returned. For 1635 the Superiors were just then organizing another mission band, and hundreds of Jesuit ambitions, inflamed by the letters and appeals contained in the latest *Relations,* were focusing on membership in this select group.

Toward that distant mission the mind of Regis also was drawn. Hours and days of prayer finally convinced him that he could do better and more effective work in that faraway vineyard of the Lord. And so, on December 15, he took up his pen and indited the following letter to the Father General:

My very Reverend Father, *Pax Christi:*

I am consumed with so vivid a desire for the mission of the realm of Canada that I should be my own greatest enemy, and should fear to be unfaithful to God's appeal, were I to hide from your Paternity the emotions I feel. Freely, therefore, I manifest them and beg you with most insistent petitions to heed my prayers. I have, moreover, so great a confidence in your goodness that I do not in the least doubt of the success of my attempt. Your Paternity knows, I think, that I have robust strength; would to God that my virtue were as strong! But virtue is made perfect in infirmity. Mine will be strengthened, I hope, with the aid of God, in the miseries that cannot but be frequent in the midst of that corrupted nation.

Your most Reverend Paternity's son

and most obedient servant in Christ,

John Francis Regis.

Crossing this letter in the post somewhere along the wintry roads to Rome, were two letters from the General, both dated December 4, 1634. In one to Father Verthamond occurred these lines: "It has displeased me greatly that Father John Francis Regis has given so many evidences of simplicity and indiscretion during the visitation of the diocese of Viviers with the most illustrious and most reverend bishop he accompanied, and I do not yet see how he has made reparation." To Father Martin, Provincial of Toulouse, the other letter commended the following instructions for handling matters at Le Puy: "It is not sufficient that Father Francis Regis be recalled to the College from the mission in which he conducted himself so badly, but he must be punished in proportion to his fault."

By the time the Superiors in France received these dispatches, they possessed full knowledge of the case and were assured of the bishop's complete change of attitude toward Regis. Both the Provincial and the rector, no doubt, kept these letters under consideration pending the receipt of further news from Rome.

Vitelleschi, in the course of the next month, was apprised

of the true state of affairs. Letters from the Provincial and from the bishop allayed his fears that the conduct of Regis might lead to another tempest and might estrange still another bishop from the Society. In fact, he perused with pleasure the words of de Suze that thanked the Jesuits for having furnished him with a man "so powerful in work and in words." After praising the prudence, zeal, energy, charity, holiness, and effectiveness of Regis, the bishop had concluded: "The only thing in which we were never able to agree was this. I always reproached him with doing too much for souls, and he always pretended that he was not doing enough for them. I place him back in your hands; it is for you to use your authority in order to oblige him to take care of a health so precious, and to prevent a man who is most charitable toward others from being so severe on himself."

In a spirit quite unlike that condemnatory one of his letters to Regis' Superiors, Father Vitelleschi wrote to Francis an answer to his request for the Canadian missions. It closed the book on the misunderstandings of 1634. Under date of January 30, 1635, appear in the registers of Vitelleschi the following words:

Your noble ardor for the divine glory and for the salvation of souls pleases me, and I give most lively thanks for it to Him who inspires it in you. When it has properly matured, we will duly consider it. In the meantime, foster it by prayer, and strengthen it by the practice of virtue; thus you will prepare yourself to combat future difficulties, then no longer remote, but met at close quarters and in hand-to-hand conflict. I add that, since these desires come from Heaven, you ought with all fidelity to preserve and nourish them, inasmuch as they are undoubtedly purchased at the price of the Blood of Jesus Christ. In the hope that you will apply yourself to this with more care than I can counsel, I further recommend myself to your Holy Sacrifices.

Regis had not awaited this reply. When it arrived he was

again in the mission field of the Vivarais, laboring for the people in the diocese of Viviers. He was already convinced that God had taken providential care of his reputation, and had rewarded him for submitting silently to that brief period of cross-bearing entailed by his social crusade. The whole affair was now settled. But it had served a special purpose in confirming Regis in his call to be a crusading missionary for life.

CHAPTER V

MARCHING FOR CHRIST

LATER in December, 1634, after he had dispatched to the General his request for the Canadian missions, Regis was changed by his Provincial from Le Puy to the College of Aubenas. To manifest still further his full appreciation of the missionary's worth, Father Martin assigned him a part in the *missio ambulatoria,* "the mission on the march," that was to be sent north from Aubenas into the Boutières Mountains.

Before the start of the mission, Regis knelt many hours in prayer at the tomb of the martyrs of Aubenas. That the heroic lives and deaths of these men were constantly in his thoughts at this time is evident from one significant fact. The phrases and even the very wording in parts of the letter containing Francis' petition for the foreign missions are identical with those of a letter written by the martyr of Aubenas, Blessed Jacques Salès, to Father General Aquaviva for the same purpose. The close similarity between the two suggests that Francis had a copy of the martyr's letter either in his mind or before his eyes as he was composing his own. As a theologian in Toulouse, Regis had no doubt been impressed with the text of the letter in the story of Salès' life and death published by Odo de Gissey just before the outbreak of the great plague there. His acquaintance with the blessed martyrs was further supplemented by the living traditions still extant about them in the various houses in which he had resided. Salès was the current hero of the Toulouse Province, the object of holy envy and emulation on the part of all the enthusiastic, Christ-loving Jesuits of the Midi.

It is plain from his letter to the General that Francis, in plunging into the Boutières region that had been a shambles for hundreds of priests besides Salès ever since the outbreak of the Religious Wars, had in mind the purpose of following in the footsteps of that valiant martyr of the Eucharist. Indeed, the dauntless courage with which he faced the hostile mountaineers among whom he was to preach the Gospel points definitely to the notion that he was seeking a rendezvous with death for Christ.

Less than five years prior to this winter, another priest, Father Jerome de Condrieu, had met a fearful martyrdom at the merciless hands of the Calvinists in this very region. As a chaplain in the armies of Louis XIII, he had come with the king's forces for the siege of Privas, June, 1629. In an effort to revisit his monastery at Valence, Father de Condrieu had secured leave of absence, and was on his way thither when captured by a roving band of Huguenots. With a savagery worthy of the contemporary Iroquois, they tortured the priest to make him abjure the faith. They sliced off his nose and his ears. They slashed his cheeks in the form of a cross. They gouged out his eyes. But still the heroic priest remained steadfast. Finally, the Calvinists completed their gory work with a *coup de grâce* of five gunshots.

This martyrdom had proved conclusively that the smouldering hatreds of the Protestants for the Catholics were still as intense as they had been during the savage wars of the previous century. One finds it hard to realize that the stories told of those times are not tales about some aboriginal Indian tribes who had never known civilization. The unbelievable atrocities committed on defenseless men, women, and children rival those perpetrated by the American Indians of the period on their enemies and captives.

We are told that in the Boutières no age, sex, or condition of persons was spared by the savage Huguenot fanatics. Strong men were seized and bound to stakes. Their heads were then encircled with ropes or chains used as torques which, when twisted, caused the eyes to split and burst from their sockets in a refinement of cruelty. Still other men were buried alive up to their necks in mud, where they rotted to death amid unspeakable sufferings. Others had their feet cooked in grease to bring on a slow, lingering death from gangrene or blood poisoning. Starvation was perhaps the least unmerciful method used by these blood-lusting were-wolves. Women and girls were subjected to unmentionable indignities in the very presence of their husbands, fathers, or mothers. Even young children were not spared. Those who were not killed outright were roasted on spits, strangled, or held for a high ransom. Some had their heads bashed in. Others were hanged by the legs from the doors of their homes where no one was left alive to rescue them before they bled to death. The Huguenots played ball games with the heads they had cut off, or diverted themselves by string-ing them together into a mock rosary.

That Regis had the fearlessness to brave such possibilities as these will seem less strange if we bear one thing in mind. He was a product of the same school of French Jesuit asceticism that was even then preparing and sending to Canada those giants of courage, St. John de Brebeuf, St. Isaac Jogues, and their companions. These daring Black-robes were destined in a few years to astonish the effete minds of that decadent generation with their incredible achievements and sufferings for Christ.

In his dreams, Regis envisioned the likelihood that he might soon be associated with them in the New World. His letter to the General had pledged his all to the hazards of life among the savage nations of Canada and New York, should he be chosen for the work. Meanwhile, Francis began spontaneously to anticipate Vitelleschi's advice that he steel himself against the type of hardships later to be demanded of him.

This new field of action, the Boutières, would furnish occasion amply sufficient for the testing of his courage by the actual endurance of perils every way comparable to those of the Huron Mission. For Francis, there will be no more hiding in hayricks to escape possible torture or even the danger of a violent death at the hands of the Huguenots. These months of midwinter missioning will reveal to him whether he is fit for the mission to Canada, whether he can face willingly for Christ the martyrdom that mission connoted.

With his eyes lighted by the gleam of an ambition soon to be realized, Regis and his companion took leave of their brethren at Aubenas. Along the snow-packed road to the north the two missionaries pressed apace, ascending the ice-sheathed ridges that lay between them and their destination, Le Cheylard. The Count de la Motte, Sieur Bayle, had invited the giving of a mission among his subjects, and had promised shelter for the Jesuits in his mountain château.

Soon the Jesuits beheld the heights of Le Cheylard where the great mountain rose from its central position. Around it, as if silently fixed forever in a picture, churned and whirled the colossal waves in a vast ocean of petrified lava, now covered with its wintry mantle of snow. The crests of these lava waves were the ranges of hills and mountains that radiated out in all directions, rising even higher than Le Cheylard in the region toward the west where soared the loftiest summits of the Cévennes. On the peaks in the immediate vicinity perched the feudal châteaux of the local barons and lords who at times defied even the royal authority, so secure did they feel themselves to be from any attacks.

Internal discord had been responsible for the capture and recapture of Le Cheylard six times during the Religious Wars. Its church had been demolished, while the neighboring priory of Aric, formerly the nucleus of religion in the district, had been ravaged. The town, situated on the opposite side of the Dorne from the château de la Motte, had become a hideout for outlaws and criminals of all classes. Buccaneering noblemen who made their livelihood by plunder could find a safe haven in the mountain fastnesses near by. They and their retinues invaded Le Cheylard for amusement and carousing. The place became a byword for crime and lawlessness. Gun battles, in which a dozen might fall, were not uncommon in the streets. Again, we are told, three or four of these murderous sportsmen had been arrested that year by the king's special justice. The charge against them was that of indulging in one of their favorite pastimes. On a bet of a few sous, they had shot some mountaineers from a distance, as though they were picking off birds on the limb or on the wing.

Regis and his companion learned the unsavory details of this hardy mountain life from the Sieur Bayle, at whose château they made their headquarters. But though the Count de la Motte was able to supply full information about the natives of Le Cheylard, he could venture no more than guesses about those thousands of people who lived in the surrounding country, in inaccessible villages and hamlets at the end of trails that seemed to lead nowhere.

Like the missionaries of New France, Regis and his companion dauntlessly flung themselves into the midst of these primitive people. It was frontier mission work. The Jesuits were obliged to build up their teaching from the very fundamentals of the faith, since a whole generation had passed with no instruction save that of an occasional priest who passed through on his way elsewhere.

Under the direction of the Sieur Bayle, Regis and Broquin

first sought out those families who had Catholic forebears, and who still retained their Catholic sympathies despite the inroads of the Religious Wars. These Francis, with great difficulty, persuaded to trudge with him through the snow to the château for instruction. Some classes were formed there and at other central places in the neighborhood. Gradually the practice of the faith was resurrected and gathered impetus as it progressed.

No sooner had the straying sheep of Le Cheylard been herded back into the fold than Regis entrusted to Father Broquin the routine work of the parish. Off he went in search of wandering Catholics farther afield, high up in the hills or deep in the forests. Disregarding the inclemency of weather that made the snow-covered roads and paths almost as impassable as the Indian trails in Canada, Francis pushed on from hamlet to hamlet in the vicinity, often absenting himself for two or three days at a time. From one direction or another he would return with a handful of willing souls who had agreed to journey to Le Cheylard for further instruction.

The Count de la Motte was astonished by the intrepidity of the young missioner. Francis' daring sallies into the teeth of the wintry blizzards seemed to Bayle imprudent folly, but he could only admire what he could not, humanly speaking, approve.

On one occasion it seemed as if the count's forebodings were justified. Regis had departed for the region of the Château of Don, snow-capped upon a steep, precipitous mountain 3500 feet above the Dorne Valley. Not long after his faring forth, a violent sleet storm blew up. For days it continued, obliterating roads, encasing every landmark in a mask of ice. A full fortnight passed before it abated. Even then, there was no sign of Regis. As the days slipped by, those at Le Cheylard began to be apprehensive. They feared Regis had been trapped in the storm, had perhaps frozen to death. But a week later he reappeared, thinner and more gaunt than ever. His one answer to the count's worried queries and to Broquin's protests against his folly was simply: "In Canada, that would be a routine experience."

Upon occasion, too, Francis encountered still another phase of the mission work he might have to sustain among the Indians. At Le Cheylard, one evening, he was showered with a hail of stones as he passed by the house of some women of evil life whose trade he had vigorously denounced in public. Fortunately, the stones struck no more than glancing blows, and so Regis was not seriously hurt. But his new converts at Le Cheylard looked upon his escape as miraculous. Soon they coupled it with the astounding feats of physical strength and stamina he had performed among them, and with the radiant holiness that vibrated from him; they concluded that he was a saint. To one another and to travelers who passed through the town they began to refer to Regis as "the saint."

Presently, this reputation of being a saint spread on ahead of him into districts he had still to visit. In some it merely hardened the hearts of the people against him all the more. On one of his excursions to the southwest of Le Cheylard, Francis toiled up a rugged, ice-paved hill to a hamlet called Girond. There the bigoted mountaineers obstinately refused to allow him to speak. Notwithstanding the sub-zero weather, they withheld their hospitality in a churlish malevolence more inhuman than that of the Canadian Indians themselves, who at least allowed the missionaries to spend the night in their dismal cabins. To them, Francis was a pariah, but by the time his pleadings were over, a thick winter fog had brought on an early nightfall. Even then, the montagnards were reluctant to show him the road down the mountain. They denied him the loan of a lantern, and adamantly insisted that he could not stay. Finally, however, one of these Girondese, not wishing to condemn

Regis to certain death by forcing him to sleep in the open or to wander down the slippery path to the valley, admitted him to his hut. In a few hours Francis had won him and the few score inhabitants of that snowbound hamlet by the sheer magnetism of his sanctity.

A few miles farther south, at Lachamp-Raphael, the renown of the "saint" gained him quite a different reception. Protected by the barriers of the lava ranges and the thick forests, most of the villages around Lacham-Raphael had been spared the Huguenot invasions. The news that the "saint" was coming lured hundreds of pilgrims thither. Not often did these good people have the consolation of hearing a servant of God and of making their confessions to a saint. Whole villages, we are told, transported themselves to his mission center despite the cold of the early spring. For weeks Francis plied his consoling spiritual trade among these plain, rugged people.

One morning, when Francis had just concluded an exhausting period of labor in the church, he left it to go in quest of a bit of food. As he walked away, a troop of soldiers marched up the steep street and halted before him. Regis stopped, puzzled as to the meaning of these unexpected arrivals. Approaching the priest, the leader of the soldiers doffed his hat and declared: "Mon Père, we have come from a great distance. We have marched the whole night, traveling thirty miles through the woods in order to profit by your instructions. Are you going to refuse us?" Unhesitatingly Francis opened his arms in welcome. His fatigue was forgotten. "Come, my children," he exclaimed; "I press all of you to my heart!" And in the ensuing hours of his priestly ministrations, soldiers and missionary were amply rewarded for their exertions by the blessed peace God breathed upon them.

The essential virility and the winsome humanness of Regis' character become more and more apparent during these months of strength-testing hardships and heart-winning conquests. Hardy mountaineers and hardened soldiers joined each other in paying tribute to the strong man of God who had come among them like an apparition of John the Baptist, preparing the way for Christ. Years later these men of the Boutières would come forward with their testimony to the heroism of the saint. Theirs would be one more set of voices attesting the universal appeal of the amiable saint whose great human heart embraced even the most outcast sinner, sought out the far-wandering sheep of the fold, and lavished his utmost impartially upon all.

To perpetuate the effects of Francis' lightning-swift visitations in the region of Le Cheylard, the Count de la Motte that year presented to the Jesuits an endowment of 16,000 francs for the support of two permanent missionaries. Their station was to be the same modest house at Le Cheylard that Francis had hallowed with his presence. Their duty was to be the gathering in of the harvest for which Regis had sowed such abundant seed.

The sowing in the Upper Boutières had taken eight months, January to August, 1635. Regis and Broquin, in accordance with their instructions, returned to Aubenas in the late summer for their annual retreat and for their future assignments. At the College Francis was given the encouraging letter from Vitelleschi that accepted his volunteering for Canada and advised him to continue preparing himself until he should be summoned.

An occasion for the pursuance of his missionary work soon arose. Bishop de Suze had requested that a mission be sent to that hotbed of Calvinism, the city of Privas and environs in the northern portion of his diocese. The Provincial, Father Martin, committed this to Regis and his companion. By the beginning of September, 1635, Francis was again on the march toward a citadel of Protestantism that had been authorized as such by Richelieu himself. Privas had been

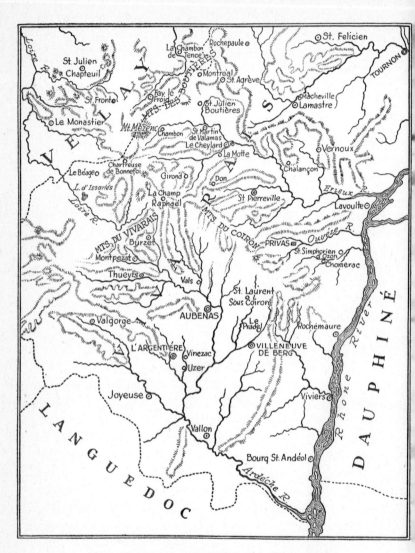

DIOCESE OF VIVIERS IN VIVARAIS

In this mountainous region of South Central France Regis
labored during the years 1634–1636.

sacked and burned by Louis XIII in 1629, and its rebuilding interdicted forever. Nevertheless, when in 1632, the
Huguenots had ingratiated themselves with the Cardinal
by siding with the crown against the rebellious l'Estrange,
governor of Le Puy but then commanding for Montmorency
in Vivarais, they were given permission to repeople Privas
and rebuild their former homes.

Father Broquin had endeavored to give a mission at Privas
some years before 1635, but the only lasting result of it was
that the Huguenots began to call their dogs "Broquin" instead of by their usual names. His reappearance with Regis
did not lend the missionaries any prestige in the city. Their
efforts at preaching in public were hooted down. Everyone
shunned them. The people of Privas were as stolidly hostile
as were the Indians in Huronia.

Nevertheless, the missioners took up their residence among
the few Catholic families that still lived on the outskirts of
the town, and planned a new method of campaign. With
the aid of some funds sent by the Count de la Motte, the
Jesuits inaugurated a silent program of charity to break
down the prejudices of the inhabitants. Working among
the needy and the ill, they quietly spread about the town
the sweet fragrance of Christian mercy. With their own
hands they tended the sick, washed their linens, dressed
their wounds, prepared their meals and medicines. Soon the
townspeople were accustomed to their presence. They were
at least tolerated without any open displays of hostility.

Like the missionaries among the Indians, Regis and his
companion gradually made conquests over the hearts of the
children. Little gifts and presents furnished by Count de la
Motte were accompanied by lessons in the love of God and
in the faith of Christ. The children naturally came back for
more. Before long, groups of them were spending hours at
the feet of the priests, forgetting mealtimes in their absorbed
interest and spellbound attention.

Parents who came to fetch their young ones remained to drink in eagerly the winning discourses of the simple priest. Regis charmed them by the obvious holiness of his speech and demeanor. It soon became a common sight to behold small groups of adults gathered to listen to him. Even the Calvinist ministers began to sense the threat that Regis and his companion now entailed for their own supremacy. In vain they inveighed against the Jesuits. Their fulminations were too obviously contradicted by the holy lives and the holy speech of the priests. By the end of their two months' stay, the fathers had succeeded in conducting a full mission, to which numbers of the Huguenots flocked. The impression made by Regis and Broquin was such that henceforth the place would at least be safe for priests and Catholics, even if conversions were not very numerous. So it was that Bishop de Suze could now appoint one of his own clergy to carry on unmolested where Francis had broken the ground.

On returning to Aubenas in November, 1635, Regis could look back on eleven months of strenuous labor in testing his virtue and physical endurance. To his mind, these months of toil, under circumstances so similar to those encountered by the missionaries in America, seemed sufficient to prove his own physical and moral fitness for that field of endeavor. With the desire, therefore, to spend himself in that particular sphere of activity, Francis again addressed himself to Vitelleschi.

Your Paternity, by a very singular kindness, has been good enough to answer, in regard to my desire for the mission of Canada, that you would take notice of it as soon as it had matured. But now, an entire year has passed since it was born; it has endured the rigor of the whole winter; it has flourished through the whole spring; it has matured all summer and autumn. It is certainly ripe. Do have the goodness to choose it and pluck it, I conjure you, mon Père, in the name of God Himself.

Many, it is true, discourage me from begging for this mission, because it seems to them impossible of attainment; whether they attribute this immense difficulty to my personal incapacity or to some fate that hangs over our Province, I leave to them to decide. For myself, in spite of all, I do not despair of this mission, especially as your Paternity offers me in your letter a great hope of soon being heeded. Therefore, give what you command me to hope for, I beg of you, and command what you will. Aubenas, November 21, 1635.

There would be months of waiting before the couriers could negotiate the difficult winter roads to and from Rome with the letter and its answer. Meanwhile, Francis was not allowed to remain idle nor to interrupt his process of nerving himself for his possible lifework among the Indians. Bishop de Suze was at hand to recommend still another project for his favorite missioner. To St. Agrève, on the northern boundary of the diocese of Viviers — the Roman road that Regis had traveled from Tournon to Le Puy — he was now sent with the commission to lay the groundwork for the re-establishment of the Church there.

The late November weather was rather mild about Aubenas when Regis embarked for his northerly destination. But by the time he had mounted the Boutières to Le Cheylard on the road to St. Agrève, winter had unleashed its chill blasts and had packed the roads in ice. A few days at the château of his good friend the Count de la Motte rejuvenated Francis, while he in turn rejuvenated the faith of his converts thereabouts.

Finally, in early December, Francis once more bade adieu to the Count and set out for the north. Resolutely he pushed on through the treacherous mountain country, reaching St. Agrève at the depths of its winter season. This crossroads town was situated on a high plateau, four thousand feet above the Rhone valley. The snow mercifully hid from Regis the depressing ruins of churches, convents, and Catholic châteaux that had been visible to his eyes ten years previously. Nor had the iron hand of Richelieu, which kept it stripped of its fortifications in retaliation, allowed St. Agrève to become again a Huguenot stronghold. The town still remained bereft of the active commercial life that was the natural outgrowth of its strategic position on the Roman road from the Alps to Western France. It was only a ghost of its former self. And it gave but a bitter, bleak welcome to the missionary. Wintering amid these hostile and savage surroundings was indeed the severest testing yet to be faced by Regis in his effort to prove his fitness for the Canadian mission.

On the edge of the town Francis discovered the small, unprepossessing chapel that the few Catholic families of that suburb had erected for the sporadic visits an outside priest might make to St. Agrève. None of the clergy were in fact anxious to be seen in this town that had been a slaughterhouse for scores of priests. No curé had resided there for the past forty years. Apart from the few nominally Catholic families, the place was still almost a frontier town, lawless, riotous, and the center of attraction for all the drunkards of the region round about.

It was not long before Francis had opportunity to witness with his own eyes the results of St. Agrève's prevailing weakness. Out of the wineshops and cabarets flowed that stream of vices one associates with the uninhibited licentiousness of primitive savagery. Men quarreled with one another in drunken frenzy, and upon the least provocation whipped out sword or pistol to settle the issue in the swiftest possible way. Half-stupefied ruffians found diversion in attacking and robbing wayfarers. Nor did they hesitate to invade homes and vent their passions upon defenseless women and young girls. It was indeed a savage town, and Regis undertook to tame it.

With his characteristic directness, Francis soon laid the ax of his endeavors at the root of St. Agrève's evils — the

drunkenness of its men. But he realized that it did no
appreciable good to storm against that vice in sermons
which the men never bothered to attend. Instead, therefore,
he carried his attack into the very haunts of iniquity themselves. One Sunday Francis boldly entered a tavern where
some Catholics and Calvinists were endeavoring to outdrink
each other. In an attempt to bring them to their senses,
Francis launched into a denunciation of their excesses,
threatening them with the direst of penalties. His words
were not without effect. But the effect was the very opposite
of that he intended to produce. One of the carousers, stung
into drunken rage by the priest's words, struggled to his
feet and lurched toward Regis. With the full force of his
brute strength, he hit him on the jaw. Francis braced himself, took the blow without flinching. Then, smiling with
a suavity that amazed all, he turned the other cheek to his
antagonist, saying, "I thank you, sir, for the blow; I assure
you I merit much more." The drunkard quickly sobered
up at this. He humbly begged pardon for his insult, made
reparation for his degrading conduct. It was noticed thereafter that men respected Francis and patronized his sermons
even more than they did the cabarets.

A month or six weeks were thus spent in reviving the
religious life of St. Agrève. For the rest of the winter and
the early spring, Francis continued his missioning in the
neighborhood of the town, along the Roman road east toward Tournon, above St. Agrève in the valley of the Doux
river, and in the mountains that flanked it. This territory
belonged to the jurisdiction of the bishop of Valence, Jacques
de Gelas de Leberon, who had heard of Regis' prowess and
had invited him to work that portion of his diocese.

Almost everywhere conditions Regis met and remedies
he applied matched those at St. Agrève. In the twenty or
thirty towns of the region, Francis preached and reawakened
the innate Catholicity of the countryfolk.

Few definite details are given in regard to these months of labor. But at one place, Rochepaule, Francis encountered an unusual obstacle to his work. Here the Franciscans had long before erected a monastery high above the Doux on the brow of a steep hill. The people in the town below had eventually tired of climbing the hill for Mass, and had inaugurated the custom of attending it in the small chapel of their cemetery. Some years before, the parishioners had petitioned the bishop that their chapel be constituted a separate parish. The Franciscans, who ministered to the priory church up above and collected tithes from all the people, vigorously opposed the separation. When their lay protector, Jean Rochette, a member of the Third Order, learned that Regis was coming to Rochepaule in the name of the bishop, he feared that the Jesuit might be bringing confirmation of the new parish. Accordingly, he circulated rumors that the unknown preacher soon to arrive was suspected of heresy and was perhaps even a Huguenot spy.

The upshot of it was a marked surprise to Regis who had come through all the Calvinist lairs unscathed. As soon as he approached within a stone's throw of the gates of Rochepaule, he was greeted with a shower of rocks hurled from the city walls. But his rendezvous with death was not yet to come. The stones and the imprecations that accompanied them simply informed him that he was not wanted in that place. Uncomprehendingly and reluctantly, he shook the dust of that forbidding town from his feet and retraced his steps toward the main road. It was not his first rebuff at the hands of good Catholics, nor would it be his last.

But compensation was not far away. He had retreated but a few miles when he met a large band of peasants from a neighboring village. En masse, they were journeying to inhospitable Rochepaule for the mission, having been drawn by the fame of the missionary. "Instruct us! Hear our confessions!" they implored. Francis was deeply touched by their ardor, but he was forced to explain that he could not take them to Rochepaule for his ministrations. That would be to risk another outbreak which might endanger their lives as well. Instead, he directed them to accompany him to his next mission station, St. André, a few miles farther north.

Along the march Francis heeded their pleas and conducted a marching mission with a happy informality. He led the simple folk in the hymns they loved to sing. When they had tired of walking, they sat upon the rocks by the wayside and listened to his touching discourses. The journey resumed, Francis drew one after another of the people apart from the rest of the singing and praying crowd. Placing his arm about his penitent's shoulder, he heard confession and gave absolution as they walked along. It is a happy insight into the character of the man who could thus become all things to all men to win all to Christ. In Regis the gentle condescension and the winsome sweetness of Christ spread through the valley of the Doux, reconquering for him thousands estranged by the warlike bishops of the recent past.

At St. André another vast crowd was awaiting the advent of the man of God. The square of the little village was packed with people who had come from towns within a radius of fifteen or twenty miles. Francis felt more than repaid for the repulse he had suffered at Rochepaule, and he devoted himself unflaggingly to the spiritual needs of his hearers. For the last two weeks of Lent he joined his mission services with the commemoration of the Passion and Resurrection of the Lord. At St. André, it was a true Holy Week that concluded the mission and sent back the people to their homes filled with the joy of the Paschal season. It seemed to be a second spring after the gloomy winter of the Religious Wars and the Huguenot disorders.

Shortly after Easter, Regis himself left St. André for his

new status, Le Puy. There he expected to find an answer from Vitelleschi concerning his request for the Canadian missions. The experiences of the past two winters had confirmed his inner conviction that he was destined to crusade for Christ among the poor and simple, even at the cost of enduring the hardships of the bitterest Canadian wilds.

At the College of Le Puy a communication from the General was handed to him. With eager fingers he opened it and read:

> It is not fate that rules our provinces, and none of them possesses anything as their own so much that they would not share it with others when it is necessary. But the mission of Canada, which has scarcely begun, is not yet provided with sufficient revenue to support as many of Ours as are begging for it by the grace of God. As soon as the occasion is presented and the Canadians clamor for new recruits, I shall remember you. In the meantime, have a care to provide yourself with the necessities of the journey, as I mentioned to you in my last letter — that is to say, with the virtues required and especially with that of patience. (January 15, 1636.)

As Francis put the letter down and thought back over the great blessings God had bestowed on his missionary work during the past two years, the words of his saintly rector at Aubenas, Father Labatut, echoed in his ears with prophetic import: "Canada for you will be the Vivarais." It soothed the sharp pangs of his disappointment at failing to achieve the ambition he had kept before himself like a guiding star through all those months of toil. True, the letter of Vitelleschi did not close the door forever on that ambition, but at least for the near future this Canada of the Vivarais would not cease to afford him equal opportunity for toil and sacrifice. If he were truly ambitious to march for Christ in America, he might still crusade apace with the Blackrobes across the sea, joining them in spirit as he tramped the wilds of the Cévennes in harvesting the fruits of the blood of martyrs like Salès and Saltemouche and de Condrieu. A less authentic saint-to-be might have lapsed into mediocrity when his high ambitions were thus frustrated. Regis, with the unerring intuition of the genuine saint, survived the crisis of this disappointment. Without another regret, he converted the full energy of his ideals and ambition into the requirements of the actual field of labor that had been revealed to him in the Vivarais.

CHAPTER VI

The Sword and the Cross

"IN THE diocese of Velay and in the domain of the seneschal of Le Puy, there are few crimes of treason, but innumerable others, more inhuman, cruel, and frequent than in all the rest of Languedoc together." Thus, in 1633, did Sieur Charles de Machault, Richelieu's intendant for Languedoc, epitomize the city and diocese to which Regis was appointed in the spring of 1636.

Machault had been deputed to investigate conditions in this region after the suppression of the rebellion of Gaston d'Orleans and Montmorency in 1632. Richelieu, though a cardinal of the Church, was interested in the reform of morals and discipline mainly because of their political import. He suppressed the Huguenot party in order to achieve the national unity of France, and he decapitated some of the most elegant Catholic nobles in the kingdom when they threatened to disrupt that unity.

Even at Le Puy there were many quaking hearts, atremble with fear, in November, 1632, after news had arrived that Machault was coming to set up his tribunal there. Besides having been on the side opposed to Henry IV during the troubles of the League, Le Puy had cherished a secret hope that Montmorency would succeed in overthrowing the power of Richelieu in his rebellion and would thereby avert the manifest threat to their municipal liberties and practical autonomy that had been contained in the Cardinal's effort to wrest to himself the taxing of the whole of Languedoc.

Machault, perhaps on secret orders from the Minister, had summarily executed the governor of Le Puy, Claude d'Hautefort, Vicomte de l'Estrange, after his capture by LaForce in a battle during the recent rebellion. At the States Assembly of Languedoc in 1632, Louis XIII deprived the dead governor of all his dignities and honors and declared the titles of his baronies to be forever extinct.

Not a few other nobles of Le Puy and Velay feared a like fate. But, nevertheless, the city prepared to welcome ostentatiously the powerful deputy. By an external show of loyalty they hoped to mitigate his known severity. Accordingly, on November 14, all the city officials in full robes, and the garrison in its military regalia assembled at the southwest gate of St. Gilles to greet Machault with a cannon salute, with speechmaking, and with a parade of escort. The wily intendant, however, slipped into the city with his contingent of cavalrymen through the northwestern entrance. Almost before the officials became aware of it, he was launching on his work of repression. Summonses were served on officials of the seneschal. Royal condemnations of various nobles were published. Swift relentless justice was meted out to numerous criminals of all classes.

By the time he was finished, Le Puy was a cowed city. Machault destroyed a number of feudal châteaux in the vicinity as warnings to the nobility. Within the city he demolished the mansion of a prominent bourgeois lawyer, Sieur Colhabaud, in reprisal for his participation in the rebellion. The electoral assemblies of the guildsmen who yearly voted for the consuls were suspended. Fines and imprisonment were imposed on scores of offenders. Finally, a Roman holiday of bloody executions marked the climax. In the Place du Martouret, where gallows, gibbets, and suitable platforms had been erected, the condemned were some of them hanged, others broken alive on the wheel, others strapped to St. Andrew crosses and burned at slow fires.

Such was Richelieu's method of securing the reform of morals at Le Puy. Needless to say, this wanton terrorism did little to eradicate lastingly the "inhuman, cruel, and frequent" crimes committed there. As soon as Machault departed, the same abuses revived, for the sword of Richelieu in the hands of his intendant was powerless to achieve even the least inner reform.

To accomplish this, there was urgent need of the spiritual and social crusading of a genuine saint. Elsewhere, God had already raised up saints for this mighty work. In Italy, during the preceding century, Saints Pius V, Philip Neri, Ignatius Loyola, Charles Borromeo, and Robert Bellarmine had been in the vanguard of the counterattack on the innovators. In Germany, the Catholic counterreform had been Peter Canisius. In France, at the very time of Regis' apostolate, the extensive influence of St. Francis de Sales and St. Vincent de Paul was being felt. At Le Puy, whither the influence of the other spiritual forces in France did not penetrate, Francis Regis was to spell the difference between the revival and the death of its moribund Catholicism.

But Regis did not descend upon Le Puy like the whirling blizzards of the Cévennes. His first sermons and catechetical instructions there in April, 1636, were like the gentle breath of spring, gradually reviving the hibernating faith of the people. At first only a few attended — those who remembered his cure of young Jacques Guigon or who had heard of his newly acquired reputation in the mountain districts. But soon the warmth of his spirit and the refreshing vigor of his discourses began to attract larger crowds. Within a short time the College church, which was still in an unfinished state, proved to be too small to accommodate all who sought to listen to him. Besides, it was impossible to hold any weekday services during the daytime, since workmen were busily engaged in putting the finishing touches on the edifice. As Brother Martellange, the lay brother architect, predicted that another year or more would be required for its completion, there seemed to be no other alternative but to turn away hundreds from every sermon.

At this juncture, Regis was summoned to the episcopal palace by Bishop Just de Serres. The prelate had undoubtedly learned from Louis de Suze the missionary prowess of the young Jesuit. But he had diplomatically waited to witness with his own eyes the effect of his country preaching on the sophisticated city folks of Le Puy. Now he was convinced that Francis was the man he needed to further the work he had been ineffectively pushing for the past fifteen years.

Like Richelieu, Bishop de Serres was under the illusion that reform of social conditions could be effected by decrees and regulations. As early as 1624, he had legislated for the establishment of the Confraternity of Christian Doctrine in the city, had decreed the adoption of the Roman Liturgy in place of the peculiar Velay Rite, and had enjoined the use of a prayer book which he had published in conformity with Tridentine instructions. But when the opportunity arose for him to prove himself another Borromeo by serving those stricken in the plague of 1629, the bishop took an ill-timed vacation and shut himself up in one of his châteaux miles away.

Withal, Just de Serres was decidedly an improvement on the former counts of Velay who had occupied the bishop's throne in the interludes between their military expeditions and their pleasure excursions. De Serres was sincerely zealous for the social uplift of his people. He had emphasized again the fundamental source of their spiritual and social rehabilitation when he issued a decree shortly before Francis' arrival, stating:

> The visitation recently made by us in the greater part of our diocese has caused us to recognize, sufficiently and with great regret, the deplorable ignorance of our diocesan people concerning

Christian doctrine and the principal mysteries of our religion. Desiring therefore to provide against an evil so general and so ruinous that almost all others take their origin from it, we enjoin on the rectors, pastors, and vicars of our diocese to teach to the Christian people every Sunday, the Lord's Prayer, the Hail Mary, the Apostles' Creed, the Commandments of God and of His Church, and the principal points of religion necessary to salvation; and we wish this to be observed in this city, in the Church of Saint-Pierre-le-Monastier, about an hour before midday, whither the people will be called by the sound of the bell. (May 24, 1635.)

Despite the fact that St. Pierre-le-Monastier belonged to the Benedictine monastery of the city, the bishop commandeered it for his catechetical program because it was in the heart of the busiest section of the town. Ten years before, he had vindicated before the Parliament of Toulouse his right to make suchlike regulations even for the churches of exempt religious orders in his diocese. Once more he exercised this right in connection with Regis.

Upon his admission into the bishop's office in the palace at the top of the hill near the cathedral, Francis was warmly greeted by Just de Serres. From the very first, the bishop conceived an admiration for the young priest and felt that he was acting wisely in committing to his care the catechetical work at St. Pierre-le-Monastier. Francis willingly accepted it, for the church was much larger than the Jesuit church, having been built in the time of the great pilgrimages to Le Puy and designed to handle the overflow crowds that could not gain admittance to the cathedral on the hilltop. De Serres had to inform Regis that even his episcopal decree of 1635 had not brought the crowds back to St. Pierre. Like many of the great churches of France, it had become deserted save for the handful of pious women who attended Mass there. To Regis was assigned the task of drawing the nominal Catholics once more to the Benedictine church and of converting them into practical, fervent ones.

While continuing his regular course at the College church,

Francis threw himself also into the new work at the "down-town cathedral." As the noon bells rang out the signal for his instructions there, burghers and peasants, artisans and loafers, nobles and beggars, and even some religious from the various convents about the town sauntered in from the crowded districts around Martouret Place and the other market places near by. Into the immense nave of the church they poured, filling spaces that had not been hallowed by worshipers for centuries. The overflow of the crowd pushed on into the tribunes, the choir, the side chapels. In the course of the next months, the Benedictines were obliged to cede their own stalls to the populace and to erect temporary pews in the sanctuary.

During the summer the concourse was even greater. The eager audience jammed into the unused balconies up above. Some even found seats on the beams and crosspieces of the vaulted ceiling and arches, where they hung silently and breathlessly upon the words of the speaker down below.

Nor were the listeners confined to any one of the social classes of Le Puy. Drawn by the novelty of a reputed saint in the flesh, the nobility came out of idle curiosity, but stayed to be enthralled by the magnetism of his personality, and thereafter returned regularly to fall under the spiritual in-fluence everyone felt radiating from the unpretentious Jesuit. The lower classes made up the majority of his congregations, but here and there appeared the finery of a rich merchant and his wife, the black habit of a priest or the traditional colors of the religious order garbs.

On occasion as many as five thousand were counted in the church at one time. During the course of the spring and summer of 1636, Francis rejuvenated the religious life of Le Puy so much so that there were few out of the 15,000 within the walls and the 20,000 in the environs who had not come under his influence. Confessions were heard in un-precedented numbers. Mass attendance improved at the cathedral, at the smaller churches of St. Vosy, St. Agrève, St. George, and St. Pierre, as well as at the other places of worship in the environs. One witness described the phenomenon as "unbelievable."

Yet, what went they out to see and to hear? What kind of a man was this new John, making straight the paths of the Lord? It was something one can easily appreciate but with difficulty describe. The people who heard Regis found it impossible to put into words the full picture of their apostle. Even before the ecclesiastical tribunal that was investigating his sanctity for beatification years later, they could do no more than testify that he had stood before them and entranced them by the hour with his simple, direct discourses. He was a holy man of God, they averred, and when he spoke from the depths of his soul with the glow of his love for God and his hatred for sin, he carried them along in a kind of transport of spirit. It was Christ speaking in him, with the same straightforward conviction, the same unerring certainty, the same heart-warming affection that had drawn those uncultured Jews of long ago and made Christians out of them.

This, rather than any exterior methods devised by human ingenuity, was the secret of his appeal. Fortunately or unfortunately, nothing of the actual text or subject matter of his catechism lessons has come down to us. But even if some of the sermons had been transcribed, it is doubtful whether the words would have caught that indefinable something which, through his simple, commonplace language, penetrated to the heart of his auditors.

Nor is any light thrown upon his effectiveness by the traditions of the methods he employed betimes. La Broue, the first biographer, mentions that he sometimes trained children to appear on the altar to sing hymns or to recite devout poems he had composed — a trite enough device at best. Again, Francis is said to have used the Socratic method of question and answer to avoid monotony, sometimes asking the questions himself, and at other times allowing individuals in the congregation to question him. Of course, these formal and informal methods did require much prayerful preparation and forethought. But like the Curé d'Ars, whose sermons were no great literary achievements, Francis spoke in the everyday language of the Gospel and of his audience, and in doing so the fruit of his long hours of solid prayer welled forth from the abundance of his Christlike heart.

To draw all things to Christ, Francis nailed his body and soul to a cross of self-denial and mortification. Like the Curé d'Ars, Regis allotted at most three or four hours for sleep at night. Long before dawn he was in the confessional to glean the harvestings of the previous day's activities. To his side penitents crowded for six or seven hours in succession, finally dropping off at about eleven o'clock. He then said Mass and gave Communion to long lines of the faithful. As soon as Mass was over, he had to hurry to St. Pierre for his midday services or to his other social work, usually without thinking of anything to eat or drink. In the afternoon at St. Pierre there was the same endless round of confessions, unless he were called away for some special duties outside. Often enough, it was five or six o'clock in the afternoon before he partook of any sustenance, and then his meal consisted of some dry bread, some apples, and some water. He jokingly asserted that the Blessed Virgin had assured him he would not be harmed by drinking water exclusively and never touching wine outside of Mass. These were but a few of the numerous details in his life of self-crucifixion that fructified his apostolate and rendered it possible for him to meet and vanquish spirits such as are not driven out save by prayer and fasting.

As Regis persevered in this costly life of zeal and sacrifice through the months and years of his apostolate, the sphere of his influence continually widened. He was a grain of wheat that fell into the stony ways of Le Puy and with his daily dying to himself and to his love of ease and comfort, his personal activity became more and more fruitful.

Out of his catechetical labor in the College church and in St. Pierre's, blossomed most of Regis' social work in the city that had been the Lourdes of the Middle Ages. He had not been teaching long before the plight of the vast number of poor in the city attracted his solicitude. Frequently, one of those bundles of rags would slip into St. Pierre while the Jesuit was preaching and would take a place in an aisle or upon a bench. The people close to him soon were made aware of the malodorous presence, and were quick in moving away, leaving the poor wretch self-consciously alone. In order to spare the poor this added humiliation, Francis arranged special services for them at the College church. There, twice or three times a week, he devoted himself exclusively to their instruction, and afterward doled out what alms he had collected for them.

As the summer of 1636 progressed, Regis began to be called the *Père des pauvres*, "father of the poor." Like Christ, he was not content merely to preach the Gospel to them, but he likewise strenuously endeavored to alleviate their deplorable destitution. Many of them who in years past had eked out a meager existence by odd jobs, were now bereft of the means of livelihood by the general depression consequent upon the formal declaration of war upon Hapsburg Spain and Austria, in May, 1635. Richelieu's campaign of aggrandizement had impoverished the whole of France. In the Velay where, in addition to the tripling of the taxes, soldiers were quartered while on their way to fight in the Rhineland, the straits to which the poor people sank were pitiful.

Still another of Richelieu's schemes multiplied the sufferings of the lower classes. This year the Cardinal renewed the policy that had delivered bushels of gold coins, to the sum of almost a million dollars, into the hands of Gustavus Adolphus in 1631 and 1632. To aid another Protestant ruler in a war on Catholic Austria, Richelieu in 1635 compacted to supply Bernard of Weimar with upwards of a million dollars a year. Nobles, middle-class people, and even the poorest were squeezed of their hoardings to meet the new obligations. The inevitable result of exporting so much money was the debasement of the value of coins. Bankers began to mint smaller denominations of money, which counterfeiters soon duplicated in great quantities. A panic of distrust spread over the country. None of the smaller coins was honored. And at Le Puy the local chronicler Jacmon lamented that in 1636, "there was a great tumult and commotion among the common people. Merchandise and edibles became dearer by one fourth. You might have seen poor artisans and peasants weeping, for they had nothing but farthings and these coins could secure neither bread nor salt nor anything else. Because of this they were dying of starvation."

Their one salvation was in the "father of the poor," Père Regis, the priest with the kindly eyes, and with ways as gentle in face of human suffering as they were thunderous against the evils of sin. As at Montpellier, Francis organized a group of charitable ladies to assist him in caring for the destitute. In a little book similar to that being used by Monsieur Vincent de Paul in Paris at this time, Francis wrote the names of his poor clients. Each of these was assigned to the care of one or other of the ladies in his organization. They were to visit the poor, to supply them with food and other necessaries. For the homeless paupers, Francis arranged that one of his richer co-workers should prepare food for them at her own home. The sign of appointment to this task was the arrival of a huge cauldron, to be used in cooking the soup or stew for the next day. This was the origin of the soup kitchen that continued for centuries to ward off starvation from the paupers of the city.

It is a distinct tribute to Francis' spiritual power that he could thus secure cooperation for the aid of the poor in such a city as Le Puy. For it had been so infested by professional beggars who in times past battened on the piety of the pilgrims to the holy shrine, that the natives had come to suspect and even refuse the deserving poor when they begged for an alms.

Nevertheless, Francis' organized charity, even when extended to the poor of the whole town during his first year, was not cursed with the evil of impersonal bureaucracy. He himself remained the guiding spirit of the whole enterprise, the sympathetic and patient listener to every story of distress, the tender father of the poor who made them feel that, in receiving this alms or service, they were but sharing in the goods furnished by their heavenly Father. In preaching to poor and rich alike he emphasized the Divine Providence of God in establishing and allowing the different conditions of men so that He might sanctify some by charity and others by poverty. Over and over again Francis insisted that God had placed the rich in their wealth only that they might be stewards of His kingdom on earth, providing for the poor who could not provide for themselves. Regis continually performed the duties of a go-between, begging from the rich to give to the poor. From door to door in the well-to-do section of the town, Francis personally went in quest of alms for the poor, and, even in the hard times then prevalent, he would not depart without some gift, either in money or in kind. For these latter, the young priest secured a special storeroom at the College. Its stock of clothes, furniture, beds, and incidentals of all descriptions was endlessly being depleted and replaced, for Francis learned that his givers were much more generous with these unneeded secondhand articles than they were with money — and the poor were equally willing to receive them.

This touch of personal service endeared Francis to the poor as a kind and generous father. Whenever they saw him threading his way through the evil-smelling slums, they would gather about him, follow at his heels, struggle with one another to be near him. Witnesses later recounted this ardent attachment as something more than a manifestation of mob greediness. The paupers genuinely worshiped their protector who brought to them besides mere physical assistance a spiritual comfort that restored some of the medieval merriment they had long since lost.

Thus, from the very start of his social work at Le Puy in 1636, Regis became an intimate part of the lives of the underprivileged and neglected "third estate." But despite his indefatigable labors for them, he managed to devote his energies also to other fields of apostolic endeavor that stemmed from his catechism teaching.

During the harvest time of that year, Le Puy was a center of bustling activity by day and gay festivities by night. The roving bands of harvesters, who moved from section to section of Velay as the crops of different altitudes matured, resorted to Le Puy as the hub of their operations during the weeks of the harvest season. Men and girls worked side by side in the fields to earn their pittances and then rushed back to the city to enjoy the many tempting diversions there offered.

Regis was not unaware of the perennial dangers to the virtue of the young peasant girls who were kept away from home for these long periods. But instead of allowing things to take their course as in former years, Francis acted promptly to cope with the situation. On Sundays and holidays, at the street corners and in the various squares about town, he assembled these transient workers and discoursed to them on their duties to be observed notwithstanding their transiency. The results were quite singular. Women and girls on their own initiative shunned the company of the dissipating men, sought lodgings in hostels away from them, and even gathered into work bands of their own in order to avoid all occasions of disaster. One particularly curious person followed up his investigation of this phenomenon and reported his admiration for the girls in this wise: "In spite of the cajoleries of brazen libertines who pursued them for miles with offers of money, they resisted with determination, so deeply fixed on their souls was the salutary advice of the servant of God. I saw it with my own eyes, and I know the rogues themselves, though I prefer not to name them."

But it had not been so in former years. In his confessional after sermons or instructions, Francis undoubtedly heard divers sad stories that had begun in the gaiety and celebration of the harvest fiesta or the Carnival season. The merry-making and dancing, the love songs and the freely flowing wine had gone to the heads of many unsuspecting girls. Forgetting themselves under the spell of the witching nights, they had lent willing ears to the empty promises and seductive entreaties of the city's experienced swains. Too late they rudely awakened to the sordidness of the slavery they had embraced.

As at Montpellier, Francis soon encountered numerous cases in which the unhappy girls appealed to him to rescue them from their sad lot. Their shame and disgust with themselves, their yearning to be freed, and their tears of contrition were, like Magdalene's, the measure and token of their sincerity. For one after another of these penitents, Francis provided a haven in the home of a rich widow who lived alone in the city. Before the summer was over, she had custody over more than ten, while a few more were likewise safely lodged with some other generous people.

Amid all of his pressing occupations Francis made time to visit these wards of his almost every day and to give them at least a brief instruction. His personal interest in their progress and welfare, as well as the mildness and mercy with which he treated them, were in stark contrast to the current methods of dealing with their correction elsewhere in France. Laws that cannot have been other than sadistic were in force at various places. In 1635, probably under the instigation of Richelieu, statutes had been enacted at Paris providing that prostitutes should be arrested, whipped in public, shaved of their hair, and exiled. At Bayonne, the practice was to slash off their noses, cage them in iron boxes, and then duck them in the river. Even at Le Puy, the law had been passed condemning them to be driven through the streets in their chemises while police and people pursued them with lashes and beat them mercilessly.

It goes without saying that these brandishings of the sword of civil authority were absurdly futile toward curbing the evil. The prostitutes were merely driven deeper into hiding in their dens of vice, and were thereby confirmed all the more in their way of life.

But in the name of the cross at the foot of which stood, among the few friends of Christ still faithful to Him, the penitent Magdalene, Francis Regis accomplished permanent rehabilitation of numerous broken creatures. He intended to push still farther into remedying the evils of the local underworld, but before he could progress beyond these initial conquests, he received another missionary summons from the bishop of Viviers, Louis de Suze.

Through the Provincial, his now devoted episcopal friend requested the services of Regis for a mission at the town in his diocese that was closest to Le Puy, namely, Fay-le-Froid. Besides, there were some towns in the diocese of Valence which Francis had promised to revisit that year. Others on the route there and back were due for missions because of their spiritual subjection to the College of Le Puy.

In September of that year, 1636, Regis consequently once more set out for a winter of toil in the mountain country.

With his companion, Brother Bensac, Francis paused at various towns along the road to preach and to catechize. Thus they plodded on by slow stages up the meandering mule path that gradually mounted up to the region of Fay-le-Froid, a thousand feet higher than the upland plateau of the Velay. Ever before them rose the highest peak of the Cévennes, Mt. Mézenc, in whose shadow lay their destination.

It was a sight to chill the heart of any but the most indomitable of men. Emerging suddenly from the forests of pine and beech and chestnut that grew almost up to the level of the town, Francis and his companion were confronted with a slatternly, harsh-looking group of squat houses, huddled together on the mountain crag for security against the wolves and marauders. Fay-the-cold it was called, and it amply justified its name. Without the least protection from the blizzardlike winds that constantly roared through it, Fay was already buried in midwinter by the early fall snowstorms and sleetings. Though the snow and the icicles, hanging like spangled pendants, softened somewhat the rough edges of the town's flat roofs, it was a bleak, dismal place.

Yet precisely with towns such as this are Regis' winter missions traditionally associated. Their rugged, fantastic scenery furnishes the backdrop for most pictures of Francis and silhouettes his figure boldly by contrast. It must be admitted, however, that Fay-le-Froid is the utmost extreme in severity of weather conditions encountered by Regis. Here indeed they verged on the incredible. Here huge stones were placed upon the housetops to prevent the snarling winds from wolfing them off. Here the large cross in the market place was held to earth only by the aid of guyropes that were anchored in the living rock. Here, too, when the months of snowing and sleetings had buried all, the inhabitants were wont to burrow tunnels through the snow from house to house in order to keep up some bit of human intercourse.

To have even ventured upon a mission during the winter here at Fay seems as quixotic as to attack windmills. It might be understandable down in the comparatively sheltered regions of Velay, but up here it was almost unthinkable that a people who had long lived in indifference to their religion could be pried away from their firesides for any purpose whatever. Still, Francis, impelled by his desire to break the Bread of Life with these soulless people, sprang into action despite the forbidding appearances of Fay-the-cold.

The resident Mass priest, Jean Nicholas, who three years before had welcomed Bishop de Suze for a brief two-day stay during his summer visitation, secured lodgings for Regis and Bensac at the house of the widow Sourdon, with whom the bishop himself had stayed. The good widow, whose husband had been the law in Fay before his death, seems to have been a most hospitable hostess, in so far as her limited means would allow. Francis repaid her in a most remarkable fashion, not by money, but by obtaining for her a gift that all of her money had been powerless to purchase for the past five or six years.

Madame Sourdon's fourteen-year-old son, Claude, was blind. Some inflammation had seized the lad's eyes when he was eight. The parents had then done everything possible to arrest the disease. Claude had been subjected to the treatment of the best doctors in Le Monastier and Le Puy. According to the boy's own words, the famous Doctor Lyonnet at the latter place had prescribed "bleedings, purges, cauteries, suction cups," and all the other maddening devices of contemporary Physick. The exquisite torments caused by these remedies had almost driven the lad out of his mind. Nor did they succeed in preventing the disease from doing its deadly work. Claude had become totally blind. Long before Regis' coming, young Sourdon had been unable to discern even the strongest lights held before his pain-racked eyes. Moreover, the malady seemed bent on destroying him utterly. Since his return from Le Monastier, where a noted Doctor Benac had pronounced his illness incurable, Claude had been confined to a bed of suffering.

One day not long after the start of the mission, the young lad was moaning heart-rendingly under the continual torturings of his affliction. Francis, who had just returned from church where he had said Mass before a handful of people, felt once more that God would hear his prayer for Claude as He had for young Jacques Guigon. Nevertheless the priest whispered to Claude's little sister, "Come, let us pray together for him." A short while the two knelt at the sick boy's bed and stormed heaven for his cure. Suddenly, the writhing figure became quiet. Claude's moaning ceased, his pains vanished. He sat up, wrenched the bandages from his eyes, and found his sight restored. His mother came running at his cry of glee. She could hardly believe her own eyes. Yet her boy was really cured. Nor could Francis escape the credit for the miracle. Claude was convinced that Regis was his benefactor. He became from that moment the most ardent champion of the holy Jesuit, and retained that ardor, as he retained his eyesight, unimpaired for the next sixty years of his life.

Soon the whole town had heard of the miracle. News of it spread to near-by hamlets as well. From one of these a helpless peasant who had likewise been blind for years was hurriedly brought to Fay over the treacherous wintry roads. Again it happened. The man's sight was restored when Francis prayed over him. He, too, returned to his home singing the praises of the man of God.

Thereafter Francis had his hands full with the crowds that flocked to his mission services. Nothing less than a pair of miracles was required to break down the prejudices of the people, Catholics and Huguenots alike. A few score years before, all Fay had been antagonized when the faith and the domination of Velay had both been forced upon the city at the point of the sword by Bishop Saint-Nectaire.

As the count of Velay, the prelate had laid siege to Fay with his troop of five hundred musketeers and his battery of cannoneers. The latter had quickly pulverized the resistance of the poorly armed natives. Forced to surrender, they threw themselves on the mercy of Saint-Nectaire who had been one of the few bishops of the realm not in sympathy with the massacre of St. Bartholomew's Day.

Saint-Nectaire had entered the conquered town in full panoply of war, drums beating, flags flying. The giant figure of the warrior-bishop arrayed in an ominous suit of black armour and astride a full-sized charger headed the advancing column. At sight of him, the crushed populace seethed anew with hatred for him and for what his heavy mace symbolized. But in stolid composure they awaited his will. The terms were soon proclaimed. In punishment for their rebellion, the people were commanded to attend his open-air victory Mass, after which the leaders of the revolt would be hanged on the forked gallows erected near the altar.

It was an unforgettably impressive scene. From the first cannon salvo that signaled the start of the Mass until the last rebel leader had ceased his futile squirming at his halter, the people stood in glum silence, only their eyes flashing the undying hate in their souls. No reverence for the Mass or the bishop subdued their spirits, but rather the presence of the triple ring of musketeers that girded the altar with guns leveled at the crowd, ready for the least show of further rebellion.

Since that time Fay had been as cold toward the Catholic faith as were the wintry winds in the face of the wayfarer. Every bit of the fire of Regis' burning zeal for the cross and all the miraculous power his love for that cross could evoke, were needed to melt that icy reserve. But just as Francis had conquered at Le Puy where the sword of Richelieu had been ineffective, so he triumphed at Fay where the sword of Bishop Saint-Nectaire had utterly defeated the purpose of the cross he wore upon his breast.

Conversions were numerous at Fay during that mission of 1636. Francis' powers were taxed to the uttermost in order to gather in the fruits of his miracles and his sermons. Claude Sourdon remembered years later how his mother used to send him to the church at nightfall in order to beg Father Regis to cease the labors he had engaged in since dawn, and to come home for some dinner. But the multitude of penitents who hemmed in the zealous missionary prevented him from leaving usually until late at night. Even then, Madame Sourdon could prevail on Francis to partake of very little in the way of nourishment, and never the least wine.

Good Madame Sourdon was hard pressed for ways of showing her gratitude toward Francis for the cure of her son. Her only recourse was to marvel at it over and over, and exult in glowing terms about it whenever Francis was in earshot. At length one day, Francis politely quieted her by remarking: "Now my dear lady, you should realize that as often as God converts a hardened sinner, He performs a much grander miracle." Nor would he allow her to indulge in boastfulness about her guest by means of allusions to the startling conversions that occurred. Francis checked her with the simple statement of fact: "It is not I who do it; it is God."

Not even the power of God's grace itself, however, could triumph over the perversity of some of the Fay inhabitants. True, Francis had remarkable success in settling family difficulties and in breaking up a number of illicit unions by touching the hearts of the couples to repentance or by threatening them with the consequences of their sins. But one particular pair in the neighborhood continued in their evil ways despite Francis' earnest pleas. Claude Sourdon saw Regis visit them often, plead with them for hours at a time, pray for them upon his return to the Sourdons', and even shed bitter tears over their obduracy. It was all in vain. Some days later, as Claude narrates, divine justice smote one of them, for in an argument with another person, the obstinate sinner was shot and killed instantly. After that, Francis had less difficulty in persuading other couples either to regularize their unions by marriage or to break them off.

Besides his work at Fay, Francis did yeoman service in ranging about the neighboring territory to give missions and to bring the Sacraments to strayed and fallen-away Catholics. Details are lacking in regard to his other stations, save for a few names like Saint-Symphorien, Chanéac, Champclause, and one of the numerous towns called Saint-Julien. Through all of them the missionary, his cross upraised, crusaded with the zeal of those medieval heroes. Even where he paused only for lightninglike visits in out-of-the-way hamlets, his memory was indelibly imprinted on the minds of the country people. Traditions of his power remained for centuries, while the memory of the military expeditions that had tried to re-establish Catholicism by the sword faded into oblivion. Once again it was true that the cross was mightier than the sword.

CHAPTER VII

To the Rescue of the Oppressed

THE winter of 1636–37 had been one of seething unrest for France. In the north, the invasion of Picardy by hordes of Spanish horsemen from the Netherlands had prostrated the population. In the east, Richelieu's push to France's natural boundaries had deluged the frontier in blood. Elsewhere, as in Gascony, Poitou, Limousin, and Angoumois, internal strife erupted into open rebellion at the excessive oppression of the taxes and the military levies. Though Richelieu had crushed these uprisings with an iron hand, the outlook was ominous. The great Cardinal for a time contemplated, in the spring of 1637, peace moves that might have spared Europe the last ten of the Thirty Years' War. But nevertheless, at the cost of untold misery for his people, the Minister doggedly pursued his wars.

Meanwhile, in April, Francis Regis, accompanied by his faithful companion, Brother Bensac, re-entered Le Puy to continue battling in the social struggle he had initiated the year before. He, too, hoped to extend the boundaries of his conquests, but by peaceful means that would rescue the oppressed from their intolerable burdens.

No sooner had he reached the city than he learned that much of the ground gained was already in danger of loss. The generous lady, into whose care Francis had committed the ten penitents previously referred to, called on him at the College, and summarily announced that he must make other provisions for his wards or else she would throw them out on the streets.

Astonished at this abrupt reversal of her good resolutions, Regis asked for an explanation. This was soon sobbed out in the midst of tears. One of the Jesuits at the College, she felt, had been disrespectful to her in some remarks he had made, perhaps in joke, about what her house had now become. Francis did not discuss the fact. He was well aware of the irresistible tendency of the French, even of French Jesuits, to utter a *bon mot*. The offense had undoubtedly been given. But still he pleaded with the lady not to take offense. "My child," he said, "why must you avenge yourself on God for the displeasure men have caused you?"

"It is not only that," she replied; "those wretched women stole from me; they were eating me out of house and home." As a matter of fact, even her relatives, who were waiting vulturelike to pounce upon her fortune when she died, had complained publicly of her lavish expenditures on behalf of her penitents. But in the end, Francis persuaded her, by an appeal to her love for Christ, to continue her harboring of these homeless girls.

The incident nevertheless pressed upon Regis the necessity of basing his rehabilitation of these women upon a more solid foundation. If they were to be properly guarded from outside occasions and from their own proclivities, they would require constant spiritual care and well-planned character training. This was impossible with ten of them in one part of the city and others distributed here and there in different places. All could not be reached by their director with sufficient regularity. Besides, the same danger as had almost thrown them out upon the streets might again threaten them each time Francis was absent on his missions.

There was only one solution to the difficulties. Francis decided to establish a refuge for his penitents where all could be grouped under a single roof, in care of a trained guardian. As a precedent and a guide, he had the example of St. Ignatius himself, who had founded the House of St. Martha at Rome as a haven for the women he snatched from its brothels.

To Bishop Just de Serres Francis first presented his proposal. This eager listener favorably acquiesced in the Jesuit's reasons and heartily concurred in the conclusion Francis had reached after long prayer and careful thought. The best interests of the people at large and of imperiled youth in particular would be well served by the establishment of this institution. It was common knowledge about the town, even among the artisans, one of whom, Antoine Jacmon, chronicled it in his memoirs, that the social diseases consequent upon the dissipation of the times were making appalling inroads on the health of Le Puy's younger generation. The house of refuge might save both the youths and the penitents from further disaster. It was a social necessity.

Bishop de Serres, already an enthusiastic admirer of Regis, gave his official approval to the project. He promised his full cooperation and aid, and instructed his vicar-general, Pierre Le Blanc, to help Regis with the details of the foundation.

When all these had been thrashed out, the financial arrangements completed, the house chosen, the directress agreed upon, Francis finally approached the rector for his advice and consent. If Father Verthamond, his former novice master, had still been at the head of the College of Le Puy, Francis would have had no difficulties at all. But in 1635, his place had been taken by a scrupulous, crotchety, suspicious religious, Father Sebastian Umeau. Regis was fully aware, as were most of the other members of the community, that Umeau would never have been appointed Superior if the plague of 1629–33 had not decimated the Jesuit ranks, thereby necessitating the acceptance of men unqualified for office both by temperament and by spiritual outlook.

Umeau, a lean, sallow-faced individual, was aware of his own shortcomings to a certain extent. He had accepted the rectorship reluctantly under protest that his health would not stand the rigors of the climate of Le Puy, nor his nerves the strain of managing the large institution. His consent had finally been given after five months of dilatory excuse-making. Exasperated by Umeau's insistence that he be commanded under holy obedience to accept the post, the General was about to appoint another man when Umeau finally capitulated and submitted to the yoke of office as a penance. For the next three years he succeeded in making himself a penance for the rest of the community as well, and upon Regis himself the weight of this penance fell heaviest.

Unfortunately, Francis had given the rector what might be regarded as ample reason to doubt his prudence. Umeau was not bound to presuppose that his subject was a saint, and yet Francis, under the impulse of perhaps special inspirations, had acted in ways that seemed most unusual. To a man like Umeau they could appear as no less than outright imprudence.

Right down the street from the College an incident had occurred that might well have immediately antagonized any superior. Two women were one day arguing vociferously — not to say blasphemously as well — in the presence of a group of passers-by. Francis chancing to come along at just that time, approached the shrews and cautiously endeavored to soothe them with words of appeasement. But not a word could he get in, no matter how abbreviated. They continued to bicker nose to nose, shaking fingers and fists in each others faces, and making the echoes ring with oaths and profanity. The blasphemies stung Francis to the quick. Stepping aside to the gutter, he scooped up two handfuls of mud (one shudders to think of their chemical content!) and then, returning to the battlers, deftly inserted the compound into the open mouth of each of the minxes. The crowd roared. The women, coughing and spewing, fled to their houses. But the public blasphemous offenses against God for which the current legal penalty was execution or the cutting out of the tongue, were stopped. Moreover, strange to say, the women later became friends. Yet one cannot doubt but that the rector was purple with indignation when he heard of this bizarre method of cementing friendships.

On another occasion, while the Carnival carousals were in progress, a masker passed by Regis and gave vent to a string of drunken oaths. Francis cautioned him to desist. But the ribald reveler merely increased his picturesque imprecations. Whereupon Francis drew back his hand and roundly slapped the culprit. Stunned momentarily by the blow, the man came to his senses. Taking off his mask, he knelt at the feet of Regis and penitently said: "Father, I am a fool; pray for me." The priest's muscular Christianity had secured still another conversion. But again, that method of spiritual therapy brought down the disfavor and criticisms of the carping rector.

Indeed, the whole of Francis' impetuous and forthright manner of acting was disagreeable to the scrupulous Umeau. Even in his sermons, Regis could be emphatic in terms that he knew to be effective, but others thought rather ill-advised. He fearlessly attacked abuses in high places and in low, thundering against them with a vehemence proportioned to their heinousness. But his critics were obliged to admit that he achieved results, and that he was a holy man, closely united to the same Christ who had inveighed in similar terms against the Scribes and Pharisees.

Umeau, cloistered like a hermit and out of touch with reality, had scant sympathy with the active life Regis led.

The rector affected a gravity and dourness he believed imperative to the religious life, and condemned as worldliness anything that was humanly agreeable. On the other hand, Francis, we are plainly told by his first biographer, "purposely wore a happy countenance, and his presence was so gay, so smiling, so frank, and so familiar that he was sometimes despised by those who judge only by the eyes. Courteous to the poor, amicable to all small folk, respectful of the great, he had an unbelievable charm and attractiveness for every kind of disposition." Unhappily, all of Regis' genuinely human and spiritual qualities were lost on the rector. Umeau remained apprehensive lest the unrestrained zeal and energy of the comparatively young priest precipitate trouble and bring disgrace upon the Society.

Accordingly, when Francis approached him with the proposal to open a refuge for reclaimed penitents, Father Umeau became a porcupine of objections. "You'll have the city up in arms against you," he stormed. Regis admitted that certain people would be inconvenienced, but it was for their own ultimate good. "Where will you get resources in these times?" the rector expostulated. Francis outlined the details for him. A rich benefactor had promised to buy the house and the appurtenances. In a short while, the place would be self-supporting. "Whom will you find to direct such an institution?" Umeau queried. Patiently, Francis mentioned those whom he and the vicar-general had chosen.

Nevertheless, the rector procrastinated. He wanted time to think the matter over. He tried to temporize for fear of displeasing certain influential persons who openly patronized the quarter, and notwithstanding this, were contributing funds to help Umeau complete the church he was erecting.

Francis pressed him with the fact of the bishop's support and approval. He urged the propitiousness of the time for beginning now a work which would have so great an influence on the spiritual and social uplift of the town.

Finally, the rector consented. He was dubious about the feasibility of the whole undertaking, but at least he could blame the bishop if it ended in wholesale trouble with the citizenry.

Armed with these official approbations, Francis lost no time in starting the enterprise that summer of 1637. The house on the Rue de Montferrand, up near the hospital and the cathedral at the top of the town, was purchased and quickly put in readiness. The zealous and competent directress was inducted into her duties, and the various girls scattered about town in the homes that had been their havens were now assembled and lodged together under one roof, and given a definite rule and routine to follow.

According to Antoine Jacmon, the local chronicler, the gendarmes of the city aided Regis in rounding up further recruits. But for the most part, Francis himself attended to that phase of the work as well. It became an *on-dit* at Le Puy that each time Father Regis was seen leaving the College hurriedly, one could be sure that there was an urgent sick call or an occasion of rescuing an oppressed girl and placing her in the refuge.

Episodes like those at Montpellier were repeated. Between his regular catechism classes at St. Pierre and at the College church, Francis found time to ferret out unwilling prisoners in the dens of iniquity flourishing in the slums of Le Puy. Oftentimes, one penitent would disclose the unhappy state of another girl who still remained in the toils of a lecherous master. In other cases, neighborhood gossip aided him. Houses crowded as close together as those that barnacled the side of Mount Anis could hardly keep their secrets from the prying eyes and eager ears of the neighbors.

One day Francis was apprised of the brutal traffic engaged in by one pander who held a girl prisoner in his house. Courageously, Francis went to the designated dwelling and called for the landlord to demand the girl's release. At first,

Regis in most civil terms entreated the man to deliver up his unwilling captive. Abashed at the proposal, the man feigned amazement, shrugged his shoulders and hypocritically disavowed any knowledge of so evil a business. Francis then requested to be allowed to inspect a certain room with him, in order to verify or disprove the accusation leveled against the landlord. But the man stoutly denied that he had any such baggage in his house, nor would he allow Regis to investigate the premises.

It was then that the French in Francis asserted itself. He felt certain that the wretch was lying. Pushing him aside, he sped into the house, up the stairs to the garret room, and there found the poor creature bolted in the dingy place. She was not the least averse to leaving her captivity, and despite the protests of the soulless pander, Francis escorted her out of the house and up to the refuge on Montferrand.

Pierre Guillelmy, formerly a pupil of Francis at the College and now an apprentice in his father's goldsmith shop, retailed his impressions of Regis' apostolate in the slums: "I myself saw the Père, in the ardor of his zeal, pursuing in the city quarter these dissipated women who, unable to resist the force of his salutary words, became docile and submissive to the voice of God. They allowed themselves to be conducted by the said priest to the house of Piety, then named St. Agatha, there to occupy themselves with the salvation of their souls. Everybody at Le Puy could give testimony to similar anecdotes."

It was the tradition at Le Puy then and for years afterward that Father Regis had an almost magic charm against that vice. Oftentimes, one word or one plea of his was sufficient to cause even the most hopelessly perverted to conceive undying aversion for their former habits.

Francis used this spiritual influence to good effect in his instructions to the inmates of St. Agatha's. In his regular sermons to them, he assisted and guided them in overcoming the tendencies that still persisted in troubling them despite their wish to be freed from their past. So efficacious and pertinent was his direction that in the course of those very months of 1637, when the novel idea of reforming prostitutes made the town's libertines and skeptics joke and await their escape, not one of the girls left the institution.

Meanwhile, Regis was continuing the same apostolic and social program he had inaugurated the year before. His work among the poor and his public catechism classes proceeded hand in hand. Crowds continued to flock to hear him, even abandoning the established preachers who regularly delivered their pompous discourses in the cathedral and in the other churches about town.

The diminution of his audience caused considerable annoyance to the Jesuit appointed as episcopal orator, Father Jean Baillard. During his course of sermons in Advent of 1636, when Regis was out of town, the preacher had attracted considerable notice and had received an invitation to conduct the Lenten course. In the middle of this series, Francis returned to resume his catechisms. The result was that Father Baillard was preaching to empty chairs in the cathedral uptown.

Later, during the summer of 1637, when Father Jean Filleau, the new Provincial, visited Le Puy for his annual inspection of the College, Father Baillard seized the occasion to complain of the rival preacher. "Father Regis," said the jealous orator, "though he is a holy man, dishonors his ministry with trivialities and unconventionalities of language. The Christian pulpit, as my oratorical experience can testify, demands more elegance."

Father Filleau, who had been rector at the Colleges of La Flèche and of Clermont in Paris, and moreover was a man of unusual insight, suspected the motive for the complaint. Nevertheless, he fell in with the seriousness of the accuser and replied, not without a bit of concealed humor: "This thing is worth being examined more closely. Come with me. We shall both go to hear him."

Together they attended the day's catechetical talk, though they had much difficulty in finding a place of vantage among the throng. During the course of the instruction the Provincial was so deeply impressed that he turned to the proud orator and whispered: "Would to God that all sermons were impregnated with that same divine unction! We shall allow Father Regis to preach in that style and to persevere in his simplicity. The finger of God is there. If I lived at Le Puy, I would miss none of his discourses."

Some months after his 1637 visitation, Father Filleau communicated to Vitelleschi at Rome his impressions. Writing from Aubenas, October 1, he stated:

> Worthy above all the others of the greatest commendation is Father John Francis Regis, ever devoted to the confessional and to the salutary teaching of Christian Doctrine. Every week children, ignorant folks, and many others gather in droves at the College Church and at another city church and experience the effects of his fruitful zeal.

The answer sent by the General contained a few pertinent remarks about Le Puy. These place in proper perspective his approbation of the apostolate of Regis.

> At the College of Le Puy much good exists which merits my congratulations. Watch out as much as you can that this advancement and progress be not hampered by the rector. I am deeply troubled that he is such as your letter depicts. Father Bonfils may resume his confessions as you see fit. As for Father Paschal — may God in His mercy make him worthy of his talents and more potent in act than in words. As for Father Francis Regis, you may notify him that his holy and strenuous work in catechism classes and in confessions is extremely grateful to us, and we appreciate him so greatly as to desire eagerly for the Society many similar workers. (November 16, 1637.)

These official opinions of Regis, in the midst of his missions and social work, must be borne in mind steadily in order to understand some of Francis' boldness in his subsequent labors. No doubt the Provincial did inform him of Father General's full approval. With the consciousness of that authority to sustain him, Francis hurtled forward undaunted by foes within the walls, whether they were jealous preachers, balking superiors, or side-line critics who regarded him as an uncontrollable free lancer, laboring on the margin of the Institute.

But while these letters were being exchanged between Aubenas and Rome, Regis was busily engaged in emergency relief work at Le Puy. His full efforts were concentrated on endeavoring to cope with the appalling conditions that arose in consequence of the famine of 1637–38.

Through Velay in the autumn had spread the terrifying rumor that the crops were failing. The previous year there had been a shortage, but, though the price of grain had risen slightly, there was still a sufficiency. This year the crops were a total loss. The merry crowds of harvesters who usually brightened the city when the harvest moon hung high descended upon it this year as a grim, hungry mob of un-employed, discouraged and despairing. Their means of livelihood was snatched away from them by the blight that had struck the grain fields. And their coming forewarned the citizens of Le Puy that a famine was in the offing.

Those who had any supplies of wheat, corn, rye, or other substantials carefully hoarded them. Some of the cunning traders at the local market bought up all available grain and held it in their storehouses to await the rise in prices. Soon wheat had doubled in price, rye had jumped from fourteen to twenty sous.

As winter set in, the famine began to spread its panic among the people. Despite the recent royal decree obliging merchants to honor the new denominations of petty coins up to the sum of ten livres, the poor were unable to purchase with their *liards* and *petit doubles* either grain at the granaries, meat at the butcher's, or salt at the salt shops. Moreover, muleteers that summer had refused to bring more salt, wine, or oil up into the mountain districts from Provence because of the small profit that would accrue to them. This final blow, due to the crop failure, completed the desperateness of the situation. The starving poor were seen daily tramping the snow-covered streets begging for food. But there was none to be had. As their last hope, they turned to their protector Father Regis with the prayer that he would save them.

This winter Francis stayed at Le Puy much later than usual before sallying forth for his distant missions. Pressing tasks confronted him there at home.

His first move to relieve the pitiable straits of his poor was to attack the wheat trust itself. With his usual directness, Francis laid the ax at the root of the extreme shortage. Approaching the monopolists who had cornered the wheat market, he fearlessly asserted to them: "You cannot profiteer on this public calamity, nor try to enrich yourselves at the cost of all this misfortune." Besides presenting the demands of common justice, he charged them further with their duty of almsgiving, even more imperative than ever in this time of extreme necessity. God would hold them guilty, he averred, of the murder of those who died of starvation while they held on selfishly to a superabundance of food.

The capitalists yielded to his forceful eloquence. Not only did they agree to put back on the market the supply they had cornered, but they also donated him large amounts of money for distribution among the poor. What meager portions were available, the poor forthwith purchased.

In his sermons at this time, Francis pleaded the cause of the destitute with supercharged vigor. His vehemence reached new heights in begging the rich and the middle classes to be doubly generous with their alms in order to help save the poor from the more severe effects of the scarcity. The response was superb. Assistance flowed in from every quarter. The city authorities practically committed the whole relief problem to Francis himself. So with the money he had gathered, he purchased large quantities of grain for the poor. This he stored in the granary connected with the home of a devout lady, Marguerite Baud, whom Regis secured as the keeper and distributor of the grain.

"La Cornilhon," as the widow Baud was called after her late husband, was kept quite busy during that whole fall of 1637, doling out the wheat to the long lines of the destitute who every day streamed up to her door. Besides those of the city, there were hundreds of others migrating in from the countryside in quest of sustenance. Most of them eventually found their way to Francis if they could not obtain relief from friends or relatives about town. And to all Regis opened the door of his heart, generously extending whatever aid he could offer. Never did he question them as to whether they had money or could borrow it from others. "It is better," he often remarked, "to be duped into giving to one unworthy pauper, than to dupe oneself in refusing alms to one who merits it."

Notwithstanding Regis' herculean efforts to provide sustenance for his poor, the granary at Marguerite Baud's home was often empty. One day that fall when the grain and the money had both given out, La Cornilhon hurried to the College and broke the news to Regis. "Your poor have no more grain," she told him simply. There was a moment of silence while Francis cast his eyes down in prayer. Then, smiling with disarming reassurance, he calmly replied, "Don't worry about it; there is still some of it in your bin." "There's not the least bit," Marguerite insisted; "just a while ago I looked there for a poor woman who came for her share."

Regis only grinned the more genially. "You have poor eyesight, my daughter," he remarked with a glint of whimsy in his eyes. Mistaking his meaning, La Cornilhon became incensed at the remark. "My eyes are not crossed, for all you may say — " But Francis interrupted her, saying firmly with good natured finality, "Go, I tell you. They are hungry, so give them a large portion."

Rather than argue further with him, Marguerite turned and walked home. Once there, she determined to show the poor themselves that there was no more grain in her bin, and then to send them with that message to Regis. She unlocked the door. As she turned the knob, the grain cascaded out on all sides. A full bushel of it emptied on the floor before she could stop its flow from the tightly packed granary.

Marguerite quickly doled out some of the abundance to the poor. That finished, she flew out in search of Regis. As she hastened toward the College she espied him walking down one of the streets. Overtaking him, she breathlessly recounted the marvel. Regis smiled knowingly and said, "God's granary will always be full."

It is noteworthy that the Curé d'Ars first gained his widespread fame in 1829 on the strength of a similar miracle. Placing a relic of St. Francis Regis in his empty loft at the presbytery, he prayed that the father of the poor work a miracle for his little ones. In a few hours, the loft was filled with grain. Regis provided for them as he had done for the poor of Le Puy during the great famine.

The mystery of the multiplication of the grain occurred at least three times during the scarcity of 1637. Marguerite Baud herself narrated another of these remarkable incidents thus: "Another time, not having any more grain in the bin, I swept it clean. When I asked the Père if he wanted me to buy some more, he told me that he should have some there. I replied that I had swept the bin and locked it with a key. Nor had I given the key — a peculiar one — to anyone else. The Père persisted and said that there was some grain in

the bin. Just to obey him, I went to my dwelling and opened
the bin and found it full of grain. It held about forty
bushels."

La Cornilhon was regarded by all as an upright, honorable woman, not prone to illuminism or illusions, but frank,
capable, clear sighted, as her depositions show. The whole
of Le Puy joined in believing her story, which the poor soon
noised about the town. Indeed, it was much more easy to
believe in this miraculous method of supplying food, than
to imagine that in the depths of the most severe winter
within the memory of men, the Père had secured some grain
from the empty or the carefully guarded granaries in the
neighborhood. The fact stands, too, on the veracity of Regis.
He could not have allowed the false impression to prevail
without being guilty of imposture himself. Those who had
opportunity to investigate the phenomenon were obliged to
confirm the truth of the miracle. In a brief, succinct declaration the Council General of Le Puy later summed up the
tradition thus: "When the grain was lacking, Father Regis
made some in order to give it away; he many times refilled
the empty granary, finding a crop and a harvest for which
no seed had been sown."

Hence we can be certain that Marguerite was stating a
simple fact that all the poor of Le Puy proved in their
persons, when she concluded her attestations with the words:
"I can guarantee you that, during the famine, I took out
of this bin a prodigious quantity of grain." God's granary
cared for God's poor. The wonder is that the paupers did
not complain to Regis for not supplying them with fish as
well, just as Christ Himself had done in Galilee.

There were many other urgent demands on Francis during
that busy fall. No human cry of need reached him but
wrung an instant response from his big, all-embracing heart.
One of the more pressing problems was that of the un-
employed harvesters. Many young girls, especially, were

stranded in the city. These added to the crisis of unemployment among the artisans and lacemakers, caused by the
hard times and the famine.

Francis quickly realized what the poverty and idleness
of these wandering girls might lead them to do for a living.
Consequently, he exerted his powers to the utmost to provide
for them. Any who had relatives in the country districts were
urged to return to them and were supplied with the necessaries for the journey. In behalf of those who were homeless, Regis put pressure on the local merchants and obtained
employment for them. A limited number were thus placed.
For the rest, Francis himself provided occupation in their
own quarters. Furnishing them with fabrics, spindles,
threads, bobbins, and other necessary equipment, he set
them to weaving, embroidering, or lacework. The products
of their skill he himself peddled after some ladies who co-
operated with him had collected them. Many a rich store-
keeper was amazed when confronted by this strange middle-
man. But he ended up by paying far more than the market
price for the goods, by way of helping Francis' wards over
the difficult period.

Still another perennial problem was aggravated by the
unwholesome conditions of that tragic winter. Already during the preceding summer, there had been threats of a
resurgence of the cholera epidemic. Not until the famine
had struck with full force, however, was there imminent
danger that the other horsemen of the Apocalypse would
swoop down upon Le Puy. The town had a remote taste
of the war when Monsieur de Polignac quartered a troop
of his soldiers upon the famished residents during October,
1637. Still more were destined to come before the winter
had passed. The town councilors, fearful lest these troop
movements bring in the contagion from elsewhere, had
ordered that the gates of the city be closed as a precautionary
measure. Everyone approaching the town was obliged to

submit to a medical examination for the dread marks of the plague before being admitted.

The hospitals nevertheless were crowded with hundreds of sick brought down by the meager sustenance and the rigors of the winter. A contemporary chronicler, Jacques de Banne, noted that "never in the lives of men now living has so much snow been seen falling and remaining so long on the ground without melting. The northern winds have been extremely cold, strong, and sustained, having done thousands upon thousands of damages." For the sick this especially meant added sufferings and woes. Francis, again the angel of comfort he had been at Toulouse, daily made the rounds of the Hotel Dieu on the Rue Siguret up near the cathedral and in the century-old hospital of St. Sebastian on the banks of the Borne in the suburb of St. Jean.

In the hovels of the poor, however, the ravages of the famine were even more unhampered than in those noisome, pestiferous dungeons that served for hospitals. The gray winter sky cast an ugly gloom over the squalor and fetid atmosphere of the slum tenements into which Francis pursued his quest for poor to aid or sick to serve. One of his brethren, who accompanied him on an excursion of mercy, averred that Francis seemed to have lost the sense of smell, since he was able to remain for whole hours in those miserable dwellings, amid diseased derelicts whose stench was nauseating. With a thoughtful charity both for his patients and for his companion, Francis obliged the latter to remain at the door while he submitted himself to the extreme mortification almost with joy.

Through those murky houses Francis toiled unsparingly, bringing a ray of light and of hope even to the most desperate cases. To his attention, one day, was called the sad plight of a poor wretch who lay dying in a lonely flat, abandoned by everyone because of the unbearable odor that arose from his ulcerated condition. Regis hurried to the

dismal hole. It was a fit home only for the myriads of
vermin that swarmed everywhere, even on the body of the
helpless man. The pitiful sight touched Francis to tears.
Immediately he fetched some linen and a fresh mattress,
cleaned the patient and the house of its vermin, and thereafter returned every day to bring food for the sufferer and
to wash his wounds. Moved to gratitude by his tender
solicitude, the poor man whispered one day with tears in
his eyes, "Ah, mon Père, you have saved my life. How can
I thank you enough?" "It is rather for me to thank you,
my brother," Francis replied. "Pardon me for having started
so late to aid you."

Upon another occasion, Francis learned of an unfortunate
woman who had been attacked by a dreadful cancer of the
face, and had gone to live outside the city walls in the
suburb of St. Gilles. So offensive and repulsive was her
affliction that no one would even cross her threshold.
Deserted by all, she was resigned to die and be done with
her sufferings when Francis came to visit her. Without
the least show of aversion or disgust he conversed with
her, allowed her to kneel close beside his chair to make
her confession to him, and in general put her at her ease
by dispelling her self-consciousness. The woman soon
regained her confidence, and lived long to cherish as a
specially dear treasure the chair that Francis had personally
carried to her home.

Nothing but the saint in Regis accounts for his heroic
charity toward these least brethren of Christ. In the persons
of these imploring mendicants Francis discerned the vision
beautiful, not in legend but in reality. He served them
wholeheartedly, not with the hope of seeing Christ visibly
in the beggars and the poor as St. Gregory beheld Him, but
in the realization that Christ was being tended in them.
This is one of the reasons why men noted that Francis
seemed entranced in his work for them, enrapt in it as

though it were a most absorbing contemplation, an all but sacramental handling of Christ's own Body. This is why nothing seemed to exhaust him, no amount of labor to wear him out. It was not labor but love, the all-sustaining love of Christ in His brethren.

Despite his absorption in his ministries at Le Puy, Francis did not forget his snowbound sheep in the hills, the flocks to whom he had been preaching his winter missions for the past few years. As soon as he was able to break away, he and Brother Bensac sallied out into the teeth of the wintry blizzards for another missionary excursion, the bitterest yet in physical hardships. Taking the road to the northeast, the courageous missionaries struck out undauntedly across the snow-packed basin of the Velay toward the great forests that crowded down out of the Meygal mountain chain and cut across the northern portion of Velay, dividing it off from the region about Le Puy. By means of almost obliterated paths, Regis and Bensac forged their way through these thick and lonely woods, emerging finally to climb up into the mountain region about Yssingeaux. Higher still they pushed toward the loftiest ridge of the upper Boutières, where stood their destination, St. Bonnet-le-Froid.

If Regis were still inuring himself for the rigors of a winter comparable to the worst to be experienced in Canada, he certainly had his supreme test on his journey. In places the snow was twenty feet or more deep. The road was barely lined by the tops of the trees that still held their heads above the snow line. In the upper plateaus and in treeless valleys, the ingenious mountain folks had planted tall stakes that now were but short markers protruding from the snow to guide the wayfarer.

Upon gaining St. Bonnet-le-Froid, 3500 feet above the valleys, Francis and the brother were accorded a warm welcome at the home of the resident curé of the hilltop town. Soon the two priests were the best of friends.

During the mission, after a day of continuous labor for the handful of people who attended, Francis, instead of retiring to rest when the others were abed, stole out of the presbytery and secretly withdrew to the church to keep vigil before the Blessed Sacrament. The curé heard him crunching his way across the snow one night, and, curious to learn his destination, followed him. What the priest saw astounded him. There in the sub-zero cold, kneeling on the stone steps before the locked door of the church, the missionary was praying bareheaded, his hands clasped before him, his legs half-buried in a snowdrift.

Amazed at the rash imprudence of his guest, the curé pleaded with him to desist from praying out there in the blizzard where he would soon be frozen to death. Francis submitted to his suggestion. But after the curé was fast asleep, he crept out again to his wintry watch.

Next day the solicitous pastor argued the matter out with Francis. None of the human reasons he proffered, however, could convince Regis that his missions would be super-naturally fruitful without those extremes of penance and prayer. The work he was doing, Francis insisted, demanded all the graces he could wrest from God. However, the curé did win one point. He persuaded Francis to accept the key to the freezing church and to pray inside instead of out where the chill wind might turn him to a block of ice. That he could pray at all, even within the ice-cold building, is still a marvelous indication that he, like Francis Xavier and young Stanislaus Kostka, felt burning within his breast a fire stronger than any natural or human love, one that needed the cool air to lessen its fervid glow.

During the few weeks he remained in that region in the early months of 1638, Regis managed to fulfill the duty incumbent on him of visiting the parish of Marlhes-en-Forez, another mountain town ten or fifteen miles north of St. Bonnet, and the site of an ancient citadel of the Knights

Templars. The miles of that journey were severe enough to impress themselves indelibly upon the stolid old lay brother, Bensac, so that years afterward the details still stood out with harrowing starkness in his mind.

The rugged mule path that was a poor excuse for a road in summertime, was now completely hidden from view. The pair were obliged to gauge their direction from the openings in the thick pine woods, and so their progress was accordingly very slow.

While they were still some miles from Marlhes, the late afternoon dusk suddenly fell like a pall upon the woods. The howling of wolves became more noticeable and Brother Bensac began to feel a chill due not entirely to the cold of the weather. Hesitatingly, he suggested to Regis that they retrace their steps to the last town they had passed, where they could certainly get lodgings for the night and then push on to Marlhes in the morning.

"We have announced the mission for tomorrow morning," Regis told him; "even though it be troublesome to us, we must not disappoint the people who have been advised of it." Bensac pressed on Regis the fact that they were in danger of going astray and being forced to spend the night in the depths of the forest. For Francis, this was no novelty, but the tone of Bensac's voice indicated that he was decidedly not enthusiastic about the prospect.

Francis reassured him. "Have a good heart, brother," he said cheerfully; "our Guardian Angels walk before us. Guided by those escorts, we have nothing to fear."

Soon, however, the lay brother's fears were confirmed. They lost the path. Bewildered by the maddening uniformity of the forest, they groped about for two full hours in the darkness, with no other gleam to direct them than the reflection of the starlight striking up from the white snow. Up and down steep declivities they clambered, and where trees crowded thickly together, they found themselves entangled in the branches, lacerated by them, blinded by the pine needles that struck their faces. Nor did the call of the wolves lend any assurance to the unstrung brother. He began to complain against Regis for having senselessly involved them in this peril.

Francis merely chided him for his lack of faith. "Why, brother, are you losing heart upon meeting this little adversity? God serves as our guide. Look upon this as an occasion heaven offers us to augment our merit." The poor brother admitted afterward that he hardly heard Francis, so great was his own fear and so loud the whining of the winds in the treetops. He imagined that he was every moment about to "roll into some abyss, to be entirely buried in the snows, or to be devoured by the wolves that roamed round about." But at length they happened upon the road again. Following it, they hastened on to Marlhes, where, a little after midnight, they arrived, "half dead from cold and fatigue."

With a prelude as trying as that, the mission could not but be consoling in contrast. A kind seamstress volunteered to mend the Père's torn cloak. Virtue went out from that garment, for some of the scraps were applied to two sick children and they forthwith recovered from their diseases. The news of these cures brought sizeable crowds out to the missions that winter, notwithstanding the intense cold. Not only at Marlhes but at other stations along the road, Francis received warm responses from the congregations he addressed. He felt fully recompensed for the rigorous cold he endured to reach them and to bring down God's grace upon them.

Upon his return to Le Puy in April, Regis had prospects of even more warming and consoling ministrations. His services were in immediate demand. The poor who lived in the lower portions of the city at the foot of the hill were visited by still another calamity. In early May, 1638, the late melting snows, coupled with ceaseless downpours of rain, converted the trickling river Borne into a rampant torrent It overflowed its banks near the city walls, flooded the lower sections of the suburbs, and rendered homeless hundreds of the poor.

Francis spent himself in the task of harboring the harborless until the flood sufferers could return to their homes. His ceaseless labors for them were a fitting climax to a winter of unstinted work for the welfare of the city. Everyone admitted that he had merited the undying gratitude of all the citizens.

But instead of this enheartening consolation, there awaited him trials and sufferings at their hands that, on his own admission, might well make him think of all his former tribulations as light in comparison. Against him, who had been the greatest single force for good in Le Puy, a concerted conspiracy was now to arise that would brush aside thoughtlessly all his great work of the past and attack him in his very person with such violence as to shorten the span of his life and bring him to an early grave.

CHAPTER VIII

Duel With the Duelists

FRANCIS REGIS had reached the fullness of his powers by the summer of 1638. Just turned forty-one, he was in his prime. Everything pointed toward long years of fruitful service in the life he had found so congenial to his character and temperament. His tall, wiry, rather gaunt figure was indeed a tower of strength and vigor, amply able to second the fervor of spirit that placed such mighty demands upon its energy. Like those lofty pines, everywhere spiring up from the soil of the Velay, Francis seemingly grew stronger under the buffetings of the winter's storms and the summer's toil. Deep rooted as he was in Christ, from whom he drew his power, Regis performed astonishing feats of physical endurance, yet never wore an appearance of fatigue.

His brethren at the College remonstrated with him often about what their human prudence considered excessive exertions. Returning from a day of ceaseless labor in the city, Francis joined in with the members of the Community for their evening recreation with a keenness and gaiety that outdistanced even the youngest among them. His buoyancy of spirit enabled him to laugh off any questions about his tiredness with the pert expression, "Why, I'm fresh as a rose." Even after a day on the road, covering twenty or thirty miles to and from the near-by Solignac, Polignac, or Bains, to supply the ministrations for which they depended on the College, Father Regis was far from assuming an exhausted mien. One of the brethren asked him, "Well, now, Father Regis, in all sincerity aren't you quite tired and fatigued?" "No, I'm not tired at all," he answered. "Why, what's a little thing like that? It seems to me I am doing nothing."

Apparently, he was utterly innocent of the need for rest and sleep that plagues most mortals, save for geniuses like Edison, and other still more unaccountable persons.

For sick calls in the middle of the night, Francis had arranged with the lay brother porter to summon him rather than any of the teachers who dearly needed their repose. Besides, more than likely the dying person requested Regis by name when he felt his end approaching. In the arms of the holy Père his devoted poor wished to breathe out their souls. One of the city doctors affirms that he often encountered Father Regis thus watching at the bedside of the dying all through the night. Yet, next morning, Francis was back in harness for another strenuous day.

It is almost preternatural that he could consistently meet with vigor and power the various situations that arose, and could turn from one task to another without more than a moment's pause for spiritual recollection. One would imagine that the lack of sleep and rest written so plainly in the large, dark circles around his eyes would proportionately cut down his efficiency. Nevertheless, by all accounts, such was not the case. The life and the deep spiritual fire that glowed in his clear blue eyes were all the more accentuated by the dark rings, and his unbroken happiness of soul, his serenity, his gay, smiling disposition, his frank, familiar attitude of mind in dealing with all, had graven a cheerfulness upon his countenance that did not disappear even when in repose. Visible in that far from handsome countenance, in the high temples, and strong Gallic nose — though not as preposterously elongated as that of his contemporary Cyrano de Bergerac — was more of greatness, of geniality, of courtesy, virility, courage, and character than ever was shown by the swashbuckling poet of Rostand's romantic dream. But of Regis could be said in very truth that he "carried his adornment" on his soul and sped through life, "caparisoned in gems unseen, trailing white plumes of freedom, and making the sharp truth ring on the stones of the old town, like golden spurs."

His energetic, quick-triggered activity stood him in good stead during his rescue of girls endangered by the loose morals of the city's gay blades. Swift action was imperative in the circumstances. Regis sprang into the fray with the speed of an echo as soon as the first cry of distress reached him. His decisions, too, were rapid, unerring; his execution of them so surprisingly brisk as to catch his adversaries unawares and leave them bewildered at his prowess. Like a skilled duelist, he thrust and parried, lunged and riposted in his battle, carrying out in all reality his part as champion and defender of the oppressed. But in thus battling for them he made his deadliest enemies.

On one occasion, while he yet doubted whether the attentions paid by a gentleman of quality to a young orphan were honorable or not, a friend of the girl rushed up to him with the news that her fall was imminent. She had already left her lodgings for an appointed rendezvous. Francis quickly learned the address of the house. With Brother Bensac and two pious ladies, he hurried to the place of assignation and rapped loudly on the door. Not a sound came from within. Francis pounded more importunately on the door. Indeed, a deal of extra knocking was still necessary before the exasperated gentleman finally opened the door, however slightly, to frighten the disturber away. To his surprise, Regis took the offensive, pushed it wide open and planted himself firmly on the threshold.

"What do you want here now, Father?" the man growled angrily. "You're entirely too meddlesome. I'm warning you,

you'd better get out of here. If you don't, it'll go bad with you."

A glance over the man's shoulder at the frightened girl who crept up behind him was sufficient for Regis. His eyes flashed to meet those of his antagonist, glinting with equal fire and superior determination.

"Is that so?" Francis fairly snapped at him. "It is I who meddle in too many affairs, while you — you go about your sinning."

Enraged, the man reached for the hilt of his sword. "Go ahead," Regis defied him; "turn your sword against me, if you will —" In an instant, it was unsheathed. The man drew back for the attack. Of a sudden the girl, filled with remorse for the danger threatening the priest who had befriended her so often, pushed the swordsman off balance and dashed out of the house into the arms of the ladies who had come with Regis.

That settled the issue. The irate and frustrated libertine recovered himself, put up his sword, and slammed the door, to have done with the whole business. But from that moment on he was an avowed enemy of the Jesuit. Interfering in a Frenchman's affairs unfailingly meant a duel to the death at that time. This first victory was only fuel on the flame. The man bided his time to carry out his menacing determination.

About this same period, Francis was apprised of the fact that a young Don Juan, notorious about town for his lewdness, was endeavoring under a mask of uprightness to seduce some girls for whom the zealous priest had made provisions and secured employment. Meeting the rake on the street one day, Regis cautioned him to leave them in peace and not to enter their home any more. The insolent pup mocked Francis' warnings, sneeringly flouted his intervention in his courtings, and stalked off more determined than ever to pursue his schemes.

LE PUY: RUE DE LA ROCHETAILLADE
Typical "rock-hewn" street, showing the cramped, slumlike
living conditions of the houses that barnacled
the side of Mount Anis.

That evening Regis himself called upon the girls in order to intercept the young man personally. On the arrival of the false-faced Lothario, Francis loosed upon him a torrent of denunciations in such wise that his evil intentions were revealed to the girls in their true light. The *roué* could not deny the facts of his past life that Regis paraded before the unsuspecting girls. His mask of respectability fell from him, and cursing the priest roundly, he abruptly slammed out of the house. While he felt no desire of returning there, his resentment at the priest's intrusion flamed into a raging lust for revenge. In his black heart he nursed an undying grudge against Regis.

In the course of those months when Francis was recruiting his Magdalenes, most of the cavaliers of the town regarded him merely as a fanatic and a killjoy. He was the butt of many an obscene joke in the wineshops, but he was not taken seriously until they realized that he actually intended to clean up the whole town. While Regis did not set himself up as custodian of public morals, his numerous conquests and conversions practically amounted to that. When finally he even stirred the smug and lethargic gendarmerie to action in aiding him to war upon vice, the city rakes became more than ordinarily alarmed. Hitherto, they had been the ones to dictate to the police the limits of their activities. Fear of the riotings and vengeance that might result from not yielding to the pressure exerted by these plumed and cloaked gangsters had prevented the gendarmes even from investigating too closely the numerous unsolved murders perpetrated by them.

Regis' appearance on the scene was a challenge to their supremacy. Besides his already recounted successes, Francis showed his power and determination in many other instances as well. On one occasion, a company of traveling actors arrived in town for a series of shows on the moveable stage in the public square. The feature attraction of the troupe was a shameless hussy whose jokes and dances and songs were as lascivious as her costume was suggestive.

As soon as Francis heard of the advertisements for the performance, and of the dangerous nature of the headliner, he forthwith clambered up the hill to the office of the consuls and demanded action against this peril to the morals of the city. The chief of the police shrugged his shoulders, hedged at committing himself, tried to evade the duty that Regis pressed upon him. But the Jesuit simply would not allow him to escape. He stormed against the man's cowardice with such cogency that the official at last agreed to interpose. With Francis he hurried down to the public square and banned the show. The disappointment of the crowd of cavaliers who had gathered for it poured more oil on the fire of their indignation.

Their fury reached new levels when the first of the Magdalenes, having satisfied Regis with their good behavior and having given proof of their change of character and their new firmness of resolution, emerged from the refuge. They were placed in respectable positions and continued leading the edifying lives they had started at St. Agatha's. Armed with the new strength of soul found there, they were impregnable to the assaults of their former admirers, who gnashed their teeth at this new evidence of Francis' ascendency.

In the cabarets, where the men gathered for cheerless evenings over their cups, they pooled their grievances and vented their wrath upon their declared enemy. His next move, they swore, would be his last. Yet Francis persisted in scoring victory after victory over them, thwarting them at every turn, leaving them often livid with rage at their impotence.

Nevertheless, Regis did not always escape unscathed. One evening while walking home in the gloom with his lay brother companion, Francis encountered another of these scented and curled ruffians half dragging, half carrying an unwilling girl through the streets. Despite her whimperings and struggles, the libertine forced her along with him. Francis was already acquainted with her sad plight, for she had told him that her repeated attempts to escape from him always proved fruitless. Her unwelcome pursuer invariably ferreted her out and hauled her back to her slavery.

This time his evil designs were destined to be frustrated. Out of the shadows of the dim street Francis appeared like a phantom, snatched the girl from the surprised grasp of the kidnaper, and told her to run for the refuge on Montferrand, while he detained the man. When the abductor recovered from his first dumbfounded reaction and realized what was happening, he tried to pursue his prey. Regis blocked his path. Infuriated, the man spouted a stream of curses, squared off and knocked the priest to the ground, kicking him violently and rolling him in the mire. Burly Brother Bensac hurled himself onto the assailant, grappling with him and pulling him out of kicking range of Regis. Arising from the ground, Francis wiped the mud off his face and shouted to Bensac to let the man free. Then, in an astonishingly mild tone he said to his attacker. "Let me thank you for the blows. For the sake of Jesus Christ, I am prepared to receive even more."

By this time, the ruffian had his fill. In a huff he made off into the darkness. While Brother Bensac helped Francis to brush off his clothes and commiserated him over the insult, Francis wryly remarked, "Considering the man's violent temper, I believe I did not get out of it in such bad shape after all."

It was fortunate for Francis that he was prepared to receive more attacks for the love of Christ. A superabundance of them soon avalanched upon him. LaBroue, the first biographer, estimated that Francis "saved no girl from disgrace without bringing down upon himself the wrath and the rage of a hundred coxcombs." While there may not have been that many for each of the scores of women ransomed during his apostolate, we know that at Le Puy there was a fast crowd of a few hundred cavaliers who practically ran the town after dark.

Antoine Jacmon, the chronicling cordwainer, informs us that in 1638 occurred a mass demonstration of the riotousness of these undisciplined nobles. A quarrel arose between the Sieur d'Aunac, brother of the consul Brunel, and the young Sieur Royet. The latter laid an ambush for d'Aunac, fired at him with his pistol, but killed instead one of his retinue. Incensed at the attack, d'Aunac organized his friends, Baron de Monreal and Sieur de Saint Germain, together with their followers to the number of a hundred or more, and proclaimed death for his assaulter. Meanwhile, Sieur Royet was not idle. He, too, summoned a few score of his friends and retainers and promised to deal blow for blow. The upshot of it was a first-class riot. The combatants dashed about the city engaging in mass duels with swords, and even resorting to gun play. The terrified townsfolk deserted the streets. Shops and houses were tightly barricaded against the rioters. The consuls ordered the city gates shut lest aid be summoned from outside by the fighting parties. Deputizing a large contingent of common citizens, and throwing the garrison into the fray, the city officials succeeded in quelling the riot, but not until the bishop intervened and used his authority in behalf of peace, did the contenders finally sign a truce.

At all events, it is quite evident that when these independent, carefree dandies grouped together, they were a decided menace. And in secret they formed a cabal against Regis that same year, 1638.

By way of parenthesis, it should be remarked that the picture of these dashing musketeers, created by nineteenth-century romanticism and projected back upon them by the fiction and the cinema of recent times, is woefully incorrect. Your seventeenth-century swashbuckling, gay-living swordsman, glorified in the persons of d'Artagnan, Cyrano de Bergerac, Bardelys the Magnificent, and others, was vastly different in real life from what their romantic admirers imagined. The story of Cyrano de Bergerac, for instance, as told from documentary evidence by Cameron Rogers, portrays the true historic figure, not as the unselfish hero whom Rostand poetically represents him to have been, but as a lecherous, murderous, villainous duelist. Life was not just a series of playful tussles with the Cardinal's men, interspersed with romantic, lovemaking escapades. The wars of the times had brutalized these men to an amazing degree, hardened them against all the amenities of civilized life, made them grossly bestial in their recreations, treacherous as snakes, indifferent to life, ready to poignard a wayfarer for a few coins, to stab a friend in order to recover a gambling loss. Despite their genteel clothes, their plumed hats, flowing capes, wide-topped boots, and perfumed, lace-bordered kerchiefs, they were in reality not the forerunners of the golden age of Louis XIV, but rather the lowest dregs in the almost empty cup of France's soured chivalry.

The gay, insidious blades of Le Puy actually did fashion their clothes and their conduct on that of the current set of heroes at Paris and in the armies. The quartering of so many regiments of soldiers on the city had resulted in a lowering of the general level of morality to their notoriously base standards. Even after the soldiers left, there remained a legion of wantons and cavalierish cads. And from the ranks of these were recruited the men who formed the conspiracy to do away with Regis.

At first they seem to have resolved on physical violence. Some of the more reckless, under the influence of a night of winebibbing, boasted that they would handle this meddlesome priest. One of them, from whom Francis had recently lured a mistress, in fact, lay in wait for him in the deserted fields outside the city. He knew Francis had left town that morning to spend the day missioning in a near-by hamlet. Estimating that the Jesuit would return according to habit at sunset, the man hid himself in a clump of trees from which he commanded a view of the road. His quarry did not fail him. When Regis reached the secluded spot, the libertine jumped from his hiding place and, collaring Francis with one hand, unsheathed his dagger with the other.

"Promise to give that girl back to me," he shrieked, "or I'll kill you here and now."

Regis' eyes clashed with those of his assailant, like the crossing of biting rapiers, steel upon steel. Francis did not cower under the threat. Drawing himself up to his full height, he showed the man that he feared neither him nor death, by saying, "Please give me time at least for an act of contrition." After a moment of prayer, Regis bared his chest to the man's dagger and defiantly taunted him: "Now strike me. But that girl is free and belongs to Christ." In the face of this sheer moral power the man's nerve failed him. He abandoned his attempt and fled.

Singly, they seemed to have had no success against the holy priest. A lawyer, well known at Le Puy, resolved to kill Regis because he had converted his paramour and thus had terminated his guilty love affair. Fully determined to do him to death at the first opportunity, the lawyer began watching the priest's movements in order to settle upon a favorable site for the deed. One day, as he stalked his prey down one of the side streets, the man was astonished to see Francis halt suddenly, spin around, and retrace his steps, going directly up to him.

"I know you are plotting my death," Regis told him to his utter amazement, "but you will achieve nothing toward it." So struck was the lawyer by this reading of his deepest secrets that he immediately forsook his plans for vengeance and was converted.

For every one he gained over to his side, however, Francis made ten new enemies. The conspirators began to realize that their strength lay in their numbers, since individually they were no match for their powerful adversary.

Accordingly, a trio, against whom Francis had allegedly tiraded in his catechism classes, decided to show their comrades how to rub out the Jesuit expeditiously. They approached the College one evening toward dusk. While one of them kept guard, another secreted himself in the shadowy recesses of the wide doorway and the third banged the knocker. On the porter's appearance, this last politely informed him that he would like to see Père Regis on the doorstep for a moment. The brother vanished to summon Francis, and minutes passed. The accomplices began to fear lest their plans might miscarry in the long delay, for someone might pass by and recognize them.

Finally the porter emerged, not from the College door but from that of the church farther down the block. He called to the visitor and told him that the priest would interview him in the church. A quick confab with his associates changed the scene of their ambush to the church door. The caller was to engage Regis in conversation, get him to walk to the door as he took his leave, and then the man with the bared dagger could knife him in the back.

Confident in the success of their new plans, the brazen murderer boldly entered the church. With a show of civility and a Judaslike smile, he nonchalantly approached Francis and bowed haughtily in greeting him. Francis lashed into him with a bluntness that jolted the cavalier to his senses. "I know your plot," he said; "I know the sinister resolution that brings you here." The man's eyes popped in surprise. "Listen to me," Francis said, changing his tone to one of appeal. "Confess your sins and return to God right now. I know your conscience is steeped in crimes, but God's mercy far outreaches their number and their heinousness. God waits to pardon you. Here, enter the confessional. Conceal nothing. It will be easy, and I promise you peace of soul." The words of Regis awoke deep repentance in the heart of the hardened sinner. He broke down, fell at the priest's knees, and sobbed out his tale of sin. After absolution, Francis lifted him to his feet and gave him a fatherly embrace.

Immediately, Francis dispatched him to fetch his confreres into church. There ensued a repetition of the almost miraculous conversion, the callous men having become, by their own subsequent account, "meek as lambs." And their return to their comrades, shriven, shamefaced, converted, was enough to make a number of them fear that the Père really did lead a charmed life.

But despite his miracles, many other efforts were made to assassinate Regis. All ended in somewhat the same manner. The priest emerged from them perhaps a bit shaken and bruised, but always with his life. On different occasions they took advantage of his charity for the sick. Once, a group of the ruffians was notified that Regis was visiting a sick person at a house down the street. While he was still within, they hurried to the door, ranged themselves in a semicircle before it with drawn swords, and were ready to attack when he should reappear. Soon Francis came out and quietly stood there, towering above them. With all the challenging courage of Christ when surrounded by his enemies in the Garden of Olives, Regis faced the crowd, eyed them with his serene, level gaze, and said simply, "Well, here I am. What is it you want to do with me?" The cravenhearted cowards looked from one to another, each waiting for someone else to make the first move. Each saw the others trembling as did he. Balked, they hesitatingly withdrew in silence, admitting they were no match for him.

Another time, one of their number pretended to lead Francis to the bedside of a dying person. After a long, hurried walk past street after street, they arrived at a deserted place where a group of the conspirators were gathered in ambush. These rushed the defenseless priest, bowled him over, rained blows upon him with their fists and with sticks, beat him unconscious amid curses and imprecations. Finally the blackrobed figure lay still as death upon the ground, blood streaming from his many wounds. They left him for dead. But somehow, Francis revived and staggered home.

A similar chase ended at the door of the supposed sick person. It was an old abandoned house, designated by the conspirators as the deathplace for Regis. But the intended assassin felt powerless to persevere with his design. He fell on his knees before Regis, avowing that he had misled him for the sole purpose of running him through with his sword, but that now he seemed restrained by some secret power.

Their pursuit of Regis even extended far beyond the city walls. A band of his enemies once laid a snare for the missionary some miles east of the city beyond the stone bridge of many arches that spanned the Loire on the road to Vals. There, in a lonely wooded section, they concealed themselves and awaited the approach of Regis and his companion. The pair were violently attacked, Regis being thrown to the ground and pummeled mercilessly until he was senseless. It was another station in his *Via Crucis,* but he arose from this fall beneath his cross and trudged on to bear even more.

Somehow or another, the news of these attacks did not reach the ears of his superiors. Francis was not the one to complain, and his companion perhaps took for granted that the rector knew all about them. Perhaps, too, the numerous martyrdoms of the recent decades had diminished in the eyes of all the incongruity of a personal attack on a priest. Indeed, if we may credit the story, St. Vincent de Paul himself had at least one similar experience in Paris. His, however, was the indignity of being struck over the head with a chair by no less a person than an irate duchess to whose son the gentle saint had refused to concede a benefice.

At any rate, the assaults continued. Francis was continually made the object of numerous annoyances even when he was not physically manhandled. The gallants delighted in pitching mud at him, in hooting and catcalling after him, in mimicking and mocking his gestures. It became unsafe for him to venture out of the house. But out he went, notwithstanding the pleas of his friends that he expose himself no longer to the murderous anger of the libertines lest they kill him or maim him for life. In his usual cheerfulness, Francis laughingly disregarded their friendly warnings. "Never fear," he said. "It would be too great a boon to die as a martyr in a Catholic city. I haven't a chance for it."

So he continued on his way merrily, facing the "volley of a thousand angry eyes," almost taking a pleasure in displeasing that chastity might triumph, sharing most willingly in the hatred that welled up in hearts that hated Christ and His purity. Alone, he stood as a bulwark of protection for the defenseless girls whom the local villains shamelessly attacked. Whatever judgment may be passed on Regis' motives and prudence in this long drawn out duel, it cannot be denied that he was the truly chivalric soul, he the one who really and selflessly loved those unhappy girls, he the one possessed of a dauntless courage emphasized even more plainly in contrast to the cowardice and meanness of those white-feathered dandies who spent their lives preying on helpless women.

After weeks of trying their skill at murdering Regis in the summer of 1638, however, the conspirators, without leaving off their persecution, hit upon a masterly scheme. Cunningly and with diabolical cleverness, they started an undercover campaign to obtain the removal of Regis from his social work by the authorities of the College. Through some devious route of gossip or chance remarks, it became known about town that the rector, Father Umeau, had many qualms about the effect of the Refuge on the future of the College. The libertines were not long in concocting a plot to confirm those fears and have Francis withdrawn from the care of it.

All around the city, criticism leveled at the futility of trying to convert the group of inveterate sinners at St. Agatha's began to be circulated. No one knew the source of the rumors, but everyone began to repeat them. It was absurd, the arguments usually went, to try to make religious out of harlots who would only return to their former ways the minute they were released from captivity. They were defrauding the deserving poor of their alms, another complaint ran, and were duping the people who contributed to their support. Ribald jests and shocking stories about the lives of the inmates and their perversions added to the horror of the good people about town. Presently they, too, were discussing the matter and handing on their ideas to the Jesuits at the College.

Some of the conspirators even took the trouble to print pamphlets and handbills on the subject. Others who still maintained a veneer of respectability on the surface, had the effrontery to approach Father Umeau personally and to denounce Regis with feigned indignation. Playing upon his apprehensiveness, they gravely informed the rector that the whole town was murmuring against the injustice of the extra imposition on their charity, especially in view of the hard times. It was even stated that the good folks who had boys at the school were on the point of turning against the College, withdrawing their boys from the rolls and refusing to allow the College to go on unless Regis were ejected.

Letters with more denunciations followed. Francis was

accused of dragging the good name of the Society into the mire from which he rescued these women. His admittedly rash and bold invasion of those dens of iniquity in quest of fallen women was held up in the glaring light of merely human judgment, subjected to scorn, to sarcasm, to vicious attack. The superior was goaded on to keep his subject within bounds, to enforce the rules that forbade religious to set foot in those places or to associate with such women as Regis led through the streets alone.

But the clinching argument was the money question. The College had an enormous debt and the church was not yet paid for entirely. Obviously, by all the laws of prudence, the Jesuits should not assume responsibility for the support of another institution. If any of Umeau's community were able to persuade rich benefactors to part with their money, it was only just that the funds should be employed in established works and not in new ventures.

Accordingly, one day in the midsummer of 1638, the rector summoned Regis to his room. With the full authority of his office, he prohibited him from any further concern in the affairs of St. Agatha's. Francis was thunderstruck at the sudden reversal of his previous decision. Yet in silence he submitted to the shattering of his plans, and left the room to pray over the matter and ponder its implications.

Regis carefully examined the state of the Refuge, calculated what it would be without his services. It was not long before he arrived at the conclusion that his bounden duty and the salvation of the souls he had won from sin demanded his presentation of the other side of the case to the rector. In this, he was fully within the provisions of the rules; yet when he did appear before Umeau to state his case, he saw from the first that it was almost hopeless. The rector hardly listened as he patiently explained all the details of the institution and their utter dependence on him as their mainspring.

Umeau remained adamant. He insisted that there were not sufficient funds for the Jesuits to support the Refuge. Moreover, he pointed out that Francis' other ministrations and his frequent absences from Le Puy rendered him incapable of handling the affairs of the institution. Finally, he ended by commanding Regis to find a man of authority and prominence in the city who might perchance be willing to take charge of the place. Otherwise, he would be obliged to inform the bishop that St. Agatha's would be abandoned. It was the voice of authority that spoke and Francis, heartbroken, retired to do what best he could, in prayer and obedience.

Obediently, but with faint hopes of success, Regis sought among his friends in the city for Umeau's elusive "man of authority" to assume the unenviable position that drew upon Regis the attacks he had suffered. No one could be found. The pamphleteers and the gossipers had amply supplemented the work of the personal assailants of Regis.

Finally, in desperation Francis again approached Umeau with a change of tactics. Tears glistening in his eyes, he begged his superior not to condemn the Refuge to extinction by removing a regular attendant priest from its care. Frantically, he urged the rector to realize that his arbitrary action would disperse the Magdalenes before they were sufficiently strong to withstand the enticements of their former lives. He warned Umeau that he was to all intents throwing them wantonly into the brothels. But in face of all his pleas, Umeau maintained his stand. Even when Regis charged to his conscience all the evil consequences of his command, the rector still persisted inflexibly. Assuredly, this was the ultimate in the stiffness of character that Vitelleschi had complained about in Umeau. The incomprehensible man repeated his absolute prohibition, and laid an injunction on Regis against ever soliciting revenues for the house in the future.

Crushed but obedient, Regis submitted to the yoke laid upon him. From then on he did not even place his foot inside the house on the Rue de Montferrand. Yet he suffered intensely from the hamstringing by Umeau. It was the bitterest cross he had shouldered. All the physical pain and toil hitherto endured seemed like play in comparison with this trial. Nevertheless, he still hoped and prayed that God would provide. Secretly, in fact, he told one of his Jesuit brethren: "I do not doubt but that this establishment will flourish now more than ever, since being crossed like this is a sure sign that it is a work of God."

Those last weeks of the summer of 1638 were marked by still more trying contradictions. Father Umeau, in an effort to please yet further those who persistently pursued their attacks on Regis, limited his other works of zeal as well. Permission to visit hospitals was refused him. Other charitable functions were regulated and rearranged. Even his instructions to the poor in the College church were curtailed. Francis was rendered practically inactive.

Nonetheless, the zealous priest did not abandon all hope. He ceaselessly appealed to the rector in the hope of persuading him to change his decisions. Repeatedly, we are told, he went down on his knees before him and begged him to "consider that, since he was without talent or virtue, he was good for nothing but to instruct and to serve the poor; that this was both the sole good he could do and the sole consolation he was able to enjoy in this life." But the only answer he received was a series of bitter recriminations for his indiscretion and his excessively active and ardent zeal.

Francis redoubled his penances and prayers. In anguish he poured out his soul for the poor people he was unable to aid in person and for those of his flock unwillingly abandoned by him when they needed him most.

By chance he heard one day that a poor man of his acquaintance, who had not been to confession for a long time, was lingering on the verge of death. In the presence of another priest, he conjured Umeau to permit him to give the Last Sacraments to the dying person. Uncannily perverse as before, the rector absolutely forbade Regis to leave the house. In all probability, of course, the dying man was attended to by some other priest. But Umeau did not inform Regis of any such fact. Hours of agony of spirit were heedlessly caused the sensitive soul of the saint. To one of his companions who tried to console him on this disappointment, Regis replied: "Feel my pulse — see, I am in a fever and will be so the whole night, unable to gain a moment's rest. I cannot go on living without serving those souls that have need of me!"

The strain of the trials and the penances, together with the effects of the physical buffetings he had endured, caused Francis to take sick for a short time — the only recorded sickness of his adult life. The lay brother who attended him was appalled at the great livid gashes riven in his back by his disciplinings. But the pain within his soul was the only one that seemed unbearable to Francis. He believed himself utterly bereft of all weapons to combat the present onslaught. With his superior, he informed one of his intimates, he could not fight save by submission; nor could he defend himself save by deference to his wishes and by respect for his opinions. To achieve this acme of self-denial required, by his own attestation, Regis' most colossal struggles. In others he was conquering alien enemies; in this case, he conquered the conqueror, himself.

The calumny of the supposed separation of Regis from the Society of Jesus was to be spread in later days. But by all human computation, if ever there had been sufficient justification on the part of Regis for becoming disgusted with the Society, that emergency would have confronted him in that summer of 1638. Yet there is not even the faintest suggestion that he dreamed of such an alternative.

The fact is that Francis was wide visioned enough to see beyond the individual superior to the organization as a whole. And he was holy enough to welcome this chance to put on the livery of his Lord and Master, seeking opprobrium, contempt, and the cross in imitation of Christ.

Meanwhile, the slow wheels of the Society's central government were being set in motion to remedy the situation. Already, Vitelleschi had warned the Provincial, Father Filleau, to "take care that the good work at Le Puy be not hampered by the rector." The Provincial, on his part, had managed to keep check on most of the complaints and to settle personally most of the grievances harbored by the community against the superior. Umeau had the pettiness to resent this interference. He even wrote to the General that Filleau had publicly disgraced him some months before by giving a very pointed exhortation to the community. But he had made peace with Filleau and during the first part of 1638, especially after receiving a congratulatory letter from Vitelleschi on the final finishing of the church, Umeau had been less troublesome. Nevertheless, in April, 1638, the General had intended to remove him from office, but was unable to do so because the priest proposed by the Provincial as his successor was equally unsatisfactory. Vitelleschi accordingly requested Father Filleau to submit another name for consideration. That of Father Ignace Arnoux, minister at Le Puy and an intimate friend of Regis, was accordingly transmitted to Rome.

Even then Vitelleschi hesitated because of Arnoux's comparative youth. In midsummer he wrote to Father Filleau, without knowing anything of the way in which Umeau had been hampering the work of Regis, informing him that he would refrain from changing the rector at Le Puy if he were now giving satisfaction.

Umeau, as we have seen, was far from doing so. At the very time of the General's letter to Filleau (July 20, 1638), many other letters were in the mails for Rome with the story of events at Le Puy. That was the last straw. Vitelleschi immediately drew up the necessary documents to depose Umeau. But those long weeks that elapsed between the sending of the letters to Rome and the receipt of the General's new appointment were ten weeks of intense suffering for Regis. It was another crisis that proved Francis to be a genuine saint. Just as he had borne in silence the temporary disgrace at the hands of Bishop de Suze, so he submitted to this new cross, wholly forgetful of his own reputation and honor, mindful only of the happiness of those to whom he had dedicated his life. It is recorded that he deliberately dissuaded some of the community from endeavoring to clear his good name in the eyes of the rector. Perhaps he realized their efforts would be futile. Perhaps also he was aware that he could crush Umeau by writing to the Provincial or even by informing the superior of the full and hearty approval of his work given by Vitelleschi in the previous year. Nevertheless, uppermost in his mind was the conviction that this trial was as far as it concerned him personally, an undeniable testimony of God's nearness to him. Francis averred that he considered these contradictions to be the proper human recompense for his labors. He looked for no reward on earth. Nor did he receive any.

Toward the end of the summer, even the prejudiced Umeau seems to have sensed the genuine humility and the sterling holiness of his subordinate. At all events, he ultimately relented in his vexatious persecutions. Admitting that he had been perhaps too willing to heed the malignant reports, he restored to Francis his permission for outside activities. "I see now that you are animated by the spirit of God," Umeau is reported to have said. "You may now act again according to the counsels of your zeal and prudence."

But it was too late. In September, 1638, the belated documents from Rome arrived. Umeau was deposed. Father

Ignace Arnoux was read in as head of the College. Sent to Toulouse, the wretched Umeau continued to manifest the same suspicious and unreasoning spirit that had made life miserable for those at Le Puy. Before his death the following year, it was necessary to change him again. Finally, the Lord took the matter into His own hands.

After Umeau's departure from Le Puy, Francis and the community realized that the former rector had in truth been a means in the hands of Providence for the sanctification of the whole house. Regis emerged from the trial in a sad physical state, but his soul was purified to the whitest in the crucible of suffering. Events that followed this period of his life indicated his achievement of the full stature of his holiness, if not as a result of the difficulties he had surmounted, at least as a subsequent development in his already superb character.

For that inner holiness, external success, length of days, even health of body were immaterial. The essential feature was that for Christ's sake he was prepared to endure even more. In fact, he deliberately chose the hard, the most toilsome, the most rugged paths. Utterly dead to himself, he lived only for Christ and for souls. Despite the tribulations connected with his work at Le Puy, Francis remarked to Pierre Le Blanc, the Vicar General: "If God left me the choice of going to heaven immediately or of working for the conversion of courtesans and prostitutes, I would choose rather, for His sake, to toil on for a long time in this apostolate."

God accepted the wish for the deed. Francis was too precious a gift to leave to the tender mercies of the ungrateful city. Two more years of life was all that God spared him on this earth.

CHAPTER IX

BROTHER HOLPEN BY BROTHER

IN APPOINTING Ignace Arnoux as rector of the College
of Le Puy, Father General Vitelleschi had designated a
superior who, far from hampering the good work being
accomplished by Regis, would assist the fervent apostle in
accordance with the Society's ideal of government. While
Umeau was one of those "dysteleological" misfits that crop
up even in the best of families, Arnoux proved to be a happy
choice for the exacting office, fitted by spiritual development
and temperament to the pattern of his patron and name-
sake, St. Ignatius, the perfect Jesuit superior.

It should be noted in passing that the wise provisions laid
down by the founder for the government of the Society
gave it a distinctive feature not common to all similar organ-
izations. Except for the office of General, which is a lifetime
position, all the posts of authority are filled by men from
the ranks. There is no ruling caste, as in military units; no
permanent, lifelong dignities, as in most ecclesiastical
hierarchies; no distinction of brother from brother, as in
even the most fraternal of brotherhoods. The idea of St.
Ignatius was that for a brief space one or other of the
brethren should assume the helm of the various Provinces
and houses in order more to help his brothers like a brother
or a kindly father, rather than dominate them like a
dictator. Indeed, in the first years of the Society, it was not
unheard of that the fathers would change places every

week. Ignatius took for granted that the interior law of charity and love would guide his men. Superiors were designated primarily to give wise and sympathetic direction to this all-consuming zeal, to exploit each one's capabilities to the utmost for the greater glory of God, and to give full rein to the guidance of the Holy Spirit, and external, authoritative approbation to the impulses received from Him.

To achieve this ideal, the common life and mutual friendship existing in the Society was of invaluable aid. In the case of Ignace Arnoux and Francis Regis, there had arisen a close, intimate acquaintanceship that had grown with the passing years. Arnoux, while a novice with Regis at Toulouse, had been captivated by the winsome character of his young religious companion, and had marveled at the rapid advance he made in the Ignatian way. At Cahors in the juniorate, and at Tournon in philosophy, Ignace had witnessed the great promise shown by his confrere for a future career as a missionary. Not infrequently Arnoux had accompanied Francis on missionary excursions in the vicinity of Tournon, had seen with his own eyes the power exercised by the voice of Regis, and had assisted him in the task of gathering up the fruits of his *ferverinos*.

Together, the two friends had lived through those gloomy, plague-menaced years of theology at Toulouse, where Arnoux had still more ample opportunity to observe the full realization of the Jesuit ideal his companion had reached. Francis' perfect living of the *Suscipe* with each successive day of service amid the plague stricken after ordination, his eager desire for martyrdom to prove his love for Christ, yet his perfect obedience to the least wishes of his superiors, had all stamped him, in the eyes of Arnoux, as a perfect Jesuit.

Again during his years as minister at Le Puy, Father Ignace verified for himself Regis' reputation for consummate sanctity. He became aware of his long hours of watching and praying at night, his almost savage disciplining of himself to win the conversion of sinners, his humanly imprudent mortification in the matter of food and rest. Despite earnest pleas for moderation, for relaxation, and for a lessening of his terrific pace, Regis had sprinted on, before the eyes of Arnoux, in his wholly absorbed following of his destiny. Ignace had watched him from afar as he outdistanced all his other brethren, and had been firmly convinced that God was driving Francis toward greater achievements. With the rest of the community, he deplored Umeau's amazing lack of perception in regard to this patent fact. On his own part Arnoux had done all in his power to assist Regis over the difficult time.

Francis on his side had reciprocated the friendship of his father minister. Though he made scant use of its benefits, he appreciated the friendly gesture Arnoux made toward him when he, by a nicety of forethought and attention, had assigned Francis a room on the south side of the house, where he might enjoy some of the brightness and sunshine that came so rarely into the narrow streets of Le Puy. Arnoux was himself accustomed to life in the highlands, having been born in Auvergne. Nevertheless, he was careful to remember that his fellow Jesuit was a southerner, brought up beneath the smiling sun of Languedoc, and might perhaps feel more at home in the sunny room. But Regis utilized even more the other room Arnoux managed to let him use as a storeroom for all the donations he received — his "treasure room," as he called it. A less agreeable father minister might have scouted the very suggestion of surrendering a room for the amalgam of junk that Francis collected for his poor. But Arnoux was in full sympathy with all of his friend's projects.

Accordingly, when he was made superior, Arnoux resolved to be, toward this new Francis fired with the zeal of a Xavier, another Ignatius, at least in his own small way. Indeed,

Arnoux had his own contributions to the making of the saint, and they were worlds apart from those of his predecessor Umeau.

Vitelleschi wrote that he expected the levelheaded, robust, and kindly Arnoux to become an excellent superior, provided he could moderate his somewhat overaffectionate disposition. If he were perchance overly attached to Regis, he was merely following the path pointed out by Providence, and was showing his own steadfast devotion to the ideal of the Society. Arnoux took an uncompromising stand as the protector of Regis. Like the Provincial, Father Filleau, he realized the finger of God was upon his work. The new rector let it be known in no uncertain terms, both before the community and in public, that he championed the cause of the Refuge, no matter what might befall.

The restoral of the care of the Refuge to Regis was therefore one of the first official acts of the new regime. Arnoux personally confided to Francis full permission to undertake again all his labors for it, and to push them with vigor. Despite Umeau's previous injunctions to the contrary, and despite the warnings of his own treasurer, the superior even allowed him to attend to the financial provisions for the maintenance of St. Agatha's. Funds had dwindled considerably during his enforced inactivity, for the group of pious ladies, who went about town collecting money for the house on Montferrand, were somewhat inadequate substitutes for the irresistible Regis. Once he returned to the task, receipts trebled. Provisions flowed in. Winter clothing and fuel were acquired. In no time, the directress had enough money and supplies to last her through the winter. Thus Francis was enabled to devote these coming months once more to the missions afield.

Before leaving for his mission work, however, Regis received still another token of Father Arnoux's stanch support.

It was learned, in late September, that the annual appro-
priation assigned by the town council to the support of
the College would not be forthcoming that year. Notwithstanding the contract by which the consuls agreed to sub-
scribe the sum of 2106 livres annually toward the running
expenses and the liquidation of the debt of the College,
the city officials declared that their limited revenues could
not meet their obligations.

The default was not lost on the enemies of Regis. Despite
the fact that anyone could realize that the damage caused
by the famine and the floods of the preceding year had
curtailed the city's trade and therefore decreased its tax
collections, the ingenious conspirators openly attributed the
nonpayment to the officials' secret opposition to Regis. They
could not openly attack him, said the critics, because the
bishop, nominal ruler of the city and powerful in the States
Assembly, might cause trouble for them. But this undercover
thrust, masked by their plausible reasonings, was really aimed
at unhorsing the troublesome apostle of the slums.

The rumors succeeded in circulating into the ranks of
the College professors themselves. They transmitted the
stories to the rector, together with the gentle hint that
perhaps Umeau had saved the College by sacrificing Regis,
and that Arnoux's reinstating of him might mean the ruin
of their educational work.

Arnoux, however, postponed the crisis by the simple
expedient of borrowing some money for that year. If the
enemies of Regis actually did wield the influence they
claimed, then the events of the following year would definitely prove it one way or the other. Accordingly, to preserve Francis' work, Arnoux assumed the extra burden of
debt on the already heavily involved institution, and managed to placate the community into accepting what sacrifices
the needed retrenchments might entail.

Foiled in their attempt on the College, the conspirators

decided upon another course of action. They realized that their chances for success against Regis directly were growing fainter with the passing days. Impatient, besides, of the long wait for the expected escape of some of the inmates, they determined one night to attack the House of St. Agatha itself. Haply, one of Regis' friends overheard the plottings, and, as the crowd of angry libertines advanced up the hill toward the Refuge brandishing crowbars and pickaxes, the eavesdropper sped off to inform the Jesuit.

Francis hastened to the rector's room to ask for permission to go and defend the Refuge. "What will you do against so many fools?" Arnoux asked.

"I shall place myself on the threshold of the door and no one will enter the house without first piercing me with his sword."

"But if they harm you," the rector countered, "the public will accuse you of imprudence." Francis did not care what people said or thought — and he told the rector so with such effectiveness that Arnoux granted him the permission, feeling certain that God would take care of him as He had so many times before. The prestige of his holiness and perhaps even the power of his presence would make the mob quail as it had previously done.

But Francis realized that this might be the time for that martyrdom which had eluded him all these years. Encountering Father de Mangeon on his way out of the house, Regis appointed him provisional executor for the forty livres of alms that the treasurer still had on his books in Regis' own name. Then he scampered off into the darkness, hurried up the steep, cobbled streets toward St. Agatha's, his mind racing back over all the narrow escapes he had experienced in dealing with this incorrigible set, over all the visible marks of God's protection for the Refuge. Half hoping for the martyr's crown he had missed by inches in these dark and treacherous streets, half trusting that he might awe this unruly crowd as he had tamed that milling mob of soldiers at Saussines intent on pillaging the church, Regis sped on block after block, Brother Bensac puffing and grumbling in his effort to keep up with him.

But his forebodings were empty, for hardly had Francis turned the corner of the Refuge, when he came upon a scene quite different from what he had anticipated. The police and some doughty citizens from the neighborhood were in full command of the situation. The screams of the women that greeted the first blows upon their outside doors had summoned the gendarmes from their near-by station. With the aid of the good men who also rushed to their assistance, they had charged down upon the band of conspirators and had dispersed them into the darkness, breaking a few heads in the process and capturing some prisoners. These latter were being conveyed to the jailhouse a block away when Regis arrived. There was nothing for him to do but to be thankful for the rescue. The gendarmes assured Francis that they would keep watch over the institution from then on, and would fend off any further attacks.

It was thus with a peaceful mind that Francis was able to depart from Le Puy for his months of apostolic toil in the mountains. This year his itinerary was plotted to reach even farther north from his base than on any previous expedition. Along the way he and his companion, the faithful coadjutor Bensac, stopped off to revisit some of the stations of his former journeys. Everywhere, but notably at Marlhes, Francis received an enthusiastic welcome and conducted missions that were blessed with abundant fruits. Marlhes was but a typical example of what was repeated elsewhere.

"Everyone ran after him," Father André, pastor of Marlhes, assures us. Drawn by the reputation of sanctity he had acquired through the miracles of the preceding year, people for miles around trudged through the snow to hear his fiery words. In one month there, the curé asserts, Francis heard more than two thousand confessions, most of them general ones. The crowds for Holy Communion were so vast that Francis was kept at the rail until four in the afternoon. On some days it continued "until after the lighting of the lanterns at five or six o'clock, for the sake of the penitents who remained fasting until night-time."

These missions were replicas of those of previous years, except that now people spontaneously converged toward the mission center as soon as the news of the missionary's arrival was bruited abroad. Francis was no longer obliged to canvass all through the little snowbound villages and hamlets snuggled closely together on the lee side of the wind-swept mountains.

Father André, nevertheless, became alarmed at Regis' labors. This year they seemed to take a greater toll of his physical strength than they had in past years. What with his continual fasting, his hearing of confessions day and night, his devoting to prayer whatever time he could snatch from the importunate peasants, the apostle seemed often on the point of dropping from exhaustion. Father André began to fear for his devoted friend and, accordingly, he wrote to Father Arnoux asking him for authority over Regis in all that pertained to his exterior life. The rector readily granted the jurisdiction for the unusual request. Armed with these powers, the pastor obliged Francis to take a bit of relaxation and to eat some nourishing food.

Father André was deeply impressed by the prompt and unquestioning obedience of the missionary. Even when the concourse around his confessional was very great, the curé had only to show him the letters from his superior in order to force him to leave all and return to the presbytery for necessary rest, refreshment, or recreation.

But the people were reluctant to allow their spiritual consolation thus to be impeded. On one occasion, after Regis had suddenly been ordered to quit the confession box, his line of penitents trooped out of the church toward the presbytery in his wake. One of them, a peasant who did not want to lose his place in the line, hurried over the slippery path without sufficient care for the sureness of his footing. Stepping on a patch of ice, he lost his balance, fell upon a rock, and dislocated his shoulder. The others took compassion on him and, picking him up, bore him to Regis in the priest's house. Father André allowed the unfortunate man to come within the presbytery, from which he emerged, "confessed, consoled, and entirely healed."

Signal favors like this, coupled with the other remarkable cures of the sick, exorcisms of the possessed, conversions of the hardened, elicited deep, reverent admiration for his guest on the part of good Father André. He began to observe Regis very closely and to note the outstanding characteristics of his sanctity. Later, his statements concerning the heroic holiness of the Jesuit missioner would be among the most authoritative in the entire group of witnesses for beatification. Besides joining with other eyewitnesses in testifying to the miracles that indubitably demonstrated Regis' great worth in the eyes of God, the priest added his own personal recollections of Francis at prayer. "He treated with God in a most intimate and sweet fashion. How many times did I see him, in absolute recollection, falling, to all appearances, into ecstasy — speechless, insensible, entirely beside himself." Whole nights were passed thus, the curé asserted, without sleep, in rapt converse with God. Yet so anxious was Francis for a consummate purity of soul that, with the sublime candor and childlike humility of one of his own penitents, he daily received the Sacrament of Penance from Father André. It is small wonder that the memory of Regis lingered on like a precious heritage in that little town where people and pastor were transformed by the saintly missionary.

On his part, Francis cherished a delightful friendship for

the "very worthy curé of Marlhes." To him Regis penned
a letter that is proof of this sincere affection. At Monastier,
the following year, Father André took sick while on a visit
to his brother, Canon Antoine André. Learning of his illness, Francis wrote to his friend from Le Puy, August 8,
1640:

Monsieur,

If I had power over the air of Monastier, I would make it so favorable to your health that in a little while you would be again in your full vigor. I learn that almost daily your health is improving, and for this I give thanks. Nevertheless, the great desire I have of seeing it perfect again would make me rather impatient, if I did not know that the Master of the weather and the air is caring for the issue. I will not cease, however, to beg it of Him, while calling myself, Monsieur,

Your most humble and affectionate servant in our Lord,

John Francis Regis.

Thus did Francis return the thoughtfulness that Père André had shown about his own health at Marlhes. Unfortunately, once he left the hospitable roof of André, Regis seemingly forgot about his physical welfare. With scant consideration for his comfort or rest, he continued to labor through the regions to the north and east of Marlhes. But the premonition of his friend began to be justified. Francis was exhausting himself indeed. Whereas he should have spent the winter recuperating from the effects of the physical violence he had suffered in Le Puy, he nonetheless pushed on courageously, heedless of his own personal good, thinking only of the needs of these strayed and scattered sheep in the hills.

Ten or fifteen miles north of Marlhes in Forez, lived an admirable Christian lady, Isabeau de Cremeaux, wife of the lord of Feugerolles, Gaspard de Capponi, and niece of the archbishop of Narbonne. Hearing of Regis' renown for holiness, she had invited him to her château, where, in her own chapel, he might give a mission to the family and the tenants of the large estate. Francis wrote her from Marlhes, accepting her invitation and fixing a date for the mission.

It was one of the most consolingly Catholic regions in which Francis had worked. No strident controversies with the Calvinists disturbed the peace of the neighborhood. No ugly ruins of churches marred the landscape. The people still lived in the pastoral simplicity of the Middle Ages, happy to be under the suzerainty of their feudal lord, honoring his lady almost as their queen. Isabeau was indeed a model Christian mother. Besides rearing her twelve children excellently, she found time for two hours of daily meditation. Her communions thrice a week, her fastings and austerities, her charity to the poor had already won the respect of her neighbors and the blessings of God. This visit of Regis she afterward cherished as one of God's most valued favors. As a result partially of his mission and partially of her own life of piety, a number of her sons afterward became holy priests, shining contrasts to the usual products of the French nobility who became clerics only to bleed the Church of her patrimony.

Turning south again from this, his most northerly point of activity, Francis paused for a mission at the little town of Coing, hidden in a pocket of the Upper Boutières some miles east of Marlhes. Later, out of devotion to the missionary, the town changed its name to St. Regis du Coing — the only one in France bearing the name of the saint.

Other stopping places along the route included the quaint towns St. Julien-Molin-Molette, St. Appolinard, Bourg-Argental, St. Saveur-en-Rue, Clavas, which he called his "Bethany," Vanosc, St. Julien Vocance, and others in the diocese of Le Puy itself. Each one of these meant miles of tramping in the snow, days of physical hardships which, though forgotten in the spiritual stimulation of winning so many souls to Christ, nevertheless sapped his strength and undermined his constitution.

On the last lap to Le Puy, Francis passed by Vorey, a hamlet on the banks of the Loire, a few leagues north of the city of Mary. The pastor at this village was Maurice Boyer, a former pupil of Francis at the College. On his request, Regis consented to preach there also. For four days he tarried among the enthusiastic people, "incessantly and

unrelentingly occupied in preaching, catechizing, or confess-
ing the people of the parish, both day and night," as Boyer
reported.

Like Father André, Boyer was perturbed at Regis' superhuman exertions. He feared they exceeded all limits of
human prudence. In his kind solicitude for the well-being
of his beloved teacher, Maurice remonstrated with Regis on
this matter at the end of the mission. Francis appreciated the
human motives that impelled his devoted pupil to express
concern over his physical fatigue. Nevertheless, he confided
to Maurice the reason why he deemed it unfair to spare himself in working for the service of God. Francis narrated how
he had visibly felt the effects of Providence in this regard.
Once, while traveling toward his mission in the country
during winter, he had slipped upon a treacherous slope, had
tumbled down into a ravine, and had broken his leg. Despite
this accident, he had struggled on for two more leagues,
assisted by his lay brother companion, and had made his
way through the slush and snow to his destination. Upon
his arrival he had yielded to the importunings of his clients
and had hobbled straightway to the confessional. Hours
later he emerged entirely cured.

Upon his return to Le Puy, though utterly fatigued by
his months of exhausting labors, Francis resumed his routine
labors in the College church, in St. Pierre's, and at St.
Agatha's. Meanwhile, Father Arnoux had been careful to
assure the possibility of his continuance in the type of work
that fitted him so well. To offset the influence of those who
opposed Regis even inside the community, Arnoux wrote to
the General in defense of the zealous apostle, February
9, 1639:

My most Reverend Father,
    I do not doubt that some have written to you against Father
Regis and against the pretended overhastiness of his zeal. I beg
you not to allow yourself to be caught unawares by the false pictures

that may have been painted of this holy man. He is an indefatigable worker who breathes only the divine glory. He combats vice with the zeal of an apostle and is not held back in his ministry by any human consideration. It is this alone that has aroused against him many scandalous sinners and even some fathers of the College who are alarmed by the rumors spread through the city by these sinners.

I am able to assure you with truth that I see nothing in his person that is worthy of blame. On the contrary I see in him many eminent virtues, worthy of all praises. If he makes war against scandals, it is always with as much prudence as zeal, ever pursuing sin and yet treating the persons of the sinners with all sweetness and charity possible.

Father Regis conducts public catechism classes in the church that is called Saint-Pierre-du-Monastier, to the admiration of all, and with an almost incredible success. In fact, one could see every Sunday for the past two years, save for Lent and Advent, five thousand persons of both sexes and of all conditions packed in there, filling not only the nave, which is very vast, but also numerous tribunes and the temporary seats that were of necessity constructed; and even under the portico and at all entrances, heads were held cocked to hear him. I add that he is an obedient religious and that he is commonly called a saint.

Unfortunately, the original Latin text for this letter is not complete; only the last paragraph has come down to us. The first two paragraphs are presented on the authority of an early biographer, Daubenton, assistant to the General and postulator of the saint's cause. Whatever may have been the actual words of Arnoux, the effect he wished to produce was achieved. Not long after Francis' return, he was able to show him the following communication from the General:

I am pained that there exist between certain fathers some jealousies, and that only one has made amends. I beg you therefore to examine the matter and to inculcate seriously into the others the ugliness of this defect. Show these fathers how opposed it is to charity, to gravity, to the reputation of the Society, to the quiet of soul each is deprived of, and to the peace of the community; finally, how much it hurts the good of souls. I greatly felicitate Father

Regis on his very fruitful and very holy apostolate of Christian doctrine; and my most ardent desire is that the fruits of it may be more numerous from day to day. (April 15, 1639.)

In the same letter, Vitelleschi had approved the manner in which Arnoux was handling the matter of the College finances. He urged the rector to be generous in dealing with the city councilors, in view of the disturbed conditions of affairs in general, and authorized him to override the wishes of the procurator even without his knowledge. The General further counseled liberality as in accord with the poverty of religious rather than opposed to it. Grave harm, he warned, was to be feared if the Jesuits insisted on the letter of the contracts that involved money.

This new approbation both for Regis and for Arnoux was an added incentive to Francis for the pursuance of his accustomed tasks. Still a dynamo of activity, Regis moved about the city more wraithlike than ever, worshiped by the poor, admired by many of the nobles, and even feared by the libertines.

These latter seem to have relented somewhat in their petty persecution. Once in a while Francis was the victim of physically violent attacks, but these were not multiplied with the savageness of the previous summer. The nobles and the swashbuckling element alike had new troubles to occupy their minds. Richelieu had decided to take Roussillon away from Spain and as commander-in-chief of the army had ordered Condé to assemble an army near Narbonne. The seneschal of Le Puy, Charles de Clermont, Seigneur and Baron of Chaste, received instructions to convoke an assembly of the nobles of Velay at Le Puy, May 15. In the refectory of the Dominican monastery the nobility met and listened to the royal decree that assessed each one a certain amount of money and conscripted certain of their number for the army in the south. Heavy penalties were imposed upon evaders. Besides, Chaste was obliged to conscript a whole regiment of militia from the Velay. The gay blades of Le Puy, having enjoyed the sport of battling with defenseless women and an unarmed man, were thus given a chance to prove whether the color of their backbones was different from that of the blond hair of their courtesans.

It was a weird summer. Snow fell abundantly in May and in June to slow up the mustering of the troops and to add to the woes of the common people. Supplies of food and clothing were requisitioned for the army, so that scarcity again threatened the town. Francis was allowed no respite from the never ending service of the poor and was kept continually bustling about in behalf of their numerous needs.

As before, he was ingenuity itself in aiding them. Even when one of his paupers ran afoul of the law and was lodged in one or other of the jails in the upper part of the town near the cathedral, Francis was summoned. If, as often happened, the prisoner had been jailed for nonpayment of debts, Regis lost no time in pleading with the creditors or even with the judges themselves. His effectiveness as a "lawyer" won freedom for many unfortunate victims of circumstances in whose defense otherwise no voice would have been raised. We are told that he was particularly eloquent in his vindication of the rights of widows or orphans or poor workmen who, in their ignorance of the law and in their general illiteracy, had been swindled out of their savings by the shysters of the city or had been evicted from their farms by the unscrupulous landlords in the country. So adept was Regis in reconciling quarrelsome parties and in settling family disputes that his name became a synonym for peacemaker. It later grew proverbial among the citizenry to remark, whenever they wished to indicate the impossibility of being reconciled with an enemy, "No, Père Regis will not come for you!"

As the summer progressed, Francis gradually regained the prestige he had lost when cast into the shadow by Umeau the preceding year. He became again an integral part of the city life, so much so that it was the usual thing for the gossips who gathered at the riverside on washday, or who in picturesque groups sat in the sun making lace, or who simply passed a tidbit of news along the grapevine route, to append to the account of any accident, scandal, quarrel, or fight, "Of course, Father Regis was there!" This extraordinary faculty of being on the scene whenever there was urgent need of him began to be regarded by the people as another miracle in his already portentous existence.

Not without reason was his uncanny knowledge currently attributed to a divine intuition that forewarned him. His intense prayer and his close union with God afforded him a supernatural insight, similar to that so strikingly noticeable in the Curé d'Ars. We have recounted above how disconcerting to his would-be assassins was his unmasking of their evil intentions, without the least outward sign to betray them. In a parallel case his intuitive powers were manifested in an equally striking manner. To a wanton hussy who refused to heed his urgings that she abandon her ways of sin, he prophetically said, "Beware! On the part of God I warn you that, if you continue, you run the risk of being chastised by a sudden death in the midst of your sins!"

Unabashed, she returned to her affairs. A few days afterward, while she was calling to one of her lovers from her low balcony, a jealous rival leveled his gun at her, and shot her through the head, killing her instantly.

Francis used his extraordinary powers with better results in the guidance of souls he encountered in the confessional. One penitent in particular volunteered, at the inquiry for beatification, the evidence of his own case in this regard. For long years he had been troubled by exactly those temptations against which Francis had warned him years before,

as constituting the gravest obstacles to his salvation. Regis'
good advice had enabled him to anticipate these difficulties
and to nerve his soul for the combat.

But it was especially for his poor that these rare gifts
were bestowed upon the "father of the poor." One night he
matched his knowledge of the future with a doctor's, after
the eminent physician had declared that a young sick girl,
whom both were attending, would live no more than three
hours. Francis approached the bed, seized the girl by the
hand, and prayed a moment. Then, just as Christ had done
for the daughter of Jairus, he cured her immediately and
completely.

Upon another occasion, he visited a young matron, Catherine Boutard, who had been on the verge of childbirth for
days amid excruciating sufferings. At the end of her tether,
she abandoned hope of living, made her confession to
Francis, and then begged him, "Father, do not leave until
I am either dead or delivered."

In the next room, Francis gathered together the family
and knelt down with them to recite the litany of the Blessed
Virgin. Some minutes later the baby came into the world
in perfect health.

Betimes, he invoked the aid of individual saints, just as
the Curé d'Ars did with St. Philomena, to receive the glory
and credit for his cures. Calling upon St. Ignatius and St.
Maurice one day, he touched a dying woman, who, though
enceinte, had burst into a fit of anger that resulted in an
unstoppable hemorrhage. As soon as she felt his hand upon
her, the woman realized that the flow of blood ceased. She
became another of his bounden debtors, a faithful worshiper
of the very footprints he left in the ugly mud of Le Puy's
streets.

But despite his ever spreading fame, and despite the
miracles he worked before the eyes of all, his avowed
enemies, with the obduracy of the Jews of old, continued

to hound him and to cry for his expulsion from the city.
Toward the end of the summer, after the conscript regiment
of more than 800, only three score of whom were men of
Le Puy, had marched off for the wars, the libertines renewed
their attacks. Again this year they pursued the same course
of tactics used before, circulating rumors that the College
of the Jesuits would be closed unless Regis were banished
from the city.

Victory seemed within their grasp during the fall of 1639.
Once more the city councilors announced that they could
not meet their obligations to the Jesuits. Funds were short
again. The demon of war had invaded their lands and
their purses. The doubly heavy taxes levied on the Velay to
fill the war chest of the monarch and his chief marshal,
Richelieu, had depleted the resources not only of the nobles
but also of the bourgeoisie and the lower classes.

The local Jeremiah, Jacmon, himself a former councilman,
wailed out a threnody on the occasion that was at the same
time an echo of the sentiments of the present city officials.
"Ah, poor country!" he writes in his memoirs, "to what
have you come that we see you deprived of so many fine
people, no fewer nobles than men of lesser degree; and
of all our means by taxes, quotas, and many subsidies. What
excesses has our misery not engendered — treacheries,
murders, seizures of gold and silver, thefts, larcenies,
forgeries, violations, wantonnesses, willful litigations, in-
justices, false witnesses, false oaths, and many other evils.
. . . And to make so little profit and have so little business!
And nevertheless, never has there been more ostentation
before the world of so great a kingdom, in which all is ruin
and waste. I pray God to have pity on us. O Holy Virgin,
pray for us. All you saints, intercede for us and give us
a holy peace! Amen."

Jacmon justly blamed the ills of the townsfolk on the
war. But the inveterate libertines slyly whispered to the

friends of the Jesuits that their trouble was caused by opposition to Regis in official circles.

The crisis came to a head when the collections of the 4000 livres from the lands and benefices assigned to the College as endowments fell far short of that total. All through the Velay and the Vivarais these farms and estates, destined to support the free school at Le Puy, had been smitten by the blight of the previous year and had not recovered fully. Moreover, requisitioning of their crops and man power for the army in the south had impeded the regular marketing of the produce. The net result was that the College authorities found it impossible to run the school on the scanty revenues.

Accordingly, the day for the opening of school passed without a resumption of classes. In a neat burst of miserly bourgeois logic, the councilors protested that the failure to open the school was a "scandal to the public," and was endangering the youth of the city. Upon being summoned to appear before them, the procurator, Father Jean La Motte, presented a statement of the College expenses and receipts, and pointed out how utterly unreasonable it was to expect the Jesuits to conduct the institution on this reduced amount of revenue. Enraged, the councilors tiraded against the superiors for allowing hundreds and hundreds of livres to flow into the Refuge of St. Agatha, an institution for whose running they had signed no contracts and assumed no obligations. That revenue, the officials intimated, could well be applied to the College itself, now that it was in these tight straits.

Father La Motte carried the remarks of the councilors back to the rector. The procurator joined in with that faction of the community which suggested the plan of sacrificing the Refuge for the sake of the College. All the old arguments were revived again to deride the Utopian plan of endeavoring to reform incorrigible prostitutes while

the education of youth, a practical, imperative foundation
for the future welfare of the State and Church, was being
imperiled. Eventually, some members of the community
became confirmed in their belief that the present straitened
circumstances of the school were due to the machinations
of the libertines. They put pressure on Arnoux to force
Regis into surrendering the work, if not for the sake of
saving himself from the wrath of the murderous libertines,
at least to spare the College from its impending doom.

Rumors of the rift in the Jesuit community began to leak
abroad. Throughout the city, people began to speculate on
the outcome of this new condemnation by the Jesuits of
their own colleague, the apostle of the fallen. To quash
these conjectures Father Arnoux next Sunday appeared in
the College church and preached a sermon in which he
publicly eulogized Regis for his great works, urged him to
continue them, and promised him in presence of all the
full support of his authority.

That public attestation of faith in Francis dispelled the
new clouds that were gathering about him. Soon afterward
the financial difficulties of the school were also settled. The
College opened on a somewhat restricted basis for what
was to be a year of great festivity — the celebration of the
hundredth anniversary of the Order, first approved as such
in 1540.

Those hundred years had thoroughly tested many of St.
Ignatius' masterly provisions, had proved many of his laws
to have been inspired. But the inestimable value of his
system of government had been doubly demonstrated anew
by the events at Le Puy that year. The permanence of the
office of General at Rome had maintained a consistency of
policy toward the work of Regis that survived the local
changes. Yet the substitution of a new Superior at Le Puy
had rescued that work from the perils threatening it. Moreover, under the sympathetic, friendly, and understanding

supervision of Father Arnoux, Francis had pursued his zealous activity with renewed vigor, and had been protected against the assaults of his wily enemies. Far from cramping his style or smothering the spirit she had mothered, the Society aided Francis to achieve heights of personal and apostolic perfection he would never have attained elsewhere. Once more the eternal truth was vindicated: "Brother holpen by brother is like unto a strong city" (Prov. 18:19).

CHAPTER X

WIDENING HIS CONQUESTS

IT HAS remained for Regis' latest French biographer, Père Guitton, to mention for the first time the particular circumstances that guided Francis in most of his missionary tours. Because of the fact that he seemed to be working directly under the bishops, Francis has come to be regarded by many of the Jesuits as a free lancer, adventuring on the fringes of the Society. Many priests, and some Jesuits even, influenced by the Jansenists, actually believed that he had been on the very point of expulsion from the Society, and that only his death prevented the serving of the papers of dismissal.

The letters, both of the Provincial and of the Rector of Le Puy, it is true, describe his missions of the winter of 1639-40 as having been decided upon directly by the bishop, Just de Serres. But this fact, as alluded to by them, indicated merely the reason for their own orders. It was by these alone that Francis was actually sent afield into towns and districts which he had not covered on his former missionary journeys.

His various itineraries, annually assigned him by the rectors of the College of Le Puy, had one definite purpose in view. This was to meet the obligations resting on the College toward the benefices assigned for its support. The College of Le Puy, as just previously stated, was wont to derive about 4000 livres a year revenue from the benefices attached to it. But pope and bishop, in connecting these properties to the College of the Jesuits, had also imposed certain spiritual duties to be discharged toward these dependencies. Besides, the rector of the College had the privilege of naming the curés or chaplains who were to fill these positions, and also had the great pleasure of paying for their keep. Still other material obligations toward the dependent parishes included the contribution of alms to the poor, the repair and upkeep of the churches and presbyteries, and the furnishing of the sacristies with linen and vestments.

So far as external arrangements were concerned the College was thus established much along the lines of medieval monasteries. The rector of the College was equivalently the prior of these subject parishes, even though they might be in different dioceses. His duty, resting on him more directly than on the bishop, was to look out for the spiritual well-being of the parishioners entrusted to him. Only in case that the rector neglected this obligation — so the Council of Trent decreed — was the bishop himself responsible for the instruction of the faithful in the truths of salvation and of the Christian life. The choice of catechists or missionaries for the parishes devolved, therefore, primarily upon the rector. In fact the Sacred Congregation had even legislated in regard to the granting of faculties for confessions by the rectors themselves. The only approbation required from the bishop was permission to exercise these faculties already obtained from the rectors, such permission not involving the validity of the administration of the Sacrament, but only its liceity.

These complications sometimes resulted in lawsuits which were carried to the very Parliament of Toulouse, as when a forgetful bishop appointed a priest to a parish which had an incumbent already designated by a rector.

Ordinarily, however, things moved smoothly enough. Thus, in our present case, the rector of the College would confer with the bishop of Le Puy about the appointment of one of the bishop's own men to a curature, since the Jesuits

lacked men to staff the parishes themselves. Besides the four
dependencies in the diocese of Le Puy, however, the College
held benefices also for eight parishes in the Valence diocese,
for one in Viviers, and for four in Vienne. Accordingly, the
rector had much correspondence with these other worthy
prelates as well. This complicated even more the task of the
treasurer or procurator of the College. Spring, summer, and
fall, he was on horseback, traveling from one of these places
to the other, haggling with the tenants about the tithes, and
so trying to scrape together enough to keep the College
running and to meet its financial obligations. While the city
of Le Puy, as we saw, had contracted to pay something
toward the upkeep of the tuition-free school, yet the bulk
of the revenue was to be derived from those outside properties that constituted its endowment.

For the spiritual care of the parishes, the rectors of the
Colleges usually kept two or three "catechists and missionaries" on their staff. The work of these men was just as
much a part of the College work as was the teaching of
classes, and indeed, they were sometimes put to teaching
when one of the regular professors fell sick. Francis himself was requisitioned to replace his fellow Jesuits from time
to time during his years in Le Puy when Umeau was
rector, but Father Arnoux had tried to spare him exclusively
for his missionary work.

To lighten the burdens of the missionaries from the
respective Colleges, the superiors sometimes exchanged the
care of distant parishes with like ones of another College.
Thus, Francis, though attached to the College of Le Puy,
gave missions at Andance and Saint-Sauveur, which
belonged to the College of Tournon, and at Saint-André,
subsidiary of the College of Lyons. Nor did he complete
the full circuit of all of Le Puy's dependencies. Some of them
were attended to by the Jesuits of Aubenas and of Tournon.

Three of the four priories of the Le Puy diocese, Regis

attended to directly from the College during the spring and
summer months. Solignac, Polignac, and Bains were within
a few hours' walk of the city. To them Regis paid frequent
visits all during his years of work at Le Puy. He also passed
through Montregard, the other College dependency, on his
way to and from his more distant missions in the diocese
of Valence and of Vienne. But his most famous mission
there was given in the year 1639.

Following the advice of the bishop that year, he set out
first by going south of Le Puy through some of the diocesan
parishes in that hilly region. Memories of his missions are
preserved at Le Monastier, where the bed he purportedly
occupied has furnished relics to cure the sick of the neighborhood ever since; at Saint-Martin-de-Fugéres, where the saint
converted to Catholicism many families led astray by heresy;
at Freycenet-la-Cuche, on the same road, and at Le Beage,
just across the diocesan line in the Viviers territory. At the
last-named place, his cultus is just as much alive as though
he had but recently been canonized.

Across the mountains to the west of Le Beage and the lake
d'Issarles, Francis followed the mule path to Pradelles, the
town that marks the southernmost extremity of his work
in this region. In his footsteps, two centuries later, Robert
Louis Stevenson and his donkey Modestine were gingerly
to pick their way and would give testimony — Modestine
mutely by her truculence, and Stevenson eloquently in his
Travels With a Donkey — to the difficulties encountered in
negotiating these mountains in the late autumn. What were
the hardships to be overcome without a donkey and in
midwinter, Regis and his unheralded lay brother companion
fully experienced. But scenes such as they witnessed near
Pradelles in 1639 amply rewarded them for their trouble.
At the crossroads of Le Geray, the parishioners from Pradelles and St. Etienne had all gathered to hear his words.
From the steps of the old church of St. Clement, built back

in the days when the Roman road was first pushed through, the missionary spoke in his unforgettable earnestness, and the cross erected by the grateful peasants has kept his memory before them throughout the centuries that followed.

That year, 1639, Francis also journeyed to the northern extremity of the diocese to the town of St. Julien, on the Ance River, some miles north of Vorey, where he had given a mission the year before. Ten miles farther to the east, at Monistrol, the traditions of the saint, however, are much more distinct. In that neighborhood was an old castle called the Tour-Maubourg. To this imposingly turreted home Regis was bound by special ties of affection, for here lived the daughter of his close friend, Count de la Motte of Le Cheylard, now the wife of Jean de Fay. At their fireside Francis was a frequent guest, bestowing his benediction on the home and the family, and especially on their young son Jacques, who sixty years later would transmit into the records of the beatification inquiry all the traditions the family had preserved about the mission work of Regis both here and at Le Cheylard.

One of the stories that particularly took his fancy, as a young man who loved the saddle and looked on horseback riding as the only practical way of covering that uneven country, Jacques de Fay narrated thus: "On a certain occasion, when Regis had yielded to the pious insistence of a good man who obliged him to take his horse and his lackey, in order to travel to the end of his mission trail, the Père forced the footman to mount the horse, while he himself went on foot as always." While the story is another glimpse of the missionary's ascetic rigor, it also affords us an insight into the consideration shown by him to others. We can easily imagine his uneasiness at seeing the poor footman straggling along in the snow. It was only a matter of getting out of sight of the generous host's home when the Père dismounted, pressed the reins into the footman's

protesting hand, and urged him to mount the horse. Francis
could well insist that he had trudged these snow-paved
mountain trails for five winters in succession and still lived
to tell the tale. Surely a few miles more would not hurt him.

East from Tour-Maubourg, on a line with St. Julien and
Monistrol, is another village that witnessed the human side
of Francis' lovable character. At Saint-Pal-de-Mons a cross
marks the place where the vagabond priest, while engaging
in an informal mission to the crowd gathered by the roadside, paused to eat a bowl of soup. Tradition has it that
they would not let him leave at the invitation of a good
housewife, whose home was just off the road, so she carried
the steaming bowl out to him and served him in the open.
He was thus able to refresh himself, just as the countryfolk
would do when their noonday meal was brought to them
where they ploughed the fields. Gestures like these let the
simple peasants know that the Père was one of them, that
he did not stand on ceremony nor disdain their frugal fare.

South of St. Pal, at Raucoules and at Labrosse, on either
side of the road from Le Puy to the College's benefice at
Montregard, are traditions of Francis' visits. One of those
indispensable conveniences for which, however, Francis
seems to have had scant use, a bed, is pointed out as the
one he occupied at Raucoules. In the home of the Juge
family at Labrosse is cherished the great mission crucifix
Regis used in preaching. It was this year graciously
donated by him to his hosts here in pledge of gratitude, as
his most precious gift. This unusual token commemorated
some equally unusual event, which seems to have been the
conversion here of his most remarkable conquest, a young
Huguenot widow of near-by Montregard.

To this village, with its beautiful name of "Mountain
View," overlooking the jagged whorl that girded the
horizon, Francis had come almost every year of his missioning in these parts. His spiritual obligation toward the inhabi-

tants, due to the dependence of their church of St. Jean upon the College of Le Puy, had drawn him here. The people's attachment to him, in turn, frequently kept him here some time over his schedule. But in the château of Girodon which stood on the high eminence, to the northeast end of the village, he was not welcome. The lord of this château, Etienne de la Franchière, had inherited the property and the errors of Calvin from his apostate father, and had married a Huguenot lady of Le Chambon-de-Tence, Louise de Romezin, daughter of the lord of Les Mazeaux. Both families had formerly been Catholics, the Romezins having abandoned the faith when the Wars of Religion began. That it was which gave the grandfather of Madame de la Franchière the chance to seize with impunity the local church lands.

Similarly, the de la Franchières had been ardent Catholics. Their ancestors, in fact, had built one of the chapels in the church of St. Jean at Montregard. But they also went over to Calvinism, and their doors were shut to the missionary who in former times would have been welcomed heartily at the château.

Cold enough had been one welcome Francis had received at Montregard.

Late one winter afternoon, as the gray of the sky was darkening into night, Francis had arrived at Montregard, drenched by the sleet and snow that had melted on his clothes. Without first seeking shelter and a change of clothes at the presbytery there, he had gone straight to the church to pay his respects to his Sacramental Lord. Finding it locked, he had thrown himself on his knees on the doorstep and bared his head in prayer to the Prisoner within. Some passers-by, attracted by this strange sight, had surprised him at his orisons, had shaken him vigorously to bring him out of his numbed condition, and finally forced him to seek shelter and warmth in a near-by house.

But the winter of 1639 was comparatively mild. Regis made of the town the center for his missions and sallied out thence to the places in the neighborhood that eagerly awaited his coming. Montfaucon and Raucoules to the west, Marlhes and St. Sauveur to the north, St. Julien and St. Bonnet to the east, St. André and Tence to the south — all had their missions of a few days, either in pairs or individually.

Besides facilitating the movements of Regis this year, the mildness of the weather, and the promptings of curiosity brought out to his mission at Montregard that winter a distinguished auditor, the chatelaine of Girodon, whose husband, Etienne de la Franchière, had died only the past July. To escape the bitter memories of his death the young widow had moved out of the Montregard château and had shut herself up with her young son Louis in the château of Marcoux, about a mile above the village. There, behind the walls of the manor and in the woodland solitude that surrounded it, she brooded over her loss and wept for her dead husband.

But even this seclusion could not keep out the news of Francis' mission and the reputation he had of being a saint. The peasants and servants of the Marcoux household were all Catholics, and on the days when Regis was conducting his services at Montregard, Madame de la Franchière could not find them around. Upon their return late in the evening, the mistress of Marcoux demanded an explanation of their absence. The fervid words of the usually stolid servitors were the first introduction she had to the existence of this "holy Père." Day and night, as she learned, he was working for the sanctification of the rough countryfolk in spite of all the ravages of the weather and the discomforts of his journeyings up to this mountain district. Averse at first, the chatelaine nevertheless became curious about him, especially when she heard of his patience, his kindness, his devoted-ness to the poor, his unequaled goodness toward all. He was indeed an anomaly.

But what intrigued her most about him, by her own admission, was the magnetic force that seemed to draw all of her people irresistibly toward Montregard, even before dawn or after sundown. Her curiosity eventually *got the better of her aversion. She decided to investigate this phenomenon of mass hypnotism and wholesale illusions, and thus enable herself to free her household from the influence of this magician.

One evening she learned that the next day, before sunrise, Regis would preach at Montregard. Shrouded by the veil of darkness and by her own heavy wrappings, she ventured out into the cold morning and made her way over the short distance to Montregard. Instead of finding a Calvinistic imposter, the chatelaine experienced a pleasurable surprise. Here was a man speaking simply to the simple countryfolk who hung on his every word, and yet conveying to them a strange sense of the peace of God as he spoke with undeniably divine unction. The former Louise de Romezin, who had felt no horror when her own chaplain some years before had settled an argument with a priest by killing him, now found another priest whose words touched her deeply. She felt so near to God as he spoke that, on returning to her château, she resolved not to miss another of his sermons. She would not, of course, abandon her own religion for the errors of Rome, but she could derive love of God and of her neighbor from the unctious instructions of this marvelous speaker.

Her presence at the sermons was quickly noticed. The good people brought the news to Francis that the noble chatelaine, who owned two châteaux in the district, had come to hear him. He consequently sought her out after one of the sermons. A short conversation with her made him realize her unusual intelligence and education, while Louise herself admitted that she was charmed with the exquisite modesty of the man of God.

Soon, with the aid of some friends, and still without letting her family know of her whereabouts, the lady of Marcoux arranged to have some extended discussions with Francis, probably at Labrosse. With a condescending superiority, she displayed her own knowledge of religious subjects by engaging Francis in arguments about some controversial points. The simple answers she drew from him only afforded her further opportunity to quote the standard Calvinist objections and the garbled texts with which her ministers had filled her mind. Francis was patience itself in bearing with her feminine failings. With an unantagonizing gentleness he heard her out, never suggesting by his manner or his answers that he suspected her of either pride or arrogance.

Her strong point, both in the number of her arguments and in the vehemence of her convictions, was her aversion to the mystery of the Real Presence of Christ in the Holy Eucharist. Francis imperturbably endured all of her blasphemous assertions on this subject, excused them on the grounds of her invincible ignorance, and then with a few words, grace-laden and compelling, presented the truth to her prejudiced mind. Immediately, the fog of her unbelief was lifted. Her doubts and arguments vanished. She believed. Sixty-three years later, in 1702, when she was giving her testimony before the board of inquirers, she still retained the vivid memory of this signal conquest of grace over her heart, and she still venerated the saintly missioner who converted her "almost with a single word."

From that time onward, she was a Catholic. Francis dispelled the rest of her doubts, instructed her in the points she needed, and baptized her that year. But to save Francis and the peasants from the wrath of the Huguenot nobles, who might have made trouble for them if they learned that he had bewitched the defenseless young widow, Louise kept her secret to herself for the whole of that year. Even during her visit to her parents at Le Chambon-de-Tence she did not reveal it, and felt safe from their wrath only when she had married, some time later, a Catholic nobleman, Annet de Banne de Boissy, who also lived at Montregard.

Another secret that she kept for threescore years afterward was the wonder of Regis' amazing influence over these rough mountain folk. She was deeply impressed by it during that winter and the next while she followed Francis around on his mission tours, eager not to miss any chance of hearing the enthralling message he delivered with ever new attractiveness. Her analysis is based on what she saw and felt herself, and it sums up quite fully what his other listeners in these parts, including the uneducated country priests, could not capture in words.

The first thing that struck her, and the thing that she noticed was most striking in the eyes of the Montagnards themselves, was the missionary's astounding physical endurance. To appear among the people here, in these months of blizzard weather and subzero cold, proved to the peasants that Regis was eager to speak to them. They could not think of anyone coming out from a distant place, during a time when they spent their days huddled around their fireplaces and their nights buried beneath blankets, unless he had a startling message to deliver. And the fervor that made possible Francis' triumph over the cold was in some way communicated to these hearth-bound folk, so that he was able to make them forget the weather, abandon their firesides, and follow him to the cold churches in which his audiences gathered. Pulling these mountaineers away from their fires in winter was a greater feat than stirring a mountain bear out of his lethargic sleep of hibernation.

For the peasant, too, Madame de la Franchière noted, the winter was a time of rest, of prolonged sleep, of inactivity. By contrast, the ceaseless labors Francis engaged in for long hours of day and night service seemed to them something superhuman, almost miraculous in itself. One day, when he returned to Montregard from a mission in an outlying place, he was met by a group of strangers come from a distance in the opposite direction to make their confessions to him. Without a moment's rest, he welcomed them with his habitual pleasantness, gave them what instructions they needed, heard their confessions, and then bade them adieu as they left to return home. Everywhere he went, Louise remarked that the importunings of the multitudes and their wearisome demands on his attention were met with unchanging kindness and invincible fortitude. It was a wonder to all how here he found hidden sources for his bursting energy, just as at Le Puy he had found hidden sources for his supplies of grain in the famine.

What impressed the people still more in his physical prowess was the fact that, despite his fatiguing labors, he never took sufficient rest or nourishment. In the course of time, Madame de la Franchière became solicitous in her own way about her friend. She states that she prepared some nourishment for him at Marcoux and sent it on to him or took it to him herself when she went to follow in his path. Traditions around the neighborhood pointed to the little sack of flour which the Père carried on his back when he went out for a couple of days on a distant mission. From this he prepared his frugal meal, mixing the flour with water and heating it over some fire. In vain the lady of Marcoux tried to add to that repast some of her upper-class substantials, some expensive vegetables, some good bread or pastry. But Francis always gave them to the poor, as she found out later, and contented himself with the hard, black bread of the mountaineers, with a little milk if they had some to offer, some herbs, or a bowl of soup. Louise did not even send him any meat, for she knew from the peasants that his rule of life interdicted it absolutely for himself.

How he drove himself on to his long journeys and his varied undertakings with the scant nourishment allotted his poor body, was a mystery to his devotees. But that, too, lent a supernatural air to his mission, for he lived on the Bread of God that he preached and in the strength of it he walked through their mountain lands to draw them all to the mount of God.

For these men as Frenchmen, and still more as mountaineers, the ordinary source of their interior fire, especially for warmth in the winter months, was the wine that came up from Burgundy or from the west by the roads called exclusively the "wine roads." Their amazement consequently reached its height when this fiery missionary appeared among them, drinking no wine nor any other of their warming beverages, but still burning interiorly with a fire that surpassed their own enthusiasm. It in fact became, in Louise de la Franchière's eyes, one of the minor miracles of his ministry, that Francis could so enthrall these wine-loving folk as to keep them away from their own wine bouts for whole days at a time.

But when she essayed to describe the inner core of the secret power that Francis wielded over the hearts of these people, Louise was at a loss for explanations. Before the mystery of God's grace working through an instrument that presented it with no obstacles, she could only "say with truth that all his actions, all his words breathed only God; he labored without any relaxation for His glory and brought everybody to give himself to God." That, after all, is about as much as can be said. Francis came among them breathing God in actions that pledged his sincerity, in words that sprang straight from the heart, and went straight into the minds of these simple people through their rustic Cévenole patois which he used so unassumingly. No flowery language, no studied eloquence, but the Gospel simplicity and directness guided his tongue in his apostolate among these people.

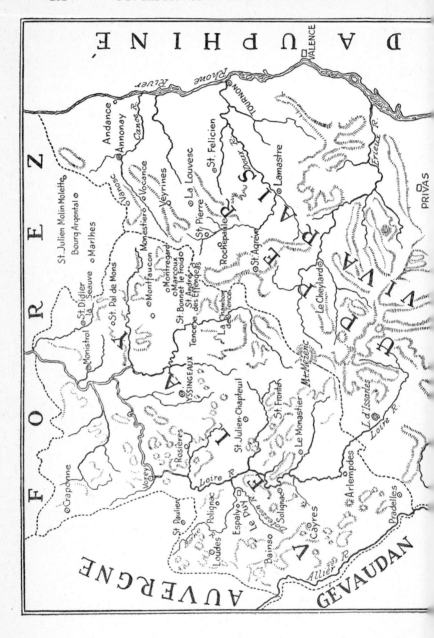

Regis won their hearts completely, unreservedly. The countryfolk felt instinctively his sincere devotion to them, despite the fact that he had been born a nobleman. He retained just enough of the affableness, the suavity, and the gentleness of his cultured background to give an elevated tone to his work amidst this rough-mannered gentry, but they never found in his manners the least condescension; they felt that he was one of their own, their master in the things they prided themselves on — hardiness, physical endurance, and tenacity; their leader in the supreme task of seeking first the kingdom of God and His justice.

They were proud, too, that the saint preferred them to the cityfolk, as he so patently did. For all their boorishness, they appreciated the fine sterling of his true worth, the tempered steel of his character. And they learned from his miracles that he would and could do anything at all for them. In him and through his hands, Christ came to the Cévennes once more, just as in the person and the deeds of another Francis, Christ had lived again in Umbria centuries before. And the line of the advance of heresy in these regions is marked by the line of Francis' missionary operations. The Camisards to the south would make no headway against these stanch Catholics when they would rise up later, and the waves of rationalism and irreligion would wash in vain against their faith, as solid as the mountains of rock that surrounded them.

As the year 1639 drew to a close, Francis decided to take advantage of the mildness of the winter in order to summon to a central place all the people of the surrounding territory to make a full profession of their faith and so constitute an impressive demonstration of their strength for the benefit of the Huguenots. For his rallying place, Regis chose the town that was the seat of the government in northeast Velay and a converging point for the main roads of the territory, Montfaucon.

Just a few miles from Montregard, situated upon the same high plateau that overlooked the Lignon river, this town of Montfaucon had been a citadel of Catholicism all through the Religious Wars. The walled and turreted fortifications, that were girded by a moat, gave to the town and its castle a strength superior to that of any of the surrounding places. And to this material redoubtableness was added the special protection of the Blessed Virgin, whose power had saved it from the attacks of the Huguenots on more than one occasion.

The date for the gathering was set for sometime after Epiphany, January 6, 1640. All arrangements were made for this historic meeting that could prove the vitality of the Church in these regions. The local priest, Louis de Lagrevol, assisted Francis in the management of the crowds that came pouring in from everywhere. People arrived even from the neighboring dioceses of Vienne and Viviers to be present at this special mission, and the response that Francis felt as he preached to them gladdened his heart and made the untold labors he had expended to gather in this harvest seem light indeed.

The mission had progressed some days when still another arrival made his appearance in Montfaucon, probably from the most distant point of all — Le Puy. But to Francis' chagrin, he bore a message from Father Arnoux summoning him back to the College, immediately, to replace a professor who had taken ill.

It was like a bolt from the blue. Here before him, waiting for his words was a crowd such as he had never assembled at Le Puy, and he was asked to abandon them to teach grammar to a handful of inconsequential boys. To Louis de Lagrevol, whom Regis advised of the message, the order seemed preposterous. He urged Francis to put off his departure at least until he could let the Rector know of the true state of things. He insisted that the order was just a wish, subject to change, offered Francis a hundred reasons that would have made any other Jesuit disregard the summons. But to no avail. Despite the great sacrifice demanded of him, and despite all the disappointed hearts, Francis submitted to the command like the true man of God he really was.

He realized that Arnoux had made many sacrifices for him at Le Puy, and had even risked the College's existence to maintain him in his work. And above all he knew that the voice of his Superior was the voice of God for him in these circumstances. The hand of God that had been over him in his former disappointments would prove again that the shadow cast over his life was but a forecast of that Hand's benevolence for the future. After the dark hours of his first missionary rebuff from the bishop of Viviers, and after his withdrawal from his cherished work at Le Puy by Umeau, the Provident Hand of God had poured balm into the wounds of his disappointment. So once more he faced the apparent calamity in full faith.

Calling together his flock, assembled from far and wide, he informed them that his duty ordered him elsewhere. He promised that they should see him again in a little while, for he would return in the autumn. He prayed God to give them all the graces they would have earned in the course of the mission, and then he bade them adieu.

The same day Francis took the road down toward Le Puy, deeply affected by the untoward interruption, but obedient and submissive.

Another of the crises that do not make a man but show what he is had passed over the life of Regis. He had acted in full accord with what he had preached. The sequel would show that it was but another shadow of God's Hand "outstretched caressingly."

CHAPTER XI

In Hoc Signo Vinces

THE cross that crowned the summit of Mount Anis above Le Puy, where stands today the gigantic Notre Dame de France, signaled to Regis late next day the goal of his return journey and symbolized what his recall indeed was for him. As he and his lay brother companion trudged through the late January gloom into the wintry city, there occurred to Francis the thoughts he was to express afterward in a letter to the General — thoughts of bitter regret that he was obliged to abandon the spiritually starving people in the country for routine tasks in a place where there was an oversupply of priests and religious and even lay folk who might do the work he was summoned to fulfill. None of them could have replaced him on the mission. It was a severe cross indeed. But as before in his life, the shadow of the cross athwart his path presaged future conquests that would compensate him for his sacrifice.

Upon his arrival at the College, Francis reported to the rector and was appointed to the teaching of the class conducted hitherto by the sick professor. It was one of the lower grammar classes of the school. Francis submitted to the hidden life and monotonous grind it imposed upon him, content to have his light shaded by a bushel if that were God's will.

The financial condition of the College probably prevented Arnoux from hiring a lay teacher to fill the vacancy. Besides, the whole economic life of Le Puy had recently suffered a rude jolt. With the College so deeply in debt, the rector could afford absolutely no more outlays. We are certain, at all events, that Arnoux did not recall Francis for any secret disapproval of him or for any official objections to his ministry. A few days before summoning him, Arnoux had written to the General a letter that admits of no doubt as to the high esteem in which he held Regis' missionary achievements:

From the most reverend bishop, our Father Francis Regis has obtained a special mission to the country villages of the diocese. And here, what has this intrepid worker not accomplished! His confessions, for a certainty, are heard from three hours before dawn up to late in the night, with such ardor and constancy on one side and the other that the crowd of penitents never fails the priest, nor the priest the penitents. Besides, it has come to be almost a daily custom for a great number of people to deprive themselves of all corporal nourishment until, purified by the Sacrament of Penance, they are able to receive at nightfall the most sweet and divine nourishment of the Eucharist. (January 8, 1640.)

Directly to face about, just a few days after writing this letter, and summon Regis back to Le Puy, must have implied ample reason on the part of Arnoux, without any other alternative in sight. But even did he not have sufficient grounds for interrupting the marvelous missionary work thus described to the General, the Providence of God justified his move, for consequent upon it came even more triumphal achievements, not the least of which was the masterly conquest of himself by Regis in submitting to the recall.

News soon spread around the city that Francis had returned. His friends and devotees were not long in demanding him for confessions and for sermons in addition to his classwork. Some of them, moreover, looked to him for the solution of a still more important problem.

As has been mentioned before, lacemaking was Le Puy's main industry, the means of livelihood for thousands of its inhabitants, the particular source of more than 600,000 livres worth of trade a year. It was to Le Puy what the home-weaving trades were to the cities of northern France and of the Netherlands. It meant security and even subsistence for hundreds upon hundreds of families, and was the old-age pension for numerous old folks who otherwise would have been destitute or a burden to the community. It has been estimated that 40,000 women and girls throughout Velay were occupied in that trade. At Le Puy, the number of girls attracted to this work was so great that the townfolk and nobles could find no more serving girls to do their house-work and cooking for them. The upper classes even com-plained that, because of the widespread wearing of laces, no distinction existed any more between them and the small folk so far as clothing was concerned. In fact, no distinction of this kind even existed between the nobles and their horses, since they, too, were richly caparisoned with costly laces, interwoven with gold and silk threads. The livery of their footmen, servants, and lackeys was also amply sup-plied with lace trimmings, according to the prevailing fashions of the times.

Le Puy had built up its immense lace trade upon these ever increasing demands for more and costlier laces, re-quired by the current fads, and had based its social and economic security upon that trade. Anything that interfered either with the fashions or the trade would strike an eco-nomic deathblow at the city. And that blow had fallen in the first month of 1640, just before Francis' return from Montfaucon.

On the last Monday in January, trumpeters and the herald of the seneschal had appeared on the main streets and squares of Le Puy to proclaim and post a new edict of His Majesty. The people paid little heed to the rapid and unintelligible vociferations of the herald, but crowds soon gathered around the places where the printed copies of the edict were hung up. When those who could read had interpreted the decree, the people would not believe their ears. Yet it was true. His Majesty, Louis XIII, had just promulgated another sumptuary law and this time the law had been passed also by the Parliament of Toulouse. Hitherto, such laws had been ineffective for Languedoc because Parliament had always resisted the royal power on a point so vital to the well-being of the province. But now it had succumbed to the threats of Richelieu. It was an ominous day for Le Puy.

The details of the decree were soon known to the entire city. The new law was to forbid that any person, no matter of what sex, quality, or condition, should wear any sort of lace, either of silk or cotton thread, on any clothes at all. Lace was forbidden for all robes, mantles, neckbands, sashes, belts, sword belts, scarves, garters, bows, ribbons, or other kinds of apparel. Included also were all adornments, buttons, designs, hems, ornaments, chains, strings, threadwork, pendants, spangles of gold or silver, whether real or fake, or any suchlike embroidery enriched with stones or pearls. As for the equipages of the nobility, their livery was to be stripped of all silk cloth, or bands of velvet or satin. And for womenfolk, even their private trousseaux were to be stripped of lacework, fancywork, undergarments of fine cloth, or embroideries of silk or linen.

For once, the women were more vehement than the men about a political question. The fury that this edict raised among them raged up and down the city all day and far into the night. And what added fuel to the flame of their wrath was the fact that no evasion was possible. The king's agents were instructed to levy heavy fines against offenders, if the law was not complied with inside of the eight-day deadline proclaimed.

Merchants and lacemakers alike waxed wroth over this new imposition. They had been paying taxes of every kind to finance the imperialistic ambitions of Richelieu and the King, and now their very means of income was being summarily stifled. That same clutching after the very least sources of revenue had forced the King and his minister to ban the use of gold and finery in the elegant clothes of nobles and commoners alike — gold that might be minted into money and kept in circulation. Yet, much of the laces made, especially the more elaborate kinds, was being exported, thus bringing revenue into the country. The witless king and his penny-wise minister were savagely criticized for killing the goose that laid the golden egg. For with the death of this industry, whole sections of the country would not be able to pay their taxes. It was a ruinous decree, and the people of Le Puy and its environs soon made their minds known.

By the time Francis arrived at Le Puy, the whole town was agog with indignation, but was frantic at its powerlessness to resist the strong royal decrees. They had seen enough examples of the fate to which those who resisted Richelieu were destined. And when a whole city rose up against his iron rule, as did Montpellier, Privas, and others, the place was ruthlessly besieged and its fortifications destroyed.

In their hour of need they turned to Regis and asked him, who seemed to be able to accomplish anything, to pray for them, even if he could not intervene politically. Delegations came to Le Puy from other cities affected. One of them, from Saint-Paulien in Auvergne, approached Regis and gave him an opportunity to declare publicly in a tone of assurance: "This decree will not last. The making of lace will take its course again. This trade will not be destroyed, but on the contrary will be increased."

Right on the heels of this prophecy came the startling news that the decree had been suddenly withdrawn, after having been in operation only that short time. The impossible seemed to have been achieved, and the people with one voice ascribed to Regis the achievement of that unexpected boon. Although he did not, as some have said, travel to Toulouse itself and secure action from the Parliament on the matter, we can be certain that he did plead the cause of the poor and the middle class before the disaffected nobles who had demanded the passing of the decree as a blow at them.

Whatever may have been the circumstances, the traditions of the lacemakers unfailingly maintain that Francis did obtain the recall of the decree. Further than this, they believe that he obtained also the fulfillment of the other part of his prophecy, namely, that the trade would increase with the years. Through the Jesuits he is said to have secured the opening of the markets of Spain and the New World to the laces of Le Puy, thereby enabling the trade to regain its former prosperity.

The truth is that Francis prayed for the increase of the trade and that his prayer was heard some years later when Louis XIV issued another sumptuary law against the wearing of any lace not made within the kingdom itself. That meant the exclusion of the more famous Italian laces, and led to the development of the national pattern, French point, after the economic protectionism of Colbert had gone into effect.

To the 40,000 lacemakers of Le Puy and its environs, Francis was a savior. Their confidence in him remained undiminished through the years, and whenever a crisis would threaten the trade again, they would have a Mass said in his honor either at Le Puy or at the place where he died.

The moral effect of Francis' prophecy in restoring the calm of the people and strengthening their courage in those early months of 1640 was probably as conducive toward the withdrawal of the decree as were his prayers. Had the people refused to obey the decree, had they revolted or resisted the royal authority in any way save by voicing their minds, the iron fist of Richelieu would have smashed them just as it had smashed the followers of Montmorency. By patiently biding their time, they won out, for Richelieu probably realized that the decree would only make him that much more unpopular, and would cut that much more of revenue from the taxes on the lacemakers and on all the allied commerce that they occasioned.

Whatever was the actual motive in the withdrawal, the people could never be persuaded that Francis was not the major cause. The tradition was so strong that it has even been accepted as fact by some writers of economic history in France. The kernel of truth that underlies most of the legendary accretions of the story is still another tribute to Francis Regis' power as a social force, even if his effects were achieved exclusively by prayer.

In the midst of the confusion caused among the lacemakers by the sumptuary decree, the libertines of Le Puy were not idle. While the attention of the police and the magistrates was diverted to the quelling of the rage of the people affected, they made another attempt on the Refuge of St. Agatha.

This time they were not to be denied. They resolved that the annoying shortage which had taken much of the pleasure out of the Carnival celebrations in the past two years would not be repeated this year. They laid their plans well and kept them secret until the night of February 1, the date set for the assault.

Thirty picked villains crept up Montferrand street in the early hours of the morning, armed with sledge hammers and pickaxes to batter down the most vulnerable spot of the wall that ran around the back of the house. By the light of their carefully shaded lanterns they selected the

spot, and, all the preliminaries having been expedited, they
smashed the bricks and mortar with a volley of rapid blows.
The wall caved in. The thirty villains rushed for the interior
of the house. In a few minutes each one had seized his
prize and had carried her off to his old haunts in the underworld. It was a coup so swift that, when the police did
arrive, they found only the directress in the house. She, too,
was packed and ready to leave by the time Francis himself
was summoned. She had had enough to do with those
hussies. Regis would have to find another matron to take
care of them.

To Francis, it looked as though his labors were completely
wiped out. The critics who had opposed him at home and
outside now wagged their heads and vahed at his idealistic
credulousness in believing that he could rehabilitate that
crowd of sinners. It would have disheartened anyone else.
But Francis merely set about the whole task from the beginning once more.

In search of another directress, he went to one of his
friends who had formerly kept some of the girls at her
house before the Refuge had been founded. Despite his requests, she would not accept the thankless task. She would
help him gather them back, but would not take charge of
the house. Finally, Francis admonished her: "My daughter,
I see well that I am not of much account to you, since you
comply so little with my exhortations and my prayers. But
there shall come a time when you will have need of them
and you yourself will come a great distance to seek me."
The prophecy was verified soon after the death of her great
friend. The lady was rudely beaten one day by some ruffians
from whom she had rescued some girls. Notwithstanding
the efforts of the doctors, she remained completely helpless
until she remembered the saint's words and had herself
carried to his tomb. There she was cured.

Eventually, Francis did find someone to conduct the

house for him. He had the broken-down wall repaired, and then set about retrieving his lost sheep.

The struggles that had marked his first conquests were repeated once more. The women came willingly enough at his first pleas, but their captors were loath to let them go. As before, they resisted with threats, with violence, with personal insults and injuries. Four of them attacked him one day as he stepped out of the Refuge after depositing therein their former prey. The wrathful villains rushed him, threw him to the ground, pounded him with their fists, kicked him ruthlessly. But the Père survived it all and pursued his work undismayed. He soon had gathered all of the former inmates, even before the end of the Carnival season, February 20.

The aftermath of this new achievement was the renewed efforts of the libertines at revenge on the holy priest. This time, in addition to their physical violence, they tried some original insults, worked out elaborately during the height of the Carnival celebrations. Behind the protection that the accepted follies of Mardi Gras afforded them, and also behind the anonymity that their masks gave their cowardly hearts, the libertines turned mimics of the actions and characteristics of Regis. In a street masquerade they paraded, dressed like the Jesuit, caricaturing his tone of voice, his manner of walking, his preaching methods. Perhaps they hoped to make him the laughingstock of the city, to chill his zeal, or cause him disgust toward ungrateful Le Puy. But the saint himself merely joined in the laughter. "Provided that God is not offended," he remarked, "what does it matter?"

Part of the act, however, boomeranged on the jokesters. In order to rouse a laugh at Francis' expense, they planned to draw him out of the College to rescue a "fake" maiden in distress. One of the masqueraders, attired garishly and painted heavily as a woman, climbed up to the top of the

Rock Corneille, a natural platform high up above the city, visible to all. There, in full view of the merrymakers and the citizens "she" strutted enticingly, until she apparently lured a well-dressed dandy to come up and make love to her. The act proceeded to amazing lengths and aroused the indignation of some pious women, as the maskers hoped. They hurried to Regis with the news that a public scandal was about to take place and that there was no time to lose.

On hearing the report, Francis merely laughed. The women were astounded at his reaction. "I assure you," one of them said, "it is so; I saw them with my own eyes." But Francis, having recollected himself for a moment, answered: "They are just two maskers playing a carnival farce. No offense of God is to be feared." He did not stir out of the College.

Meanwhile, the two buffoons were awaiting his arrival so as to be able to jeer at his ill-timed zeal for law and order. They had visions of him rushing up with the police, only to have the gendarmes themselves guffaw at him when they unmasked the whole ludicrous plot. But hours passed and still nothing happened. The joke was on them. They had to wait until nightfall before they could descend and slink down some side street to avoid the jeers of the people.

During the Forty Hours' Devotion, held throughout the last days of the Carnival season to make reparation for the excesses of the masqueraders, Francis was kneeling in adoration at the back of the College church near the confessionals when another episode in his conflict with these troublesome wretches occurred.

A group of maskers, equipped with drums and other noisemaking apparatus, stopped before the Church to serenade him. A crowd gathered about them and increased the uproar to deafening proportions. Francis soon emerged from the church, stood on the steps, and mildly tried to coax the clowns to be on their way. He whispered that their diversions, elsewhere unobjectionable, were disturbing the prayer and adoration of the pious folks within.

His pleas were met with redoubled beatings of the drums and with even more noise from the accompanying din makers. The band leader, after he had thus increased the tempo of their raucousness, turned upon the priest with vile imprecations and struck him a stunning blow that knocked him down upon the steps. The crowd dispersed as quickly as did the maskers for fear of the police.

When the report of the outrage finally reached the officials of the city, the councilors sent a deputation to the College to make amends and to seek the identity of the culprit. Upon being admitted to the Rector's office their spokesman immediately declared that the criminal outrage would not go unpunished. This was the first news Arnoux had heard of the whole affair. Into the presence of the magistrates he summoned Francis and questioned him about the attack. But to their amazement, Regis would not reproach the young man with anything, nor would he prefer any charges against his assaulter. "No, he did me no evil, and I really have no complaint to formulate either against him or against anyone else," he said. M. Blanc, the spokesman, had to retire without having secured even the name of the offender. But when the story of the priest's Christlike forgiveness was told about the city, it reached the guilty man, touched his heart, and changed him into an ardent admirer of the priest he had assaulted.

Regis had paid dearly for his achievements in behalf of the Refuge, and one cannot be certain that these attacks on his person did not continue all through this his last year at Le Puy. The violence had taken its toll of his physical strength, but had also served as confirmation of the heroic moral fiber of his character. The unembittered patience with which he had endured the insolence and effrontery of those hotheaded rakes had been a sure token that his heart and mind were steeped in the true spirit of the meek Christ, silent and uncomplaining under His sufferings.

Francis seems to have had but one regret about the whole trying series of attacks. They had exhausted his bodily stamina and threatened to cut short his work among the country people. It was this thought of the greater good that could be accomplished outside of Le Puy that led him to seek to be relieved of his work in the city.

Sometime during the spring, probably in late March, Father Arnoux was able to show to Francis a letter from the General which gave him high hopes in this regard. During January, Arnoux had written to Vitelleschi a letter already quoted, suggesting that Regis' missions among the rustics be established on a permanent basis with a fixed annual revenue in order to preserve and increase the abundant fruits he described therein. The General's answer gave enthusiastic approval to the project. He characterized the news of Regis' apostolic successes as a joyous and magnificent Christmas present, the announcement of which abundantly compensated for the disturbing news Arnoux had to tell him about two of the other Jesuits at Le Puy who were on the point of being expelled from the Society.

Accordingly, on the evening of Palm Sunday, 1640, at the conclusion of a Lent that might have been spent most fruitfully on the missions, Francis took pen in hand and wrote to Vitelleschi the following letter:

Very Reverend Father,

I know that your Paternity has greatly at heart the one project for which I implore you in this letter with the utmost earnestness; it is that I may be allowed to travel through the country villages with one of our brothers and to consecrate to these missions for the salvation of the peasants whatever of life is left to me. Of a certainty, I am unable to explain the fruits that missions of this type produce. I would hardly be convinced of them myself, unless I had gathered them with my own hands, not very often, it is true — a thing that is a great sorrow to me. May this at least be allowed me,

I conjure you for God's sake, each year to labor thus for five or six months.

The lord bishop of Le Puy has given me the fullest powers by letters patent for the whole extent of his diocese. Some pious persons will furnish money for this purpose, and have already furnished some for me. The superior has one hundred and fifty francs destined for this use. Without difficulty I could find some other money for me and for my companion, since it would be necessary in order not to be a burden to the colleges or to the pastors; freed from the worry of expense, these latter would receive us with joy. Many among them have on repeated occasions and long since called on me for this ministry. Their prayers have been incessant but in vain, for the Superior of the College retains me in this city of Le Puy. For four years I have been occupied here in teaching catechism classes, either in our church or in another, often with all the display and pomp possible. Consequently, is it surprising that I am exhausted? Besides, here there is bread in abundance, while the unfortunate peasants are dying of frightful starvation. I hope that it will not be with this mission as it was with that of Canada, but I promise it to myself with full reliance on your most reverend Paternity.

Your Paternity's most humble servant in Christ,
John Francis Regis.

From Le Puy, the Calends of April, in the year 1640, the first centenary of the Society, the jubilee year of great happiness for all Jesuits, and may this permission render it full of jubilation for me.

By this letter, Francis was giving the General full opportunity to confirm or disapprove his whole missionary life, and to furnish documentary evidence that would remain for years to solve the questions as to whether or not he came under official disapproval in the last year of his life and was on the point of being expelled from the Society when he died.

In the meantime, Francis went about his regular classwork at Le Puy and, when school closed, resumed his catechism classes at the College church and at St. Pierre. Bishop de Serres changed his admiration for Regis only to increase it as the time went by. During this year, the happy

thought occurred to him of having a portrait made of his
saintly catechist. For this purpose, he secretly commissioned
one of the local artists, the most clever in the city, to study
Regis in action at St. Pierre and to produce a living portrait
of him. To church, accordingly, the artist took his sketch
pad, and there while Regis was preaching or saying Mass,
he made some preliminary drawings. Of course, it was out
of the question to ask Regis to sit for the picture. Perhaps
it was better for the painter to catch his characteristics as
they were revealed in true life and not be hampered by an
unnatural pose in a sitting. When he had finished and presented the work to the bishop, it served as still another
occasion for the grateful prelate to laud the fruitful apostolate of the Jesuit. In fact, Just de Serres remained until
the end a stanch believer in and supporter of his missionary
friend, and was unfailingly vehement in praising him in
spite of his maligners and critics. Even in the very presence
of Regis, the bishop openly praised him, going as far as to
re-echo the popular cry, "the saint," that had been used to
designate the holy priest.

Nor was the bishop unaware of the stories that were circulated about the marvels that were marking Regis' ministry
with the sign of God's special blessing. From mouth to
mouth it was told how he had been called to the bedside
of a dying woman to ease her passage out of this world,
and instead of helping her to die, he had restored her to
health. Another time, he had issued a simple command,
"Fever, leave this woman, for she needs her health to earn
her living," and the patient was cured. Still another time,
he had cured the mother of a large family despite her wish
to die. She had refused to heed his exhortations that she
pray for her recovery, had said that she preferred to die
rather than ask for a miracle. Next day, when he again came
to visit her, she was up doing her housework and ready to
upbraid him for his pious ruse.

Of his spiritual marvels there was no end. Not the least of these was the upright life led by the girls whom he had discharged from the Refuge once he was satisfied with their reformation and strength of character. Without exception they took up honest ways of living and bravely went to church despite the suspicious looks that always met their appearances in public. They were living proofs of the efficacy of Francis' methods in dealing with their type; his unfailing sympathy, coupled with an attitude of deference and respect that restored their own self-respect, made them realize the fullness of Christ's forgiveness, and gave them something to live up to in the future. Some had criticized him for dealing with them "as though he were talking with queens," but they, too, had to admit the effectiveness of his program from a purely natural point of view, even though the true source of his influence over them was his supernatural closeness to the Christ who had charmed Magdalene into repentance and had made a new woman out of the one taken in adultery.

Much more light would be thrown on his apostolate in this matter if the correspondence he kept up with the directress of the refuge had been preserved. We are assured that whenever he went out on the missions he first came to give a farewell bit of advice and instruction to his penitents. And it was a standing rule that the directress was to write him each week concerning the behavior of her charges. Only one of the notes he wrote to her is extant, addressed to "the governess of my penitents."

The Peace of our Lord be with you!
My dearest sister,

I beg you to believe that I do not fail to remember you and all of your children, even in the midst of my most pressing occupations. Salute them for me and assure them that I am their, and particularly your,

Most affectionate servant in our Lord,
John Francis Regis.

He was indeed their only affectionate servant and friend at Le Puy. After his passing, no one else was found immediately to take care of their material welfare while they were working for their spiritual improvement. The institution lapsed for four years before being taken up again, but the spirit of Regis hovered over it through all its vicissitudes. Half a century later the bishop of Le Puy built a vast plant of seven buildings to house the Refuge, which, under the direction of the religious of our Lady of Refuge, lasted until the Revolution.

The final impressions that Francis was to leave at Le Puy all give witness to the social fruits of his amazing love of God. Everyone was certain that he was driven on not by any earthly motive but only by an absorbing passion for Christ and for the least of His brethren. Canon Pierre Le Blanc, the vicar-general of the diocese who collaborated with Francis in many of his undertakings, observed that "his countenance breathed so much devotion and piety that at the first glance one felt himself conscious of the indwelling of God in him. His example enkindled the love of God in all hearts. I experienced it myself and my confreres of the chapter with me." Hugues de Pradier, one of the confreres, gave his confirmation to the same verdict: "The fire of charity that animated him outshone all his other characteristics. Others have remarked it like myself. . . . One could not converse with him without immediately sensing a communication of the divine fire with which his heart was inflamed."

Besides the clergy, the nobles of the city also went on record with their impressions of the holy priest who worked among them. Five hundred nobles, assembled for the General Council some years after Regis' departure, signed a statement that embodied the experiences of the older persons and the traditions handed down to the younger. "Our churches, our prisons, our hospitals would speak if we did not. Our churches would say that he was a man of God through and through; our hospitals that he was a man of the poor; and our prisons that he carried mercy into the house of justice. He was a rich pauper. Having nothing, he nourished the needy. . . . He has taught us charity for our neighbor. One had only to be wretched to see Father Regis at his side; he poured himself out for the poor, and if he had possessed as much finances and supplies as charity, he would have made works of mercy come to an end for lack of miseries among the poor."

But the poor and the simple folk of Le Puy gave the most symbolic witness to the influence that Francis had exercised among them. Most of them could not write their impressions of their "Père," but once he had gone they still flocked to the institution that had been the source of their most valued social blessings from him — his confessional. They venerated it as a chapel. Each day hundreds would come to pray beside it, to kiss its wood, and to implore the continuance of his apostolate among them.

This achievement of a personal holiness that radiated God back into the hearts of his people was the greatest triumph for Francis Regis, a triumph he secured by accepting with heroic constancy the crosses that were laid upon his humble shoulders.

CHAPTER XII

THE LAST CAMPAIGN

IN THE autumn of 1640, while Father Jean Filleau, the
Provincial, was residing at the College of Le Puy for his
annual visitation, Regis received an urgent summons to his
room. Francis thought at first that it was merely the usual
call for an interview such as was held every year during
the visit of the Provincial. But Father Filleau had a special
surprise for him. A packet of letters had just arrived from
Rome, and among the letters was one addressed to Francis
Regis. With a smile of happy anticipation, Filleau handed
the sealed envelope to his fellow Jesuit, and sat back to
watch him open it with trembling hands. Francis quickly
glanced through the contents of the letter, and then with
unconcealed joy read it aloud to the Provincial as follows:

Your holy and greatly to be desired plan of evangelizing the villages meets with my full approval and my highest esteem. By this
same courier, I am now recommending it to the Provincial expressly
because of the great good for the glory of God and the salvation
of many I hope for from it. Of course, this business cannot be
undertaken without the direction of the Provincial who, I think,
will wholeheartedly concur with you in promoting it. On my own
part, in any case, I shall not fail to help you by all the means I
shall deem possible, and I earnestly exhort you to notify me if I
can aid you in the future for the development or stabilizing of this
magnificent work. Meanwhile, I recommend myself to your holy
prayers and sacrifices. (June 8, 1640.)

Father Filleau shared with Francis his beaming, glowing

consolation upon the receipt of so emphatic and unreserved an approval as that contained in the words of the General. To add further to his joy, the Provincial took up another letter that lay upon his desk, and in turn read it to Francis. Line after line increased the joy in the heart of Regis as he heard once more the approving words of the General of the Society of Jesus:

> This present letter concerns Father Francis Regis who wishes to evangelize the country villages, together with a lay brother companion, for five or six months each year. Since he has at hand some money (so as not to be a burden to anyone), has the ready consent of the bishop, and finally — a thing that I do not by any means doubt — has great hopes for spiritual results, I on my part fully approve this holy plan. Unless your Reverence sees anything opposed to it, I wish it to be established for a long period if possible, and strenuously carried on, not only by that father, as long as his strength lasts, but also by many others after him. Your Reverence will communicate to him what you deem best in the Lord concerning this matter, and afterwards, as soon as possible, inform me about the whole business. (June 8, 1640.)

Rome having thus spoken, Father Filleau was happy to assure Francis that he could continue in what God evidently intended to be his lifework. He urged him to persevere in the zealous tasks he had already so faithfully and courageously been fulfilling these past seven years in the mountain districts. Finally, giving him his blessing, the Provincial dispatched him to make the necessary arrangements with Father Arnoux.

Francis immediately hurried to the rector's room to break the good news to his stanch friend and supporter. Arnoux joined eagerly in Francis' enthusiasm upon perusing the two letters again. He rejoiced at this official approbation since it indirectly vindicated himself also for his fidelity to Regis in all of his enterprises. But, on examining his friend more closely, noting how thin he seemed beneath his loose-fitting and patched cassock, how gaunt his features despite the spiritual glow of his eyes, the rector realized that there was indeed basis for Vitelleschi's reference to the exhaustion of his strength, and for his hinting that others be appointed to carry on after him. Nevertheless, as Arnoux was conscious also of the fact that one man afire with the love of God will accomplish the work of ten, even though his very fervor burn him out prematurely, he concurred with Vitelleschi's decision that Regis should not be put on the shelf but be allowed to continue his work "as long as his strength lasts."

Father Arnoux and Regis accordingly spent many hours arranging the itinerary for that winter's missionary tours. Included first of all was the place Francis had left so abruptly in January — Montfaucon. From there Francis was to traverse the northeastern part of the Le Puy diocese and then cross over into Vienne territory to administer to the spiritual needs of three of the parishes there that depended on the College of Le Puy — Veyrines, St. Pierre, and Lalouvesc. Other calls at various places he had visited before were also indicated.

Early in September Francis and his lay brother companion bade farewell to the rector and the community and departed for what was to be Francis' last campaign. Arnoux had serious misgivings about the state of Francis' health after his strenuous past winter and his months of battling with the local libertines, but since none of his missionary excursions had begun with more official approbation than this, the rector allowed him to go whither his destiny and God's explicit will were summoning him.

A little over a month later, Arnoux received a final communication from the General. Like the other two letters cited above, this in no way crippled the wings of Francis' ardent desires, but dealt one more blow to the Jansenist assertion that Francis was to be expelled from the Order. This final testimony of Vitelleschi does indeed treat of dismissal from the Society, but not of Regis. It reads as follows:

To Father Ignatius, Rector at Le Puy:

Concerning the coadjutor Beissar's dismissal, I have received up to the present no information at all. But concerning the fruitful excursions of Father Regis, I have long known of them and have felicitated the Society and myself, and especially your College, which should greatly rejoice in the accomplishment of works so necessary and so holy. (September 8, 1640.)

These three letters were full and final reparation for the hasty and mistaken condemnation Vitelleschi had issued in 1634 anent the "simplicity and indiscretion" Regis had shown on his first missionary crusade through the mountain villages of the Cévennes. That same simplicity and an equally courageous indiscretion had marked his unsparing efforts in behalf of the spiritual welfare of those Cévenole peasants for the subsequent six years. But now, instead of the ill-considered disapproval of a young, hotheaded prelate, Francis enjoyed the full concurrence of his bishop, Just de Serres, with all his undertakings. This plus the reiterated approbations of his local Superiors, Fathers Filleau and Arnoux, fully corroborated Vitelleschi's conviction that Regis was a "worker most worthy of the Society." Though the General had failed to heed Francis' request for the Canadian missions, he had afforded him, in God's providential way and time, a field of activity equally challenging to his gigantic zeal and equally capable of testing the sterling character of the heroic holiness of the missionary. Vitelleschi had put the seal of his office upon these "necessary and holy" works. His letters still exist in the archives as standing refutation of the legend that the General was about to cut Regis off from the Society in the latter months of 1640.

So sudden a reversal of the General's attitude toward the missionary would have been impossible, unless some untoward event actually had occurred within the last months of Regis' apostolate. Nothing of the sort is recorded. Rather, there is full and compelling evidence that Francis fulfilled the prescriptions of the General with unshaken constancy. To the last ounce of his strength, he devoted himself to his apostolic work.

We therefore find Francis back at Montfaucon in September, wearing himself out in laboring for an overflow congregation that had gathered at this center of marketry and commerce, determined to regain what they had lost by the interruption of their mission nine months before. With somewhat of a premonition that this might be one of his last appearances among his devoted faithful, Francis toiled unstintedly for their spiritual consolation. He poured out the fullest expressions of his zeal for them in the sermons delivered by him three times a day, as well as in the catechism classes for the children. The rest of the hours he spent in the confessional, in comforting the poor and the sick, and in giving the Bread of life to those who came from great distances for Communion, arriving late in the day but fasting for it nevertheless.

Louise de Romezin almost made Montfaucon her home during these days and weeks of grace. When Francis moved his headquarters to the mother-parish of Montfaucon, Raucoules, she followed with the long train of people that accompanied him.

At Raucoules, where Regis missioned for the rest of October and part of November that year, another incident occurred that proved his gift of prophecy. Marcellin du Fornel, a young man from St. Didier, grandson of the lordling of that place in northern Velay, had come to Raucoules to treat with some friends who were in process of negotiating a marriage for him with a lady of distinction. The nineteen-year-old noble encountered Regis one day and in the course of the conversation Francis asked him his intentions for the future. Marcellin replied that he would continue his law studies at the University of Valence for the purpose of obtaining a doctorate there. "Very good," said Regis, "but what after that?" "I think I'll get married," Marcellin answered; "an honorable engagement is being arranged for me. It will be completed shortly."

Regis eyed the young man intently and then declared, "You will obtain your doctorate but not your marriage. God destines you to enter our Society and to illumine it by your eloquence and your virtues, if you are faithful."

The young man dismissed it lightly as though it were a joke or merely a pious fancy. Never having dreamed of entering religion, he prosecuted his efforts to arrange for his marriage. Francis furnished him an added motive — to prove that the pious prophecy of the priest would never be verified. But, as events later showed, Marcellin only proved Regis to be correct. The marriage negotiations were frustrated a short time afterward. Immediately, du Fornel departed for Valence to drown his sorrow in his studies for the doctorate during the next session. But before the twelvemonth had elapsed, he had not only received his degree but had also been admitted to the Novitiate at Toulouse. His untimely death thirty years later plunged the whole province in grief, for he was, as Francis had predicted, a shining light in the Society both for his superb sermons and for his holy life.

The region of Montfaucon and Raucoules was hallowed by Regis all during the late autumn. Finally, after the Feasts of All Saints and All Souls, his center of activity was changed to St. André, a dependency of the College of Lyons. There again, despite the bitterness of the winter, Francis lavished himself on his ministerial works. The graces that had flowed out from him during his mission there in 1636 were repeated and multiplied.

But down in Le Puy the severity of the winter was alarming Father Arnoux. If the weather was so bitterly cold in the sheltered basin of Le Puy, Arnoux reasoned that it must be impossibly inclement on the other side of the woods up in the Boutières. Accordingly, in his solicitude for the health of Regis, he dispatched a messenger, a servant of the College, to propose to him that he postpone the rest of the missions and return to Le Puy until the worst of the winter had passed. However, the rector left it up to Francis' own judgment, since he was the only one who could estimate his own strength. But, at all events, Arnoux would have afforded him authority and justification for a break in the months of continuous labors, if he should deem it advisable.

Whatever may have been his motives, his messenger did not reach Francis until another dread messenger had come into Velay.

Meanwhile, Regis had pushed still higher up into the mountains. It is not known whether he had hitherto visited the little towns of Veyrines and Lalouvesc, high up in the ridges that overlooked the La Roche river, but it is at any rate certain that he climbed up there by way of the slippery, steep-graded roads to give a mission in late November, 1640. In charge of both churches was Father Bayle, the pastor appointed by the rector of Le Puy to these incumbencies, and this good priest had scheduled missions at both places. However, Francis had not finished evangelizing Veyrines itself before the messenger from Father Arnoux arrived, during the first days of December, to inform him of the superior's wishes.

Despite the fact that Arnoux's message, unlike that of the previous January, contained no strict command, Francis complied with his wish to the extent of postponing the mission of Lalouvesc until the latter part of December and setting out for home.

On his way down the mountains, however, Francis passed through the crossroads town of St. Bonnet-le-Froid where he had given missions before. Here he heard the appalling news that happy Montfaucon, which he had just left a few weeks ago, had been visited by the plague. Some of the populace lay stricken under the relentless epidemic. One whole family had already been wiped out. Even the local doctor had succumbed. Merchants and muleteers had brought word that Father de Lagrevol was toiling alone among the plague victims, most of the other inhabitants having fled from the walled town at the first approach of the dread calamity.

Confronted with this urgent need of his services, Francis promptly forgot about himself and his superior's paternal solicitude for his health. It was no time for vacations, now that some of his flock were imperiled. Without hesitation, he directed the messenger to return to Father Arnoux with the news that he would be delayed, and he himself turned his steps toward Montfaucon. Perhaps now in this ill-fated city would be that elusive rendezvous with martyrdom he had pursued at Toulouse, at Le Puy, and up and down these mountains for the past decade. Guiding him like a brilliant star in the night, this thought that he might now consummate his years of ceaseless sacrifice for these mountain folk by a supreme act of heroic charity drew him with increasing speed toward the city. All night long he and his companion trudged through the snow. Next morning, as dawn was breaking, the gloomy walls and crenelated towers of Montfaucon appeared against the first streaks of light. Francis hurried through the deserted gates and down the dark streets to the presbytery.

"Your people are in distress," Francis said upon greeting the pastor. "I have come to aid you."

Happy as he was to see his good friend, Father de Lagrevol nevertheless feared lest the plague might indeed rob his people of the apostle whose future ministrations would mean more to them than the little he could do now against the ruthless pestilence. Fortunately, most of his flock had fled, and he was well able to care for the spiritual needs of the few dozen who were stricken. Already he had conducted the funerals for the first victims. And there still remained in town some valiant souls to assist in the nursing and physical care of the stricken. Hence, de Lagrevol was unwilling to allow Francis to risk his life.

"You have no right, Father," he finally said to Regis, "to expose yourself thus. The bishop and your superiors have given you permission to preach to our people and to lead them back to God, but not to serve the plague stricken. I cannot go beyond their wishes."

But Francis was not to be put off so easily. In his eagerness to serve the afflicted, he volunteered to remove de Lagrevol's scruple, saying, "My superior lives only six leagues from here. If you are willing to accept my aid for the sick, I promise to obtain his permission." The pastor smiled at Francis' estimate of the distance to Le Puy, shortened by his earnestness to half of what it really was. But notwithstanding this, de Lagrevol remained fixed in his determination. No motives Francis could adduce were able to shake his firm resolve. Moreover, de Lagrevol insisted that this was the mind of the magistrates as well, and to verify his assertion, he left Francis in the presbytery and strode across the square to the home of Jean de Chabanacy, one of the councilors.

"You know as well as I do," the priest told the magistrate, "the charity of Father Regis. If we yield to his demand, he will expose himself without regard for the contagion; and this very holy man, so useful to the people of Velay and Vivarais, runs the risk of being stolen away from us to the great detriment of numbers of souls."

De Chabanacy was in full harmony with the pastor's opinion. He even feared further that the widespread popularity of the Jesuit would have more power to draw people thither than fear of the plague would to keep them away from Montfaucon. Thus, unwittingly, his presence there might contribute to the propagation of the epidemic among the crowds who would undoubtedly assemble at least in the vicinity.

Louis de Lagrevol returned to his guest to render the final verdict. Thanking Regis wholeheartedly for his charitable offer, he begged him to aid his prostrate parishioners by his prayers. But he could not stay at Montfaucon. Under no circumstances was he allowed to serve the plague stricken.

Obediently, Francis submitted. Putting on his hat, whose broad brim was battered and frayed, and adjusting his tattered cloak, he bade farewell to his friend. Together the two walked down the narrow street to the eastern gate of the town. By the time they reached it a small group of townfolk, including the councilor de Chabanacy, had joined them as an escort of honor for their great friend. Out of the city and a short distance along the road to Montregard, the little company conducted Regis and his associate. No one spoke, for Francis was rapt in the deepest prayer, his sighs almost as rhythmic as his footsteps.

At the bottom of Montfaucon's hill Francis paused, cast his glistening eyes up toward the gray walls of the city on the heights, and with his upraised hand slowly traced the sign of the cross while calling down God's blessing upon afflicted Montfaucon. The large outlines of his blessing seemed to stretch wide as possible to embrace the whole extent of the town and each suffering victim of the plague.

With a sigh for those tortured victims whose agonies he could not personally alleviate, he turned sorrowfully away and slowly paced onward toward the brow of the next hill. His escort seemed loath to leave him. Together they toiled up the rocky path behind Regis, their silent sympathy attesting their appreciation of this coming. At a curve in the road near the heights, Francis again stopped to pray over the city and bless it slowly and solemnly. Again, upon reaching the summit he halted, made the sign of the cross with large and feeling gestures over the stricken city.

In silence the little bodyguard awaited a farewell word. Of a sudden, they saw Francis' eyes light up with an unearthly glow. His face became suffused with color, such as men had often before noted when he prayed intensely, totally rapt in the consciousness of God's nearness. Then, with a smile of assurance, he turned his tear-filled eyes toward the group that had accompanied him and said in a voice choked with emotion, "Have courage. The contagion at Montfaucon will go no farther. The rest of the inhabitants will escape it. The plague will cease immediately."

With a few words of farewell to Father de Lagrevol, Francis took leave of his friends and of Montfaucon. Pastor and people hurried back to the city with the good news of the saint's prophecy. It was indeed verified by the sequel. Only thirty out of the six hundred inhabitants died of the plague during the entire three months it raged. Before the end of the next month, even those suspected of contagion had recovered. In other places, notably farther north in Forez, towns where Francis had not been were kept under the pall of the plague for four years. The inhabitants of Montfaucon justly felt grateful for the intervention of him whom they considered their savior.

In the interim, Francis was not idle. The Providence of God once more afforded him opportunity elsewhere for fulfilling that very ambition he had sacrificed. Leaving Montfaucon, he traversed the environs which he had scoured so recently in quest of strayed sheep. Here and there he discovered snowbound dwellings of those same sheep, now stricken with the fearful visitation. For these isolated cases, Regis was a godsend. Without his succor they would have been left utterly unattended, and had he stayed at Montfaucon where there was a comparative abundance of spiritual and physical aid for the victims, he might have missed the chance to be a good samaritan to these neighboring hamlets.

For the next two weeks Francis made his headquarters at Montregard. There, too, he found some abandoned poor who had contracted the plague but had not been cared for properly. By calling the attention of the authorities to these unhappy paupers and to those prostrate under the plague in their huts out in the hills, Regis accomplished much more good than he could have done in Montfaucon. Yet despite his incessant toil in the midst of the most contagious cases, the crown of martyrdom as a victim of charity eluded him. God once more accepted the desire for the act, and reserved to Himself the choice of the day and the hour.

Toward the middle of December Francis in his prayer received an intimation of the approach of his appointed time. Under the impulse of this light from above he suddenly slipped away from Montregard and hastened down through the woods past Yssingeaux on the road to Le Puy. It was somewhat of a strange compulsion that drove him on, though to his lay brother companion the reason was simply that he wished to comply with Father Arnoux's suggestion.

Early in the afternoon of Thursday, December 13, the pair approached Le Puy. Nevertheless, because he wished to spend the coming days in prayer and solitude, Francis did not immediately enter the city. He would have been forthwith recognized, besieged by multitudes of penitents, required to preach and hear confessions. Accordingly, he and his companion turned off the road in the vicinity of Cheyrac, near Polignac, and moved toward the College's country house. There they joined a group of fathers and scholastics who had taken advantage of the break in the weather to spend the regular weekly holiday outside the city.

The community had been looking for Francis' arrival ever since the return of the messenger. But it was quite a surprise for him to appear so suddenly and at the villa whither he had seldom retired since his days as a young teacher in the

College. Nevertheless a warm welcome awaited him among his brethren. Taking his place before the roaring fire, he joined in as one of them and passed the afternoon in pleasant converse. Forgetful of his fatigue, he willingly answered their solicitous queries about his adventures on the missions, and participated in the laughter and gay banter with which they whiled away the hours.

As the group broke up to return to the city in the evening dusk, Francis took aside one of the priests who was a close friend of his and confided to him the reason for his sudden reappearance. "I have interrupted my mission," he said somberly, "to dispose myself to die well."

His friend was shocked at the revelation, but Francis quieted his protestations before they were voiced. "I have reserved these next three days for myself," he continued. "I wish to make a confession of my whole life, very exactly, for I have the assurance that this will be the last. Be good enough to aid me in this important matter. I wish to have you for my director."

More than surprised at the choice of himself, the priest nevertheless loyally accepted the charge. "You could certainly choose a more experienced guide," he admitted, "but you could not find one more devoted to your interests."

With his newly chosen spiritual father, Regis walked back toward the city, following in the footsteps of the rest of the group who filed along two by two on the wintry road. Shrouded by darkness, they entered Le Puy and hurried silently and secretly toward the College, as though concealing their much sought for colleague and smuggling him in without the people's knowledge.

Apparently, Father Arnoux was not at the College for that last week-end Francis was to spend there. It seems likely that he was himself exercising the ministry outside the city, since the Ember Days and the Feast of Christmas demanded much extra apostolic work throughout the diocese. At any rate, there is no mention of his presence, nor any record of his reactions to Regis' return under the influence of his approaching death. Nor was the rector there to compel Francis to stay at Le Puy until the depths of the winter had passed.

Little enough, too, is known of the actual events that passed in the mind and soul of the missionary during those last days at Le Puy. His silence and solitude were interrupted only by his conversations with his director and by his general confession.

After that was finished on the last day of the Triduum, and his friend had pronounced the words of absolution over the almost stainless soul of Regis, the confessor felt emboldened to pry further into the nature of Francis' foreknowledge of his coming demise.

"When do you intend to return to your missions, mon Père?" he asked Francis in a noncommittal fashion.

"Tomorrow morning," Regis answered; "they are waiting for me over there."

His good friend endeavored to parry for a delay, possibly until the rector could return and forbid him to go. "But the renovation of vows is approaching," he urged. "Remain here. Our young brothers will be so happy to have you for their feast."

"The Master does not wish it," replied Regis, with certitude in his tones.

"The Master?" his confessor rejoined, feigning not to comprehend. "Why, I know the intentions of Father Rector. He would be glad for you to wait until this solemnity."

Regis repeated his statement with conviction. "No, mon Père, the Master wishes me to depart tomorrow morning."

The renovation of the vows was to be held on the Epiphany. The confessor therefore strove to approach the matter from the other end. Not being able to prevent Regis from going, he might at least draw from him a promise to return before the rigors of the winter sapped what little strength he had in reserve.

"Then it won't be for long, will it?" he queried. "You'll return for the renovation, will you not?"

Regis paused in thought for a moment. "No, I will not," he stated with finality. "But my companion, Brother Bideau, will be back here by then."

"But how can you send back your companion?" the confessor pursued. "Will you remain all alone on the mission? You should not dream of acting that way. It would be most blameworthy."

Francis merely reiterated his remark. "Nevertheless, so it is," he insisted. "Brother Bideau will be here. I will not." And again, after some seconds of prayer, "No, Father, I shall not return."

Regis had faced death so often in his meditation and in his spiritual activities that it seemed tedious to delay longer on the matter. There were other things to be attended to before his departure. A few little debts he had contracted for the poor were paid. What records, if any, he had kept of his spiritual life were summarily destroyed, even his sermon outlines and preaching notes. There was the round of farewells to be made among the members of the community, including those who had been misled into opposing his activities in behalf of the House of St. Agatha. The rest of his affairs Francis left in care of the kindly Providence of God that had watched over him all these years.

Mute witnesses alone remained behind him. The frightening discipline with which he lashed his back to do penance for sinners and win them back to Christ, the iron chain that tortured his flesh, the little hairshirt that he wore about his waist were his only surviving possessions. Perhaps he forgot to dispose of them, for during wintertime he did not need them. Out on the missions the cutting winds lashed him more severely than the discipline, the biting cold gnawed at his vitals more insistently than hairshirt or iron chain.

Besides these mute witnesses, only two or three of his Jesuit brethren were allowed to raise their voices in testimony to the holiness of their saintly comrade. The archbishop of Vienne, in charge of the process of investigation into Francis' sanctity, thought it best to permit the spontaneous attestations of the people themselves to canonize Francis, rather than depend on the statements of the Jesuits, since the Jansenists, so active among the French clergy at the time, would accuse them of partiality. As a consequence, very few incidents survive concerning the community life led by Regis, his dealings with his brethren, and even the exalted spiritual gifts that may have been noticed in him during his life at Le Puy. Father de Mangeon's words can with certainty be taken as summing up what was the common consensus of all the Jesuits of the College: "He heard with the same impassivity those who condemned and those who approved his conduct, unaffected by either, just like a completely mortified man, neither desiring nor fearing anything, so utterly had the divine love annihilated in his heart everything it could have had of the human and the earthly."

Francis had lived for twenty-two years among these men whose ideal was to be "men crucified to the world, to whom the world itself is crucified; new men, who have put off self, that they may put on Christ; dead to themselves that they may live to justice." It was still in the service of these brethren and of the College that he departed from their midst to die. Lalouvesc, his goal, was as closely a part of the College as was the College Church itself in Le Puy. Enigmatically, though outside his regular residence, Francis was to die in a Jesuit house, despite all the efforts of the Jansenists to prove that he did not.

CHAPTER XIII

Toward the New Jerusalem

LIKE a mighty river, gathering momentum as it rushes
nearer to the ocean, the lifestream of Regis became a raging
torrent of energy the closer it approached the end of its
course toward the tideless sea. No longer now the sparkling
trickle of life that had emerged from the covered spring
of Fontcouverte, nor the quiet, happy brook that had flowed
serenely through the meadows of Languedoc. From his first
years of Jesuit life, Francis' vitality had bounded forward
with increased impetus, recklessly, daringly, with the heedless onrush of mountain rapids, hurtling along through
cataracts of difficulties, intrepidly plunging into what for
others would have been "titanic glooms of chasmed fears,"
streaming onwards toward his destined consummation.

The consciousness of his approaching end spurred him
and Brother Bideau along the mountain roads to their distant
mission after they left Le Puy on December 17. Since the
mission of Lalouvesc had been postponed until the twenty-
third, Regis broke his journey at the place he had abruptly
forsaken the week before, Montregard. There "they were
waiting" for him, the suffering plague victims for whom
he had provided earlier in the month. Once more he was
their good shepherd, seeking them out in their snow-trapped
dwellings, traversing the frozen fastnesses of the vicinity to
bring a word of consolation to the sick and dying, appearing
like a visiting angel, so thin and transparent were his features

and the gentle, bony hand he raised in benediction over them. The depths of his tenderness for these rugged people, the boundlessness of his devotion to them, often obscured amid his feats of physical endurance, were once more revealed to these appreciative mountaineers.

Those last days passed all too rapidly for his devoted clients. At the end of the week he moved on to Raucoules, mother-parish of Montregard, to say Mass for the Sunday assembly there. Crowds packed the little church at Raucoules that morning, December 23; everyone was eager for his words, his blessing, for another glimpse of him saying Mass, another chance to receive Holy Communion at the hands of their saint. All morning long he was constrained to tarry among them. The good folk continued coming with no regard for the snowstorm raging outside. After those hardships of the way, Francis could not allow himself to disappoint them by tearing himself away without having satisfied the entire congregation.

It was early afternoon before he had finished. Emerging from the church, he discovered that a heavy blanket of snow overlay the entire landscape, concealing paths and roads, landmarks and even familiar houses beneath the drifts. Nevertheless, since he had given his word that he would be at Lalouvesc on Mount Chaix that night, he determined to venture forth. Already the mountaineers from the more distant points of Father Bayle's parish were stirring abroad on their way to the mission. He, too, must push on. Brother Bideau and he muffled up tightly in their lamentably thin cloaks and plodded out into the last flurries of the heavy fall of snow.

Progress was exceedingly slow. The six or seven miles to St. Bonnet-le-Froid seemed that many leagues as they bent double, battling their way into the teeth of the wind. By the time they gained that crossroads town, the day, one of the shortest in the year, was losing what little gray light it cast upon the half-buried houses. Still, Francis and Bideau did not stop. Though they realized that more than half their journey remained to be made in the darkness, they pressed on across the frozen rivulet and plunged into the whitened woods and hills on the other side. Both had journeyed over this road earlier in the month on their way to Veyrines on the northern slope of Mount Chaix. It was but a matter of keeping to the same road until they reached the Mount, then turning in a southerly direction to Lalouvesc.

But the snowstorm and the darkness upset their calculations. None of the familiar road markers protruded from the snow. Fences, hedges, stone walls were all hidden. Even the natives themselves were known to lose their way home after a snowfall such as had that day occurred, and to perish from the cold within hailing distance of their homes. It is not surprising, then, that these newcomers soon went astray. For hours they wandered through the thick, hilly woods, repeating for Regis the harrowing experiences of a similar night near Marlhes. More maddening than anything was their inability to find any human habitation at all in the seemingly endless woods. They could not ask for information and so were obliged to guide themselves by the direction of the stars, and to grope their way feebly by the reflection of the starlight on the snow.

By the middle of the night Francis and his fellow traveler had abandoned all hope of reaching their destination. All they sought was a roof to shelter them from the zero weather, lest they be frozen to death as they walked. Not until they had tramped on through the crunching snow for many more miles did they win out to a semblance of a refuge from the piercing cold. An old deserted shack loomed up before them. Too exhausted to go any farther, they dug away the snow from before the door and threw themselves into the dank place. The roof and walls, dilapidated though they were, were nevertheless enough to fend off most of the snow and to slow down the icy blasts of the blizzard. It was a blessed respite from the exhaustion of their walking, from the terror and pain of their plungings down unseen slopes, from the strain of hauling themselves up out of the rocky gullies on the slippery ice that sheathed all with biting cold.

In the damp and dismal interior no fire was possible. The pair lay down upon the hard floor to recoup their strength by a few hours of the sleep of exhaustion. Despite their wet clothes and frozen limbs, they slept.

At dawn, when he awoke, Francis felt chilled to the bone, yet at intermittent periods, a fever burned him up, even causing him to sweat. But his one thought was to hurry on to Lalouvesc where "they were waiting." The pair discovered upon leaving their shelter that they had stopped within sight of Veyrines, a few hours' journey from their destination. Without pausing to regret that they had not dragged themselves a little farther in their quest for cover during the night so as to have reached one of the fires of the village, they resumed their journey and soon thawed out their limbs with the exertions of the march.

The uphill path was climbed by the weary travelers despite their fatigue and weakness. Along their way they hastened by many of the houses that belonged to the parish of Lalouvesc, grouped here and there on the hillside in greater numbers than in the immediate neighborhood of the church up at the crossroads. The modest mountain château of the former lords of Lalouvesc stood on a fortified eminence closer to the town. Finally, at the junction of the two ancient trails where the Knights of Malta had long ago built a hospice for pilgrims, Francis and Bideau beheld the cross atop a small stone church.

Because he was intent on saying Mass for the people, Francis did not even stop at the inn to take refreshment or to moisten his fever-parched mouth. He hurried at once to the church where he found the congregation still waiting.

The pastor of Veyrines was startled to see the weakened condition of Regis. He used all his powers of persuasion to force his guest to celebrate Mass immediately so that he could take some nourishment. But the people clamored for him to preach first, to hear their confessions in order that they might receive Communion at his Mass. Their wishes prevailed. Forgetting his physical lassitude, Francis devoted himself unsparingly to the absorbing tasks of his spiritual ministry. And the hardy moutaineers lacked the delicacy of perception that would have urged them to be less importunate in their demands, if they wished to keep their saint on this side of heaven much longer.

Nevertheless, even after his Mass, they gave him no rest. Louise de la Franchière, who arrived that day to attend Regis' midnight Mass and to spend most of Christmas there, saw her great friend submitting to their unheeding impositions without the least show of weariness or impatience. She noticed that he seemed more wan than usual and she learned from Father Bayle of the sickness that threatened him. It pained her doubly to witness how he lavished his efforts on those boorish people. But she knew that no amount of urging could persuade him to desist as long as there was one penitent to be shriven. His catechism instructions and his sermons alone interrupted his confessions. The mission of Lalouvesc had begun.

The night before Christmas, we are told, was likewise consumed in absolving the endless lines of peasants. They came in increasing numbers in order to spend Christmas in a truly religious way. These new arrivals replaced those who had stayed through the night before. But no one replaced Regis. This martyr to the confessional shrank from no sacrifice to comply with the demands of the souls that knelt at his feet.

At midnight and at dawn, Francis suspended his ministry of forgiveness for the ministry of the altar. The little church was pervaded with the atmosphere of Bethlehem as those simple folk, like the shepherds of old, hastened with joy to adore the newly born Babe, and to listen to a voice beside His dwelling place that sounded as unearthly as those of the angels themselves. With the third Mass later in the day the spiritual joy of the congregation reached a new peak of intensity and that of Francis mounted almost to ecstasy. Men wondered why heaven seemed so near that day, and why their saint spoke to them with so joyous a mien. It was an unforgettably holy night and holy day for all who heard him.

But even for Christmas, Francis did not interrupt the mission. Confessions and Communions followed each other as wave on wave of new pilgrims ascended to Lalouvesc. That afternoon and on into the evening, Francis dispensed from the tribunal of penance that peace on earth promised to men of good will. His unbelievable stamina, together with an almost miraculous grace from God, sustained him so marvelously that the hours flitted by almost without his noticing them. A few hours of rest, and then next morning, the Feast of St. Stephen, again he was in the confessional at dawn. Between his sermons at the appointed times the people thronged to his box at the back of the church. It was two o'clock before he was able to break away for Mass.

People noted that he lingered longer than usual over this Mass of the first Christian martyr. Meditatively, he drank deeply of the full meaning of the Epistle that told of another who had also done signs and wonders among the people, and, full of grace and fortitude, had preached not wisely, from the world's point of view, but too well, for it had brought him to his heroic death. It was the last Mass that Regis would offer up. Four times during it he repeated, "I see the heavens opened and the Son of man standing on the right hand of God." Those words stayed in his mind like a haunting memory unto the last moment of his life.

His beloved children hardly allowed him time to unvest before begging again for confession. Crowded up into the sanctuary, they tugged at his cassock as he finished putting off his vestments. Francis acceded to their wishes without even thinking of something to eat. Unable to make his way through the packed church to his confessional at the rear, he sat upon a chair near the altar and heard his penitents one by one.

Above his position was a broken window. Through it poured in the chill December air, descending upon his bare head and upon his body to which his clothes, damp from the feverish perspiration, adhered with a deathlike clamminess. But still the peasants did not notice the danger. Jealously they watched for their turn to draw near the saint and to unload their sins and griefs into his understandingly sympathetic ear. Nor did any external change appear in his manner. He was still the patient, gentle confessor he had always been, interested in the least human ills, considerate of everyone's feelings except his own.

Late in the afternoon the incredible happened before the astonished eyes of the penitents. In the midst of a confession, the Père crumpled up in a faint and toppled from his chair onto the floor. To the amazed peasants it was as if a towering pine had suddenly fallen over in the forest. They were paralyzed with incredulity. Looking at one another uncomprehendingly, they seemed to be waiting for him to rise and continue his work. Finally, it dawned on them. Their saintly confessor was subject to human ailments after all. A few men close by took hold of the great, tall body, lifted its pitifully light weight from the ground, and bore him tenderly through the stunned crowd.

Outside, the shadows of evening were already settling like a pall over the whole landscape. The slow cortege moved over the precarious path of ice and snow toward Father Bayle's house. Up the three stone steps of its entrance they carried their limp burden, conveyed it into the small parlor, and laid it gently upon the couch before the fireplace. Behind them trailed a file of anxious parishioners who also crowded into the small room and cast apprehensive eyes toward the still figure of their great friend. Someone stirred the fire in the hearth. By its flickering light they saw Francis move, revived by the warmth of the flames that leaped to his rescue.

The quick recovery was an immense relief to Father Bayle and Brother Bideau, as well as to the peasants. Tension in the room relaxed. But the pastor was determined that Francis should have some rest. He began to herd the people out in order to allow Regis the quiet needed for his sleep. Some of the importunate folk, however, had already asked for Francis' absolution. He would not hear of dispersing them. Though his breath came with labored gaspings, he could still whisper the words of forgiveness, could still raise his weak arm in the sign of the cross.

For two more hours he persevered in the slow, racking process. One after another advanced to his side, fully twenty in all, each one sapping from the stricken priest another of his remaining ounces of energy. It was a slow martyrdom, a hidden agony of exquisite suffering. "As long as his strength lasts," the General had said, Francis was to devote himself to these rugged countryfolk. It was literally being fulfilled now.

At length, the weakened forces of the missionary failed again. The dismay of the bystanders became a frightened alarm for his life. They realized that this was no passing weakness, but that their saint was dying. His return to consciousness was delayed for long, anxious minutes as they mutely watched him. Father Bayle finally awoke to the seriousness of the situation. He ordered them to bring his own bed from the adjoining room and to lay the unconscious priest upon it.

Upon regaining control of his faculties, Francis was still very low. His strength was drained completely by the fever that reduced him to helplessness. Yet the congestion of his lungs pierced his sides with swords of pain at every fretful breath. Even so, he strove in vain to remove himself from the comfort of the bed when he learned to his disappointment that he was to die upon the soft mattress. He whispered pathetically that he wished Father Bayle to have his bed for the night, as it was the only one in the house. Pleading that he wished to die upon the straw in the cellar that served for a stable, he begged them to carry him thither. All during his years in these mountains he had not had whereon to lay his head. He wished to be like Christ even to the last. Nevertheless, when he saw the distress of his friends, he resigned himself to his lot.

By next day the news had spread all through the neighborhood. Father Jean La Motte, procurator of Le Puy, heard it while in Montregard on some business. He quickly hurried over to Lalouvesc, arriving about the same time as did three more Jesuits, Father Lascombe from Annonay, and two priests who came from the College of Tournon with a doctor and an apothecary. Every effort was made to stave off the advances of the fever and the lung congestion. But all attempts to save his life were futile. It was too late. Pneumonia had attacked his chest. The doctor could do nothing but predict death within a few days.

For two more days Regis' remarkable physique, that had endured the amazing hardships he underwent, kept him alive despite the ravages of the fever. We are told that he suffered his little children to come unto him up to the very last. He was their Père and he still whispered words of consolation to his little ones, as long as his voice allowed him.

Besides that work, he wished for nothing more. They prepared for him a bowl of rich hot broth. He refused it. It was too delicate for him. Instead, he accepted what the peasants themselves took when they were sick — warm milk. Even that was more than he really desired. His one yearning now was to clasp his bony fingers on his crucifix in prayer. With that he could die contented.

Not until the last day of the year was the end visibly near. The morning before, Father Lascombe had heard Francis' last confession, a renewal of the general confession he had recently made at Le Puy. The priest admitted later that there was not even a venial sin of complete advertence in the whole of the confession. To Regis' pure soul Lascombe soon afterward had brought Holy Viaticum, the Companion of his last journey toward the New Jerusalem. Then, while Francis communed with his Beloved, the priest anointed him with the oils of Extreme Unction to strengthen him for his departure.

The long hours of the deathwatch stretched through that night and on into the next day. Still the dying man prayed silently in the dancing firelight of the hearth. Eyes closed, fingers tightly clutching his crucifix, Francis retained full possession of his mind and prepared for death by surging toward God with all the fervor of his intense love. Yet he still carried in his heart the memory of all those forsaken sheep for whom he had been crusading these past years. Scene after scene of his toil for them rose up as he now prayed for them, and for the thousands of others whom he had failed to reach in his brief career. It still seemed to him that he had "done nothing," that he could offer up only a holocaust of unfulfilled desires, as Xavier had on the island of San Cian almost a century before. Regis had ambitioned to be a martyr of charity in behalf of the plague stricken, had yearned for the living martyrdom that was the Canadian mission, had striven to be a social crusader in Le Puy and a country missionary for life in the rugged Cévennes. Now in the failing hours of his life, all seemed frustrated. He was being snatched away just when his work

had begun. He would have chosen to live on in the service
of the abandoned and the oppressed. But God had ruled
otherwise. Only one ambition of Francis' youthful enthusiasm was being achieved. In obedience, even unto the death
of the cross, he was like Christ, humbled to the dust beneath
the cross he carried, and now stretched out upon a bed
of pain that racked him like a crucifixion. His prayer
mounted up to the climax of the *Consummatum Est*. Mutely
clasping his crucified Lord, he prayed for the coming
of death.

As the old year of 1640 was dying, Francis opened his
weary eyes and whispered to Brother Bideau, who sat at
his bedside, "Oh Brother, I have never felt worse in my
life." The intensity of his fever had risen apace with the
fervor of his prayer. Death was upon his pallid features
now, a vastly different death from that he had courageously
faced so often during the stormy years of his ministry. He
had breathed of death in the fetid atmosphere of pest-ridden
Toulouse, but now the slow breaths that he drew seemed
ages apart, and each seemed to tear his sides asunder. Un-
flinchingly, defiantly, he had looked death in the eye, had
bared his chest to the sharp blades of swords and daggers
without number. But now he felt as if all his old assailants
had plunged their rapiers and poignards into his sides and
left them there to torture each of his dying breaths. In his
ardor of love he had burned with the desire of dying for
Christ; his raging fever made of his body a burning holocaust
in consummation of that desire. Riven of all the glamour
and glory of a heroic death, Francis submitted to this final
sacrifice with the *Fiat Voluntas Tua* which had accompanied
all his submissions to the inscrutable Providence that seemed
to "char the wood" before limning with it even the divine
design.

But once more, after Francis had plumbed the depths
of suffering, God raised him to new heights. The climax

of his agonizing deathwatch had hardly passed before the bystanders noted a change in him. His eyes opened wider. His face became wreathed in a smile. And as he gazed upward, he whispered to Brother Bideau, "Ah, my brother, I see our Lord and our Lady opening the gates of Paradise for me."

They gathered quickly around his bedside. Francis' eyes remained fastened upon the vision that enthralled them, the same that had greeted the eyes of Stephen the first martyr. For moments he lingered between heaven and earth, and then breathing the words of the dying Saviour, "Into Thy Hands, O Lord, I commend my spirit," he passed into the reality of the vision he beheld.

. . . .

It was about midnight on December 31, 1640, when Regis died, thus ending the year of the Jubilee of the Society of Jesus, the one which he had prayed might be a year of jubilation for himself. That joy he had sought by requesting of the General permission to consecrate his life to the service of the missions in the country. Now his consecration was fulfilled in a more literal way than either had intended. But the future was to prove that the mighty spiritual strength of Regis could last even beyond the grave. The vast store of spiritual energy amassed during his years of self-sacrificing labors did not perish when his body collapsed beneath the strain. It, too, in another chapter of his miraculous adventures, was dedicated to the service of these countryfolk in ever widening beneficence.

Meanwhile, the body that they then laid out for burial in the early hours of the New Year still bore the marks of his ceaseless battlings for his neighbor. Worn thin by fasting, striped with his continual disciplinings, weather-beaten through constant exposure to the rigors of winter, it nevertheless remained precious in the eyes of his devoted followers. The Jesuit cassock and the priestly vestments in

which they clothed him mercifully concealed from the
gaze of his flock the frightening marks of his sufferings,
revealing only the priestliness of their beloved Père. Moreover, his countenance, instead of withering or hardening into
the expressionless mold of death, retained its freshness of
color and serenity.

News of the holy priest's death soon spread to the
extremities of his mission territory. The throngs that
hastened to Lalouvesc on the first and second of January
filed silently past his bier in the little church, all weeping
profusely for the loss of their irreplaceable friend, all marvel-
ing at the lifelike repose and the spiritual beauty of his
countenance.

For the funeral on January 2 twenty-two priests
assembled in the sanctuary and chanted for Regis the
office of the dead. After the Requiem Mass and the final
ceremonies, they watched as the coffin was lowered
into the provisional grave dug for it in the church itself,
near the gospel side of the altar, not far from where he had
last ministered to his penitents before collapsing. As the box
thudded upon the hard ground at the bottom, the peasants
burst out into loud sobs, "like children who weep for their
father, believing they have lost all in losing him."

After the burial, as the Jesuits present from Le Puy,
Annonay, and Tournon, met to discuss the final resting
place of their brother, the peasants were also gathering to
determine that they would at least not lose the treasured
relics of their saint. The provisional tomb would be his
permanent sepulcher as well, they resolved, for their Père
had chosen to live among them and to die among them.
He would stay with them forever.

Nevertheless, each of the three Jesuit houses represented
at the funeral wished to have the body. Father Lascombe
from Annonay claimed it because his residence was closest
to Lalouvesc and within the confines of the diocese of

Vienne where the Providence of God had permitted the saint's death to occur. The College of Tournon on the Rhone, not far away, also wished to possess its former pupil's remains to bury them in state within the lordly College church. But Father La Motte, who had defrayed the modest expenses of the funeral, insisted that the body belonged to Le Puy and that it should be carried thither as soon as the roads became passable in the springtime. When the thaws came, Francis would once more be on the road back to Le Puy as was his wont.

So the Jesuits decided. But they reckoned not on the devotion of Father Bayle to his saintly friend, nor on the stubbornness of the peasants who had determined to keep their great missionary's body. Father Bayle secretly resolved that Francis should remain in death a Jesuit of Lalouvesc, though he faithfully wrote in his parochial register some days after the funeral: "On the last day of December, 1640, died in my room and on my bed, the Reverend Father John Francis Regis, Jesuit of Le Puy, where he had been sick for six days."

Down in the Velay, the people of Le Puy still considered that Francis was theirs. Father Arnoux, without waiting for the spring, performed some solemn obsequies for Francis, as if for a warrior who had died in battle far from home. A huge catafalque was erected in the College church. The Mass of the dead was celebrated. A panegyric was preached. Some of the Jesuits of the College, astonished at what they construed as an uncalled for innovation, wrote to the General to complain about according such signal honors to one who was not even a Professed Father. But the sage old Vitelleschi merely confirmed with Rome's official approval the rector's extreme devotion to his dead friend. "It pleases me," he wrote, "that you have rendered him his well-deserved honors before a cenotaph." (February 15, 1641.)

In the same letter, Vitelleschi mirrored his mind very

plainly in regard to the death of Francis Regis. "He succumbed in a most enviable fashion as a true son of the Society, while applying himself to holy labors and in the heat of battle for souls against the demon and sin." *Germanum Societatis Filium,* "a genuine son of the Society," the General acclaimed Regis in this last communication in his regard. Assuredly, not a title that would have been given to one under the cloud of expulsion, as the Jansenists wishfully thought the saint to have been! In their hatred for the Society, they failed to see that Regis was a genuine saint because he was, as the General had stated, a "genuine son of the Society."

All Le Puy joined in with Father Arnoux in mourning for the dead Jesuit. Too late some of them also realized that he was an indubitable saint. But nevertheless, they still claimed him as their own. Many of the citizens made pilgrimages to his tomb despite the wretched weather. On their return they unfailingly repeated the same demand: the body of Regis must be brought back from that obscure country village to the great city in which he had labored so zealously. Here he could be honored by many more people and in a much more fitting manner than on the out-of-the-way mountain where he had died.

Spring came once more, but the body of Regis still rested at Lalouvesc. Father Balthasar Carrel, the new Provincial, insisted on the return of the remains from their snowbound burial place. But the death of Bishop de Serres prevented the necessary official action in the matter.

The peasants, meanwhile, together with their pastor Father Bayle, resolved to safeguard their treasure from any efforts on the part of the cityfolk or the Jesuits to take it away. Rumors had even spread about that the brethren of Regis had resolved to steal the body in secret. To fend off any such possibility, Father Bayle decided to transfer the remains from the original grave to another one under the very altar of a side chapel. The exhumed coffin did not appear to them sufficiently strong, and so they took an enormous chestnut tree trunk, hollowed it out, and piously laid therein the body of their protector. Lowering the trunk into its deep grave, they covered it first with crossbeams fitted tightly together as though to hold the coffin forever in the rocky grave.

Thus safely hidden beneath the altar of St. John the Baptist the body of Regis remained. His dear, simple country-folk clung to it as they had clung to him in life, feeling certain that he would still remain their protector, that he would still prefer to be among them, than to be brought back to the city where he had been treated so inhumanly. No one here would desecrate his body with savage attacks as they had done at Le Puy. Here, too, the peasants intended to build a fitting shrine for him, if the church would ever confirm with her official approbation their unerringly accurate opinion of their Père's sanctity.

The Church's confirmation came in time. From the very day of his death, Regis continued those miraculous favors he had so generously lavished on the people during his life. The little bags of dust they gathered from his tomb as a sort of relic served to bring his healing presence to those sick who found favor in his eyes. The hardy peasants even mixed a few grains of the dust in the broth or water they drank when sick, and were thus freed from fevers or other ailments.

But more notable than this material aid was the fact that, immediately after his burial at Lalouvesc, a strange post-humous social crusade of peace and spiritual uplifting began. The distress that had wrung sobs from the hearts of his dear peasant friends was suddenly soothed by an indescribable calm experienced by all who approached his tomb. As a token of his covenanted consecration to these humble folk, an untold succession of spiritual blessings followed, due to the merits and intercession of the saint.

Louise de la Franchière was one of the first to feel that
peace. She had left Lalouvesc on Christmas Day to spend
part of it at home with her young son. Not until the day
of the funeral was she able to return. Entering the church
in anguish of heart and dismay, she approached the grave
so recently closed. Already the peasants had scooped away
much of the earth that covered the coffin. She drew as near
as she could to the hallowed remains, and there was filled
with a flood of peace and exquisite consolation. Hardly able
to tear herself away from the place, she resolved to purchase a home in the vicinity that she might pass the rest of
her days at this source of spiritual benedictions. Her family
was obliged to intervene in order to dissuade her from her
holy purpose. But she joined the crowds of pilgrims who
climbed up to Lalouvesc, both before and after the institution of the process of canonization.

During the first thirty years the visitors here were mainly
natives of Vivarais and Velay who had felt the personal
influence of the missionary. Large numbers of them might
be seen before the great festivals of the Church, keeping
night-long vigil near his tomb. One year the priests in
charge actually counted a total of no fewer than 7000 pilgrims at the shrine for the Feast of the Assumption alone
— many more, indeed, than the little town could dream
of harboring. But the sturdy mountain people, untroubled
by this fact, took their scant hours of sleep within the
church itself or out in the open.

It was not, however, until 1676, with the notable cure of
an archbishop who had invoked the aid of the saint, that
the official process of the Church was instituted. Many reported miracles were daily investigated and the life of the
missionary was diligently scrutinized. On May 8, 1716, the
Beatification finally took place, and twenty-one years later
came the canonization by Pope Clement XII, on exactly
the same day this honor was given to Vincent de Paul.

The fervor and enthusiasm of the people, stimulated by
the numerous miracles that occurred, had threatened for a
while to endanger the cause of canonization. Unwittingly
the pious faithful had anticipated the decision of the Church
by according to Francis honors expressly forbidden by
Urban VIII in his regulations concerning the recognition
of saints.

At the canonical investigations many witnesses summed
up the marvels of these pilgrimages, both as to the spiritual
graces gained and the actual miracles worked. Within the
first decade of years after Regis' death more than forty
major miracles were recorded as performed at Lalouvesc.
A list of these was assembled by the first biographer,
LaBroue. By the time that Rome began its work upon his
cause, the number had been trebled.

But the really great miracle of Lalouvesc was the miracle
of the continuous train of conversions and spiritual regen-
erations witnessed at the tomb. Thousands ascended the
mount not to seek physical cures but to confess their sins,
to receive the Eucharist fruitfully, to make their peace with
God at this source of supernatural peace. Many notorious
sinners and heretics pilgrimed thither to obtain a fresh
start in life. Amid the pure air of those mountain heights
they received the ministrations of the saint even as the
people of the surrounding territory had enjoyed them during his visible apostolate.

But from Le Puy itself the influence of Regis first began
to extend beyond the boundaries of France. Before the days
of his final departure from that scene of his labors and
trials, Francis had deeply impressed in particular two young
men, one a Jesuit scholastic and the other a student at the
College. The former, Gabriel Druillettes by name, was sent
upon those missions for which Regis so ardently yearned
and became the first apostle of the Abenaquis, performing
among them feats of apostolic fervor. The other, Claude

Allouez, also entered the Society of Jesus, was sent out to New France and for thirty years evangelized the Indians, zealously spreading the civilizing influence of the gospel along a mission course of more than two thousand miles. He instructed more than 100,000 savages, mostly of the Ottawa nations, became the first priest recorded to have said Mass in what is now Wisconsin, and finally died in complete isolation on one of his journeys, during the night of August 27–28, 1689.

In the relation of this missionary's accomplishments, his Superior, Father Claude d'Ablon, wrote from Quebec:

This apostle of all the nations of the Ottawas . . . drew his first inspiration from the conversations he had with Father Francis Regis, of holy memory, whom he often assisted, taking part in the answers and recitations at the catechism classes of this very famous apostle. There he was called by God to our Society. (August 29, 1690.)

Thus, in fact, the spiritual influence of Regis reached those distant mission fields for which he had longed so ardently during his own life, and for which he had prepared himself so heroically.

At home, in the Vivarais and Velay regions, the missionary enterprise, initiated by Regis, was continued by his fellow Jesuits after his death. Along the trails he had blazed for them, a whole line of missionaries now poured ceaselessly throughout the seventeenth and the eighteenth centuries, and on even to the expulsion and suppression of the Society. So deeply impressed on them was the example of their precursor that the people spontaneously called them the "new Regises."

One thing is certain. Nothing more was necessary than only to recall to the people the words and exhortations of Regis to be effective among them. His practical application of the Gospel to the daily lives of these hardy mountaineers had been handed down with time and had become a hallowed tradition. Into the folklore of the people went little rhymes, and quaint and pithy sayings regarding him. Their great apostle, whom they looked upon as coming straight from Christ to them, was referred to simply as "The Saint," without any further qualification. Villages vied with one another in claiming mementos of their heavenly patron, and in erecting shrines and wayside "crosses of St. Regis" in places that had been hallowed by his presence or had been the scenes of special events in his life. These crosses are still to be found throughout the Vivarais, and even in certain remote regions most probably not visited by him.

So, too, numerous springs and fountains can be found piously dedicated by these humble countryfolk to their heavenly patron, while in various localities relics of the saint are still preserved as most precious family heirlooms.

Throughout the rest of France as well, Regis participated after death, as he had done during his own lifetime, in the regeneration of the French clergy. We have had occasion in the course of this sketch to note his dealings with the priests and religious who heard him at Le Puy and with the country pastors with whom he lived during his missions. In 1636 or 1637 that great force in the movement for sacerdotal renewal, M. Jean-Jacques Olier, had passed through Le Puy and observed there a congregation of ecclesiastics, mostly canons, among whom the fiery words of "the holy Francis Regis" had rekindled into new flame the spark of their priestly zeal. Later in that year, Olier, then Abbé of Pébrac and afterward founder of the Sulpicians, described in a letter to friends in Paris the work of this congregation:

These priests give examples of virtue that delight the whole province. Catechism classes are conducted by them in many places about the city; visits to prisons and hospitals are frequent here, and at present they are preparing to give missions in all the places that depend on their chapter.

Many of these same men were among the hundreds of
priests who climbed up to Lalouvesc during the early years
of the pilgrimage to draw from the spirit of Regis new
flames of apostolic zeal.

Thirty years after the canonization of Regis came the
expulsion of the Jesuits from France. Their suppression
followed soon after. But the influence of Regis stayed, and,
in fact, achieved some of its most remarkable results during
that very period of the Society's temporary eclipse. It is true
that the relics of his body were removed from Lalouvesc
during the dark years of the terror under the Revolution,
but his spirit hovered over the sacked and desecrated shrine
and still continued its spiritual crusading, which soon came
to extend over the face of the earth, mainly through those
who received their inspiration from Regis at Lalouvesc: the
Curé d'Ars, St. John Vianney, apostle and patron of priestly
sanctity in our time; Blessed Philippine Duchesne, the
Xavier of the Madames of the Sacred Heart; Archbishop
d'Aviau, founder of the Basilians; Abbé Therme and Mother
Couderc, cofounders of the Ladies of the Cenacle; Bishop
Loras, pioneer in Alabama as first president of Spring Hill
College, and in Iowa as bishop of Dubuque; Jean Abbés,
founder of the St. Peter of Luxemburg Society; Maxime de
Bussy, inspirer of the Worker-Brothers of St. Francis Regis;
and M. Gossin, inaugurator of the splendid "Work of St.
Regis," for the legitimation of marriages and children.

This posthumous mission of St. Francis Regis likens him
unmistakably to the great apostle of the Indies, St. Francis
Xavier, and to that other patron of the missions, St. Thérèse
of the Child Jesus. As with both these saints, the secret of
Regis' spiritual power is to be found, humanly speaking, in
the dynamic spiritual life he led while still on earth. And
to this posthumous apostolate, too, must one assign, in
God's Providence, the reason for the extraordinarily inimitable mode of life by which he achieved sainthood.

Perhaps this very inimitability is the reason why that inner spiritual life of Regis is shrouded in such secrecy. His exalted holiness was not bared before our eyes in an autobiography like that which the Little Flower so charmingly wrote to reveal the secrets of the King in her own regard, yet in broad outlines the secret of Regis' holiness is visible for all. "I believed, while observing him," said one who knew the saint well, "that he acted no longer according to his own spirit, but by a divine inspiration; he had only one interior force that made him act. God, or rather the love of God, was the soul of his soul."

Utter detachment from his own interests was but an effect of his complete surrender to the all-absorbing passion for Christ that urged him on. Much of his human appeal was contained in what we might call the vagabond independence of all earthly concerns which he manifested all through his life. None of the thousand futilities that cramp the spirit and clutter up the unselfish aspirations of man's soul with the demands of the flesh were allowed in any way to interfere with the free workings of the Holy Spirit in his life. Nothing chained him to earth with ties of affection, and so he could become an effective hunter of souls.

The workings of the Spirit in the soul of Francis Regis can be judged by the remarkable effects he achieved. But even in the midst of his busiest apostolate, men noticed that his mind was filled with the spiritual recollection of the most intense contemplative. Betimes, he was found rapt in prayer, ecstatic, his countenance aglow, as though caught up from this world and absorbed in God. We need but recall here that night of prayer before the blizzard-buffeted door of the church at St. Bonnet-le-Froid; those hours of prayer before the closed church of Montregard, without any consciousness of the rains or snows; that entire day of adoration in the College Church at Le Puy, without the least thought of taking nourishment. These were but a

few of the signs that indicated the mystic side of his amazingly active character. Men knew that "his riches were
Christ, Christ suffering naked on the cross. He had graven
this Christ deeply on his heart." So attested his intimate
friend, Vicar-General Pierre Le Blanc.

In canonizing Regis, the Church officially stated that his
holiness was well-nigh inimitable in these extraordinary
features, but she nevertheless proposed him as a model to
be imitated, at least in the larger principles that guided
him, by all those who feel the same compassion for the
multitude, and who wish in some little way and according
to their own abilities, to bring succor to the woes of humanity. With the words of the act of canonization we fittingly
conclude this sketch:

On this hard and laborious way entered the courageous soldier
of God, John Francis Regis. Treading down the desires of the
flesh and bearing bravely the sufferings of this life, he girt himself
with strength amid tribulations and contumelies, in labors and
trials, in prayer, fasting, and vigils. Walking in the spirit, he scaled
the mountain heights, looking ever to the author and finisher of
our faith, Jesus, who having joy set before Him endured the cross,
despising the shame. . . .

Rejoicing, then, in the Lord with spiritual joy, may we celebrate
on earth the triumph of this Blessed Servant of God, already
crowned in heaven. May we celebrate it in such wise as truly to
admire his labors, his faith, his charity, and his holy deeds. May
we celebrate his triumph and praise his victory that so in turn we
may come to love his virtues, to imitate zealously his laborious life
and holy conversation . . . and to direct according to his example
our own path in the sight of the Lord.

Narrow and thorny and hard, indeed, is that path, but illustrious
and great is the company of our fellow travelers with whom we
walk along upon it and who make easy our journey. For the Lord
Himself it was who first walked upon it; after Him the intrepid
Apostles; then the Martyrs — yea, boys and women and tender
girls! And now, in these latter days, there walked upon it also the
Blessed John Francis.

If, then, we desire a reward, a destiny, a fatherland such as he
possesses, let us not fear to imitate his laborious life.

APPENDIX

The Jansenist Calumny

IT MUST be admitted from the start that the Jansenists could find absolutely nothing to calumniate in the life of Regis himself. They did manage, however, to direct their shafts against the Society of Jesus, their archenemy.

Prosper Lambertini, the future Pope Benedict XIV, was the devil's advocate in the cause of Regis' canonization when this was undertaken in 1710. The objection brought by him against the saint was that in the processes no testimonies concerning his sanctity were given by his own religious brethren. As has been mentioned in the text of this volume, the Jesuits judiciously abstained from anything that might make it appear that they were pressing his cause. The archbishops deemed it advisable to let the people themselves be the prime movers in the popular demand for Regis' canonization. Yet the promotor of the faith insisted, at that late date, on having some Jesuit testimonies. Owing to the fact that all the Jesuits who had known Regis intimately were dead by that time, the testimonies gathered were of such a nature as to make little impression on Lambertini.

While he was still in this dubious mood, a Jansenist priest, Father Louis Maille, approached him with a startling statement. This great servant of God, he informed Lambertini, had been a Jesuit without doubt, but the Fathers of the Company of Jesus, jealous of his increasing reputation and not able to endure so holy a man who eclipsed them by the brilliance of his merits, had dismissed him and cut him off from the body of their Society, so that after quitting their ranks, he died as a curate in Lalouvesc. By implication, Maille thus indicated to Lambertini the presumed reason for the lack of Jesuit witnesses to the sanctity of Regis. But how could Maille know this? He himself, he claimed, had been born in the environs of Lalouvesc.

This statement the devil's advocate immediately conveyed to Pope Clement XI. The pontiff, in turn, ordered the seizure and examination of the official records of the Society. But the catalogues of all the latter years of the saint's life, it was found, registered him as a *bona-fide* member. Even that of 1641 contained the record of his death in the Society. Besides, the letters of the General, cited at length in the body of this sketch, confirmed beyond the shadow of a doubt the high esteem in which Regis was officially held in the Order.

The accusation, moreover, cast suspicion upon Maille himself. For twenty-two years this man had been living in Rome, consequent upon the suppression of a school at Aix, of which he had been the director. At Rome he was found to have been engaged in furthering the cause of Jansenism, acting as assistant to du Vaucel, alias Walloni, and styling himself Dom Luigi. In the case of Regis he believed he saw the chance for a Jansenist revenge on the Jesuits, since they had been instrumental in the original suppression of the nest of heresy he had been feathering for himself at Aix. As a consequence he now found himself pursued by many charges that finally caught up with him in July, 1710, when the inquisitors of the Holy Office condemned him to five years' imprisonment in the Castel Sant' Angelo.

For the Jansenists in France, however, this was but further confirmation of their original prejudice against Regis and the Jesuits. They still maintained that he had been expelled from the Society, and no amount of evidence ever sufficed to change their minds. Even to the present day their collateral descendants still think of Regis and St. Stanislaus, as well as of St. Aloysius, as having died outside the Order. But all three saints remain, as ever, brilliant examples of the sanctity attainable within the Society of Jesus.

CHRONOLOGICAL TABLE

1597	Jan. 31	Birth	Fontcouverte
1611-16		Education at College	Béziers
1616-18		Novitiate	Toulouse
1618	Dec. 8	First Vows	Auch
1619	Jan.-Aug.	Juniorate	Cahors
1619-22		Professor of Grammar	Billom
1622-25		Philosophy Studies	Tournon
1625-27		Professor of Grammar	Le Puy
1627-28		Professor of Grammar	Auch
1628-31	Jan.	Theology Studies	Toulouse
1630	Trinity Sun.	First Mass	Toulouse
1631	Jan.	Mission	Fontcouverte
1631	Mar.-Aug.	Tertianship	Toulouse
1631-32		Professor of Grammar	Pamiers
1632-34		Missionary	Montpellier and environs
1633	Nov. 6	Last Vows	Montpellier
1634	May-Sept.	Episcopal Visitation	Diocese of Viviers
1634	Nov.-Dec.	The "Great Trial"	Le Puy
1635	Jan.-Aug.	Boutieres Mission	Le Cheylard and environs
1635	Sept.-Oct.	Boutieres Mission	Privas
1635	Nov.-Dec.	Boutieres Mission	Saint-Agrève
1636	Jan.-Mar.	Valence Diocese Mission	Doux Valley, St. André
1636	Apr.-Oct.	First Great Catechisms	Le Puy
1636-37	Oct.-Apr.	Apostolate in Mountains	Fay-le-Froid, etc.
1637	Apr.-Dec.	Catechism and Social Work	Le Puy
1637-38	Dec.-Apr.	Apostolate in Mountains	St. Pierre, Marlhes, etc.
1638	Apr.-Sept.	Catechism and Social Work	Le Puy
1638-39	Sept.-Apr.	Apostolate in Mountains	Diocese of Le Puy
1639	Apr.-Oct.	Catechism and Social Work	Le Puy
1639-40	Oct.-Jan.	Apostolate in Mountains	Montregard, Montfaucon
1640	Jan.-Oct.	Catechism and Social Work	Le Puy
1640	Oct.-Dec.	Apostolate in Mountains	Montfaucon, Veyrines, etc.
1640	Dec. 13-17	Last Retreat	Le Puy
1640	Dec. 24-26	Last Mission	Lalouvesc
1640	Dec. 26-31	Illness and Death	Lalouvesc

BIBLIOGRAPHY

Arnaud, E., *Histoire des Protestants du Vivarais et du Velay*, 2 vols. (Paris, 1888).

Arnaud, J. A. M., *Histoire du Velay*, 2 vols. (Le Puy, 1816).

Avenel, G., *La Noblesse Française sous Richelieu* (Paris, 1901).

Aymes, N., *Trente Années du Grand Siècle. La France de Louis XIII* (Paris, 1909).

Babeau, A., *La ville sous l'ancien Régime*, 2 vols. (Paris, 1884).

———— *La Vie Rurale dans l'ancienne France* (Paris, 1885).

———— *Le Bourgeois d'autrefois* (Paris, 1886).

Baird, H. M., *The Rise of the Huguenots of France*, 2 vols. (New York, 1900).

———— *The Huguenots and Henry of Navarre*, 2 vols. (New York, 1903).

———— *The Huguenots and the Revocation of the Edict of Nantes*, Vol I (New York, 1895).

Baudrillart, Henri, *Les Populations Agricoles de la France. La Population du Midi* (Paris, 1893).

Bonnefon, P., *La Société Française du XVIIe Siècle* (Paris, 1903).

Boudon-Lashermes, A., *Le Vieux Puy. Les Origines de la Cité d'Anis* (Le Puy, 1923).

———— *Le Vieux Puy. Le Grand Pardon et L'Église du Puy de 992 à 1921* (Le Puy, 1921).

Bourgeois, E., et André, L., *Sources de l'histoire de France en XVIIe Siècle*, 4 vols. (Paris, 1923).

Burel, Jean, *Mémoires* (Ed. Chassaing) (Le Puy, 1874).

Challamel, A., *The History of Fashion in France* (London, 1882).

Crane, T. F., *La Société Française au XVIIe Siècle* (New York, 1907).

Crétineau-Joly, J., S.J., *Histoire de la Compagnie de Jésus en France* (Paris, 1859).

Curley, F. de, S.J., *Saint Jean-François Régis* (Paris, 1893).

Daniel, C., *Les Jésuites Instituteurs de la Jeunesse Française au XVIIe et au XVIIIe Siècle* (Paris, 1880).

Daubenton, G., S.J., *The Life of St. John Francis Regis* (Tr. Murphy) (London, 1738).

Fagniez, G., *La Femme et la Société Française dans la première moitié du XVIIe Siècle* (Paris, 1929).

Fryer, E. M., *The Hill Towns of France* (New York, 1914).

Gasquet, A., *Lectures sur la Société Française aux XVIIe et XVIIIe Siècles* (Paris).

Gidel, C., *Les Français du XVIIe Siècle* (Paris, 1911).

Gosselin, L. L. T., *Gens de la Vieille France* (Paris, 1919).

Guilhermy, E. de, S.J., *Ménologe de la Compagnie de Jésus* (Paris, 1893).

Guitton, G., S.J., *Saint Jean-François Régis* (Paris, 1936).

Hammerton, J. A., *In the Track of R. L. Stevenson* (New York, 1908).

Hanotaux, G. A. A., *La France en 1614* (Paris, 1913).

Holland, R. E., S.J., *St. John Francis Regis* (Chicago, 1922).

Hugon, C., *Social France in the XVII Century* (London, 1911).

Jacmon, A., *Mémoires* (Ed. Chassaing) (Le Puy, 1885).

Joanne, P., *Itinéraire général de la France* (Paris, 1878-1882).

Jousset, P., *La France Geographie illustrée* (Paris).

Lacroix, P., *Dix-Septième Siècle* (Paris, 1882).

Langlade, J., *Le Puy et Le Velay* (Paris, 1921).

Martindale, C. C., S.J., *Captains of Christ, II: St. John Francis Regis* (London, 1917).

Miltoun, F., *The Cathedrals of Southern France* (Boston, 1904).

Muirhead, F., *Southern France* (London, 1926).

Palm, F. C., *The Economic Policies of Richelieu* (Urbana, 1922).

———— *Calvinism and the Religious Wars* (New York, 1932).

Pennell, E. R., *French Cathedrals* (New York, 1909).

Perkins, J. B., *France Under Richelieu and Mazarin* (New York, 1887).

Perrens, F., *Les Libertins en France au XVIIe Siècle* (Paris, 1899).

Perroy, H., S.J., *A Great and Humble Soul, Mother Thérèse Couderc* (Tr. Burke) (New York, 1933).

Perroy, Marguerite, *Saint François Régis* (Marseilles, 1932).

Prat, J. M., S.J., *Recherches Historiques et Critiques sur la Compagnie de Jésus du temps du P. Coton. 1564–1626,* Vols. IV–V (Lyons, 1876).

Roschach, E., *Histoire graphique de l'ancienne Province de Languedoc* (Toulouse, 1904).

Schimberg, A., *L'Éducation Morale dans les Collèges de la Com-*

pagnie de Jésus en France sous l'ancien Régime (Paris, 1913).

Sicard, A., *L'Ancien Clergé de France,* 3 vols. (Paris, 1893-1903).

Strang, F., *Town and Country in Southern France* (London, 1937).

Tanner, M., S.J., *Societas Jesu, Apostolorum Imitatrix* (Antwerp, 1693).

Theuriet, A., *Rustic Life in France* (Tr. Dole) (New York, 1896).

Turner, H. B., *Picturesque Old France* (Boston, 1929).

Vianey, J., *Saint François Régis* (Paris, 1912).

Villat, L., *Le Velay* (Paris, 1908).

Young, A., *Travels in France, 1787–1789* (London, 1890).

Zeiller, M., *Topographia Galliae* (Frankfort, 1661).